Islandica

A Series in Icelandic and Norse Studies

Cornell University Library

PATRICK J. STEVENS, MANAGING EDITOR

VOLUME LXI

Willard Fiske

Friend and Benefactor of Iceland

KRISTÍN BRAGADÓTTIR

T0324398

Willard Fiske
Friend and Benefactor of Iceland

KRISTÍN BRAGADÓTTIR

Translated and Edited by Patrick J. Stevens

ISLANDICA LXI

CORNELL UNIVERSITY LIBRARY
ITHACA, NEW YORK
2019

All rights reserved. Except for brief quotations in a review,
this book, or parts thereof, must not be reproduced in any form
without permission in writing from the publisher.

First published as *Willard Fiske: Vinur Íslands og velgjörðamaður*
by Háskólaútgáfan (University Press of Iceland), 2008

English-language translation published by Cornell University Library, 2019
Distributed by Cornell University Press

Copyright © 2019 by Kristín Bragadóttir

Copyright, English-language translation © 2019 by Cornell University

Design and composition: Jack Donner
Cover design: Carla DeMello, Cornell University Library

A complete version of this book is available through open access
at https://ecommons.cornell.edu/handle/1813/55752

ISBN: 978-0-935995-22-0

Contents

Translator's Preface

In 2008, Kristín Bragadóttir authored *Willard Fiske: Vinur Íslands og velgjörðamaður*. Work on a translation of this book from the Icelandic commenced in 2009, and proceeded intermittently across the following decade. A host of professional obligations influenced the incremental pace of the work, during which the author, long a friend as well as a colleague of the translator, displayed infinite patience.

The original publication offered Icelandic readers a deep and coherent chronology of Fiske's enchantment with Iceland, which endured for more than half a century until his death in 1904. This translation attempts to offer English-reading audiences the same chronology, as the narrative of Fiske's remarkable relationship with Iceland and the Icelanders is also a chapter in American intellectual and scholarly history. It is also, of course, a tale intimately associated with the founding and early evolution of Cornell University, where Fiske served as the first university librarian and taught several languages.

The translation follows the Icelandic text, albeit with occasional editorial reconsiderations and flexibility in wording. A very long (and difficult) poem by the scholar Eiríkr Magnússon, written for the sendoff Fiske received as he departed Iceland in October 1879, is omitted in translation save for the first stanza (see chapter 17). Chapter 22, rehearsing the dispute between Fiske and Cornell University over Jennie McGraw Fiske's will, has experienced some abbreviation, but also incorporated perspectives Andrew Dickson White committed to his diary that reflect the first university president's sense of conciliation. The generous number of illustrations Kristín included in her book are present here in the translation. A significant modification consists of the addition by the translator of additional endnotes. In the second decade of the twenty-first century, Iceland has emerged as a prime destination for modern tourists. The rugged, stunning beauty of the unique landscape, almost haunted by its association with the medieval Viking Age, is irresistible to discerning travelers. Many of these visitors may not be familiar with Icelandic cultural and political developments of the nineteenth century; in effect, with the local history of a population that stood at one hundred thousand residents in 1900.

In the first chapter, for example, the translator has added an endnote to explain the role of the so-called "Fjölnismen," young Icelanders in Copenhagen who published *Fjölnir*, an Icelandic periodical "especially influential in shaping Icelandic nationalism and national opinion through articles on a wide range of topics," including literature, "publishing (among others) numerous poems by Jónas Hallgrímsson (1807–1845), the great Romantic poet of Iceland and a founding 'Fjölnisman.'" Icelandic high-school students know of *Fjölnir* and Jónas and the long struggle to achieve cultural and political independence from Denmark; Icelandic readers needed no explanation from the author. This revision by endnote is an attempt at cultural translation.

Inclusion of this translation in Islandica reflects Willard Fiske's bequest creating the series and the importance of the Fiske Icelandic Collection during the last century for Norse and Icelandic studies. It is a pleasure to acknowledge the kind collaboration of Háskólaútgáfan (the University Press of Iceland), publisher of the original book, in this endeavor. Finally, since the appearance of the Icelandic version, Kristín Bragadóttir retired from her administrative career in the National and University Library of Iceland and became, in her word, once again an Icelandic "schoolgirl"—earning her doctorate in history in 2017 at the University of Iceland with a dissertation on "Íslenskar bækur erlendis: Bókasöfnun Willards Fiskes (1831–1904)" (Icelandic books abroad: The book collecting of Willard Fiske [1831–1904]).

PATRICK J. STEVENS
ITHACA, NEW YORK

Introduction

A century and a decade have elapsed since Daniel Willard Fiske, friend of Iceland, passed away on 17 September 1904. This book has been written to remember this distinguished man who became infatuated with Iceland and wanted to improve as much as possible land and nation, which he demonstrated truly through his works. Fiske was a colorful personality and his life was richly varied; this narrative dwells especially on the Icelandic chapter therein. He realized his long-awaited dream of going to Iceland in the summer of 1879 and sojourned there less than four months. Afterward his thoughts were more or less bound up with Iceland and the Icelanders. In Iceland he is especially remembered for his collection of Icelandic books, the noble gifts he sent to Icelanders, and his fascination with the tiny island of Grímsey just north of the Icelandic mainland.

The influence of Fiske is still perceptible in Icelandic cultural life. In the National and University Library of Iceland, his collection of works on chess, one of the special collections in the National Section, bears eloquent witness to its donor. The collaboration of the collection with the Fiske Icelandic Collection in the Division of Rare and Manuscript Collections of the Cornell University Library has been beneficial on multiple levels. In his will, Fiske stipulated that a portion of the funds the university inherited from him should go toward an annual publication connected with his Icelandic collection. Islandica came out first in 1908 and has since been published fairly regularly (though not annually). The author of this book was for a time the Islandica series editor.

In compiling this book, I attempted to walk in the footsteps of Daniel Willard Fiske as much as possible. I sat in the Cornell University Library, where I have benefited from the excellent assistance of staff in the Division of Rare and Manuscript Collections; and likewise in the manuscripts section of the Royal Library in Copenhagen, where I studied the correspondence on the origins of his collection, and the evolution of its Icelandic component, between Fiske and Icelanders living there as well as various Danes whom he had become acquainted with as a young man in Denmark. Then there was his time in Sweden, where he developed a better acquaintance with Nordic culture, to him clearly favorable; that sojourn was always on his mind and came up often in his letters. In Carolina Rediviva, the university library at Uppsala, I spent long hours working in the same reading room as did Fiske, who frequented it a century and a half earlier; likewise I went with him in mind to Djurgården (in Stockholm), Sigtuna, and Hammarby. All these were places for which he had affection. The most significant period for Fiske's compilation of the Icelandic collecton was nonetheless his last twenty-one years, when he lived in Florence and just outside the city in the village of Fiesole. Here I have threaded the footpaths of Fiske and had a good look at his home, Villa Landor, and the surrounding grounds.

It is appropriate to name here the bibliographical sources that have been most useful in writing this book: *Willard Fiske: Æfiminning*, by Bogi Th. Melsteð, which is well known; *Willard Fiske in Iceland: Based on the Pocket Notebook Kept during His Sojourn There, 1879*, which P. M. Mitchell edited and "issued in conjunction with the Willard Fiske Commemoration [at Cornell] in 1989"; and *Memorials of Willard Fiske*, which Horatio S. White, Fiske's literary executor, compiled in three volumes in 1920–22. Last but not least it is pertinent to mention the correspondence to and from Fiske that is preserved in the Fiske Icelandic Collection and in the National and University Library of Iceland. To some it may seem that I have painted a one-sided picture of Fiske, but the letters and other sources show him unbelievably sympathetic toward Icelanders, and the these sources are followed closely in the book.

In 2002 I received a two-month research leave to explore holdings relating to Fiske outside of Iceland. I devoted the time to going through his collected dorrespondence in the Fiske Icelandic Collection in Ithaca and also letters from Fiske to various Icelanders who lived in Denmark. Thes letters are preserved in the Royal Library in Copenhagen and cover the period from 1852, when he left Scandinavia, until 1904, and it bears mentioning that Icelanders living in Denmark were ready to assist him in obtaining Icelandic materials. I remain grateful to the National Library of Iceland (where I served as an associate university librarian before retirement) for having made it possible for me to gather these research materials.

Many deserve thanks for having improved the manuscript in various ways. I thank especially Þórunn Sigurðardóttir, Þorvaldur Kristinsson, Þorleifur Jónsson, Aðalgeir Kristjánsson, and Patrick J. Stevens for proofreading the manuscript and for many fine suggestions. The late Ögmundur Helgason read most of the chapters and offered valuable advice. I also thank Jökull Sævarsson and my husband, Sveinn Magnússon, for reading the manuscript and for helpful comments. Sveinn also took several photographs that appear in the book. I thank most of all Sigríður Harðardóttir, the editor of the Icelandic version of the book, for her close proofreading and exacting emendations of the manuscript. The photographer Helgi Braga I thank for the image processing. Menningarsjóður (the Icelandic Cultural Fund) supported original publication of the book in Icelandic.

Hólavellir, 2008 and 2018
Kristín Bragadóttir

Chapter 1

Forming the Idea

Daniel Willard Fiske was born in Ellisburgh, New York on 11 November 1831. He attended Cazenovia Seminary, a Christian school, and then Hamilton College, but was too restless to complete a degree and instead pursued his longing to travel and to learn Nordic languages. Before turning twenty, Fiske had become enthusiastic about the cultures of other nations, and when barely twenty, he was of a mind for adventure, poor in worldly goods yet full of optimism and daring.[1]

Willard Fiske's enthusiasm for Iceland in particular arose from his earliest youth. He did his utmost to acquaint himself with the land and nation and every Icelandic issue in detail,[2] and read everything he could obtain about Iceland, enlivening further his interest.

Several books with descriptions of Iceland, published in various languages and locales, saw the light of day before Fiske set off on his Iceland journey, and he doubtless knew them all. Various maps of Iceland, often beautifully done and at times showing more than the island alone, were sought after at this time. Maps of Iceland were also available from travel books and descriptions of Iceland, and though the oldest of these were far from realistic, they undoubtedly aroused people's interest. The oldest maps depict whales, sea monsters, and ships at sea; the terrestrial images derive from nature, national life, even the dwellings of Icelanders. The depictions are exaggerations, showing people's ideas and ignorance of a distant land. These maps are therefore considerably more than maps of a country; one can infer much more from them.

Willard Fiske in middle age. The portrait is from about the same time as his trip to Iceland.

One book Fiske knew was *Tilforladelige Efterretninger om Island*,[3] by Niels Horrebow, which came out in 1752. The book, which garnered wide attention, was accompanied by a map of Iceland that, though there were various flaws on it, was considered a major improvement. Of significance were the first triangulated measurements, deriving from exploration of the land, as the basis for the map. He also knew the writings of his countryman George P. Marsh; these awoke his interest in Nordic culture.[4] Marsh was especially interested in Swedish literature and translated works into English. In addition he collected Icelandic materials such as grammars; travel books devoted to Iceland; and the principal Icelandic law codes, *Grágás*, *Járnsíða*, and *Jónsbók*.[5] Marsh translated the grammar of Rasmus Kristian Rask as *A Compendious Grammar of the Old Northern or Icelandic Language*, published in 1838.[6] Marsh was by then a respected specialist on the island to the north, and has been called the pioneer of Icelandic studies in America.[7] Although it is not clear how influential his writings were, it is amply evident Fiske read his works cover to cover, since he acknowledged that it had been the books of Marsh, along with *On Heroes,*

Hero-Worship and the Heroic in History,[8] by Thomas Carlyle, on Norse mythology, that directed his mind to the languages and literatures of the North.[9] Fiske was also familiar with the translation of Paul Henri de Mallet's work by Bishop Thomas Percy as *Northern Antiquities*,[10] published in London in 1847.

Fiske lived his entire life by the light of this quickened spark. He collected a number of Icelandic travel descriptions at a time when journeys and travel books literally enhanced human vistas, influencing greatly people's thinking and consequently literature, sciences, and the arts.[11] Fiske also read with enthusiasm Sir Walter Scott's abridged translation of *Eyrbyggja saga*,[12] and later, Sir George Webbe Dasent's translations of Icelandic family sagas[13] and the collaborative translations of William Morris and Eiríkr Magnússon.[14]

He also knew the works of the poet and translator Bayard Taylor,[15] who had become especially familiar with Scandinavia.[16] Taylor went to Iceland in 1874,[17] and after his journey, he labored still more intensively to spread knowledge of Icelandic culture.

Fiske also read Adam Oehlenschläger's works, enchanted by the romanticism in them:[18] Oehlenschläger sought his ideas in the ancient Norse cultural legacy, *Snorra Edda*[19] being among his sources. All these works abetted Fiske's ever-increasing enthusiasm for Iceland, and in the middle of the nineteenth century he began collecting Icelandic books himself.[20] Yet his purse was light and permitted no purchases of substance, least of all scarce or more expensive works. The dew of Romanticism lay over Old Norse literature at this time, making these works appealing to a man such as Fiske; and he became ever more determined to know Iceland through and through.

Lack of money notwithstanding, Fiske came to Copenhagen in 1850. He needed little time to come to know the city and soon felt at home there. He thought it splendid coming to Scandinavia and quickly found that these countries had their own long history and traditions different from those of the young United States.

During his Scandinavian sojourn Fiske supported himself through journalism, sending many reports on politics and literature to the United States. He reminded people of the privilege of those who have a history of their own, and wrote in a letter to the *Syracuse Star*: "Your readers, living in a land which has no Past, but a great

Present and a mightier Future, are wont to envy and admire the countries of Europe for their long history, their glorious foretime."[21] He was also employed by the American Embassy in Copenhagen and assisted with various tasks, thus earning a little money.

Fiske was vigilant for material that could offer him a comprehensive picture of Scandinavia, and he read everything he came across. His sensitivity to languages strengthened his enthusiasm for travel and for speaking with people in their own idioms. Before his life's end he spoke Danish, Swedish, German, French, Dutch, and Italian very well and other languages, such as Icelandic, Russian, Persian, and Arabic, reasonably so.[22] For a while he studied Sanskrit.

Fiske was in Denmark for a good half year. There he met many Icelandic cultural figures and came under their influence. One of the "Fjölnismen,"[23] Gísli Brynjúlfsson, assisted him in learning Icelandic, and quite rapidly Fiske mastered the language. He was pleased with the teaching, having found he made considerable progress under Gísli, and declared that with one month's sojourn in Iceland he would even be able to speak Icelandic fluently.[24] Fiske and Gísli became fast friends, but unfortunately, little of their correspondence has been preserved.[25]

Among other Icelanders Fiske associated with in Copenhagen, and who inspired him regarding the direction then being taken in the struggle for Icelandic independence, were Jón Sigurðsson, president of the Icelandic Literary Society (Hið íslenzka bókmenntafélag); Jón Þorkelsson (eldri), later rector or principal of the Learned School in Reykjavík (formally Reykjavíkur lærði skóli, often simply Lærði skólinn or Latínuskólinn, now Menntaskólinn í Reykjavík); Guðbrandur Vigfússon, a future librarian at Oxford; and Árni Thorsteinsson, later governor-general of Iceland. Fiske corresponded with these men for years. He also became acquainted with Carl Christian Rafn, who with Rasmus Rask had founded the Danish Royal Society of Northern Antiquities (Det kongelige nordiske oldskriftselskab) in 1825. Rafn, the secretary of the society, pioneered antiquarian studies in Denmark.[26]

Copenhagen had much to offer and Fiske used his time well. Among other musuems, the Thorvaldsen Collection aroused his interest, and he spent long hours there. He compiled an article on the origins of the artist and was struck at how far Thorvaldsen had advanced in his art.[27]

Fiske always remembered his Copenhagen days with great pleasure; there his enthusiasm for things Nordic had received a lift: "More than ever, now I am here, do I love this Northern land . . . to-day I feel that I am more of a human being—more *alive* than before I left home," he wrote in Copenhagen at the close of 1850.[28] Certainly his passion for Icelandic culture grew with his Danish sojourn, but he was to be even more influenced by Uppsala.[29]

During spring 1851 Fiske crossed the Sund to Sweden. In Lund he scrutinized the ancient cathedral carefully, enchanted by its architecture and history. Historical sites invariably enthused him and he always found seeing their details absorbing. Fiske also made a journey to visit the Lund University librarian, E. W. Berling; the collection at Lund was a venerable one.[30] From Lund he set out on foot for Växjö, especially to visit the grave of the poet and bishop Esaias Tegnér.[31] In a letter to Rafn he related having stood by the grave and recalling to memory "Nattvardsbarnen." Tegnér's poem, which Longfellow translated in 1841, had seduced him.

His journey continued to Kalmar. Fiske knew Kalmar Palace by reputation and set about going over it to gain a greater understanding of its history. From Kalmar he went to Visby[32] in Gotland, and though he stayed there briefly, it is evident from his letters that the visit made a lasting impression.[33] Sensitive to history, he imagined himself back in the thirteenth century, gazed out over the Eystrasalt and saw before him the old trading center with its thick, fortified wall, and the ships with their precious wares coming from the east.[34]

The days went by rapidly, and although Fiske longed to acquaint himself far better with local conditions, time was not availing, as his journey to Uppsala, where he intended to pursue study at the university, awaited. On the way north he stopped briefly at Stockholm. Having acquainted himself with notable buildings in the city center, Fiske went through Djurgården, the old royal hunting preserve.[35] He headed afterward for Uppsala, a growing and lively university town. In the distance rose the two majestic cathedral spires, and they, along with the palace, which stood like a fort on top of its slope, made the city sublime and distinguished in appearance. Here Fiske was to dwell for some time, acquainting himself with the life of the people in the city and its surroundings.

Chapter 2

Maturing in Uppsala

W illard Fiske stayed in Uppsala for a year and a half and mastered Swedish. He had long thought very highly of the outstanding Swedish men of science and culture, many of whom had worked at the university in Uppsala.[1] One of them was the naturalist Carl von Linné; Fiske went by foot to Hammarby, where Linné had lived from 1758 until he died in 1778.[2] There Linné had held lectures and furthered his own studies, inter alia creating the famous plant classification system by which he is known. Fiske also knew of the physicist Anders Celsius and his development of the one-hundred-degree thermometric scale that was adopted throughout the world. These Swedes had passed away long before, but had contributed much in the arts and sciences.

Fiske was sturdy and in good physical shape. He was a robust hiker, not hesitating to devote a day's walk between points. Instinctively curious, he took in knowledge of land and nation. The Swedish landscape suited him well; enchanted by the nature, he went past small lakes that seemed to lie like glittering gems between forest ridges overgrown with hanging birch.[3] He longed to see more places in the Uppsala vicinity and went on foot to the city of Sigtuna, somewhat to the south. In Sigtuna, which dates from about the year 1000 and is one of the oldest cities in Sweden, were an ancient townstead and ruins that testified to former fame. All that stood at the ancient core he found noteworthy, and he was captivated by the historical narratives. After an enjoyable trip steeped in information, he returned to Uppsala.

The Carolina Rediviva University Library in Uppsaka, where Fiske often studied.

In the university town Fiske felt at home and able to immerse himself in its history. He recounted in many letters going around the city and reading its history in every alleyway.[4] The Carolina Rediviva library beckoned, and he would often sit inside reading.

At its founding, from 1620, Carolina Rediviva was the Court library, and had its roots in the library of King Gustav II Adolf (1594–1632) and Queen Christina (1626–1689), who took the Swedish crown after her father. Christina had great enthusiasm for the arts and sciences and saved many items of cultural value from ruin. The collection in this period (1668) acquired one of its greatest gems, the beautiful *Edda Upsaliensis* manuscript of *Edda Snorra Sturlusonar*, partially illuminated, from around 1300.[5]

Fiske devoted his free time to looking at buildings and monuments. He later especially recollected the cathedral and the palace of Gustav Vasa[6] that stood on the slope and loomed over the town. He also went to the heathen heart of Sweden, the three burial mounds in Old Uppsala where the graves of Óðinn, Þór, and Freyr were said to be.[7] The world he longed to know better thus came into clearer focus.

The sojourn in Uppsala intensified Fiske's enthusiasm for Icelandic culture because of the great interest in Iceland at that time among men of culture there.[8] Swedes had looked upon medieval Icelandic literature as an important information source on the Swedish nation and readily searched superhumanly therein to define themselves.[9] Several Swedish voyagers had also gone to Iceland and written about the country[10]; thus the knowledge of the land and its people was rather considerable at Uppsala. Fiske adopted the disposition prevalent at Uppsala and Icelandic literature, especially the medieval, took ever deeper root in the mind of the visitor.[11]

As mentioned before, Fiske was purposefully determined to collect Icelandic books, and Uppsala offered him a copious number.[12] Icelandic sagas had been printed there before anywhere else, the Swedes having preceded the Icelanders and Danes. *Gautreks saga* was the first saga printed in Uppsala, published with a Swedish translation in 1664.

In Uppsala Fiske provisioned himself liberally, in spiritual terms, for his Iceland voyage. His sojourn in the city sparking his enthusiasm more than his stay in Copenhagen,[13] he registered as a student in Scandinavian studies at the University of Uppsala. Student life attracted him and he affiliated with a "student nation,"[14] the milieu for most student social life.[15] He chose the Dalecarlia "nation" as it was the largest and he found Dalarna,[16] where people held to old customs and even mode of dress, separating themselves in many respects from other districts in Sweden, a charming region.

Fiske worked to support his study in Uppsala by teaching English and sending dispatches to American newspapers, and by holding lectures on American literature.[17] It did not escape notice that he gave the lectures in good Swedish.[18]

After his stay in Uppsala Fiske went to Norway and attended a Scandinavian students' meeting. At its close he went back to Copenhagen in the autumn of 1852, intending to journey out to the saga island in the North, but arrived ten days late, missing the steamer for Iceland.[19] To his bitter sorrow, his Iceland journey had to await a better time.

Fiske was now more convinced than ever that Nordic culture suited his character and his interests far more than that of the United States.[20] Yet most good adventures come to an end; after two years in Scandinavia, a sojourn rich in learning, he returned to the United States in autumn 1852. He nurtured a strong and irrepressible longing to journey to Iceland during the next quarter-century, using the time to gather more material and read about the land and nation, as he wanted to be well prepared when he did set out. He was pleased with the Icelandic books he had purchased for himself, and thus had reading material to hand. It was said that when Fiske returned to the United States from his Scandinavian sojourn, he had the best collection of Icelandic books in the country.[21]

Chapter 3

Home (and Away Again)

Willard Fiske, scarcely twenty-one years of age, returned home with a stash of good memories. Now he took on various occupations: In 1853 he obtained a post with the Astor Library in New York City, serving there until 1859.[1] During 1859–60 he worked as a writer for the American Geographical and Statistical Society. Fiske had long had a passion for chess and was a good player; with Paul Morphy, he published *The American Chess Monthly* from 1857 to 1860. He published other writings on chess and, among other projects, compiled in 1859 *The Book of the First American Chess Congress*, which was held in New York in 1857. In Fiske's mind, the game of chess was an art form, and his enthusiasm for that art never diminished.

Fiske worked for a time in the diplomatic service of the United States, performing appropriate tasks, including secretarial duties. In 1862–63 he served as secretary with the American legation in Vienna.

Journalism suited Fiske well. Along with his fixed occupations, he was forever writing, and sent articles on various topics to newspapers back home. In 1863–65 he wrote for *The Syracuse Daily Journal* and in 1867 in the respected and widely read *Harford Courant*, one of the oldest papers in America. At that time he compiled a diversity of articles, many relating to culture and politics in Europe, with the Nordic countries having their place. A considerable number of the articles dwelled in an illuminating and positive manner on Iceland, and he thereby awakened the interest of English speakers in the land and nation. People were impressed

"Far above Cayuga's waters . . ." View of the lake from the Cornell campus.

by his knowledge of Old Icelandic literature, which was beyond that of most. Subsequently he was a bookseller and editor in Syracuse and for a time worked in the post office there.[2]

Willard Fiske was a refined and far-seeing man of culture and lived a varied and colorful life. His was a constant yearning for travel and adventure, and in autumn 1867 he packed his trunk once more, this time for the Near East. Of the countries he came to know in this trip, he was most drawn to Egypt and Palestine, and when he was in Egypt, he received an invitation he could not decline. He was called to the professorship of Old Norse and Northern European languages at Cornell University in Ithaca, along with the post of first university librarian.[3]

Cornell University was being organized and formally opened in the autumn of 1868. A strong cultural movement had sprung up in the United States and several new universities had been founded. There was a need for persons of culture in virtually all disciplines, and the ground was fertile.

Fiske then left Egypt for Ithaca, which now became his home town. He found living there excellent and his life became more structured as he settled down to business. Everything had to be thoroughly worked out from the beginning, as these were the university's early years. Considerable stamina and willingness to work were necessary to acquire publications and to establish the university library in good order, and to build up the language department with languages that had never been taught in the country. Fiske was likely the first to have taught Scandinavian languages at the university level in the United States.[4]

Ithaca, a small city in upstate New York, is situated in a large lake district. South of Lake Ontario there lie long and narrow dells running north to south, and in these valleys are lakes, long and slender like outstretched fingers, hence the name Finger Lakes. Ithaca is an attractive city and its surroundings uniquely variegated and beautiful. The sides of the valley in which the city lies are cut through by numerous narrow gorges with remarkable rock strata and cascading streams that give the place a distinctive appearance. Cornell University stands on the slope southeast of Cayuga Lake, and from it there is a beautiful view over the water, especially from higher stories of principal buildings on West Campus.

Ezra Cornell, founder of the university, was born in 1807 and came from a family of poor farmers. He left his parents' farm in

SAGE COLLEGE AND BARNES HALL.

The young Cornell campus, where Fiske was the first university librarian and taught Nordic languages.

Reading room of the university library (now Uris Library) and the campus bookstore.

northern New York State at the age of nineteen, self-taught in farm work and a competent craftsman. He first came to Ithaca in 1828 and thought highly of the place; he quickly took on carpentry and machine work. In 1843 he went to Georgia and then to Maine to try his luck. He acquired knowledge of electricity and proved clever in everything concerning machines and electrical current. He became acquainted with Samuel Morse, later known for Morse

Cayuga Lake and the university campus. Photograph taken from the campanile (McGraw Tower) of the university library.

code,[5] and became convinced of the possibility of setting up a telegraph network. This took Cornell many years of research, but in the end he succeeded, making himself both famous and wealthy. He was now ready to return to his family in Ithaca, where he had his wife and five children, and to advance generous sums toward the founding of a university.

Cornell was from his early years experienced in agricultural work and interested in everything that could strengthen the field, and was also an idealist with knowledge of exact sciences. He wanted to accomplish good and was now sufficiently wealthy to bring it to reality. Most of all he wanted to further those fields he had especially excelled in. The region around Ithaca was fertile and well suited to agriculture, and Cornell saw an opportunity to employ his wealth and knowledge to advancement in agriculture, mechanical engineering and other important disciplines. He had left Ithaca penurious but full of optimism and ideals, and returned hence after a thirteen-year absence. A reputation of progress and success preceded him.

The other man who founded the university was Andrew Dickson White, born in 1832, also in New York State. He came from people of substance and had received a religious upbringing. He was considered a good student and dreamed of entering Yale or Harvard. Admitted to the former, he pursued literature and medieval studies. At the end of those studies he did not cease, and as he had more money to hand than most, he decided to improve his subject knowledge on his own, studying in other humanistic fields such as history and languages. He also had a very great interest in architecture. After his studies he traveled to Europe and came under the influence of European culture. In 1856 Andrew D. White was said to be one of the one hundred best-educated men in the United States.[6] In 1864 he was elected to the New York State Senate and quickly made chairman of the senate committee on education.[7]

At this time Ezra Cornell was also elected state senator and chaired agricultural affairs. There two very dissimilar men with contrasting views and unlike emphases met each other, and after a period of acquaintance it nonetheless dawned on them that a new university was of interest to both. Together they consecrated their energetic effort to the project. Thus these men of disparate background and life perspective worked in concert, placing as a result the university on a successful footing.

The die was cast on 7 February 1865. A bill for the founding of Cornell University was placed before the state senate leadership. Ezra Cornell guaranteed funds toward its realization, and Governor Reuben E. Fenton signed the bill on 27 April of the same year. Then the wheels began to turn rapidly. Cornell selected a tract on his estate in Ithaca for the university, benefiting from the advice of his friend Henry W. Sage, who was a woodsman. The space was good and offered good possibilities for the growth of the university.

Morris Bishop, paraphrasing, summarizes Andrew D. White's thinking on academic structure as enunciated in a "Plan of Organization" submitted to the Board of Trustees 21 October 1866:

> "We shall divide our structure . . . into two parts: one, for the students who have chosen their career, a Division of Special Sciences and Arts, as Agriculture and Engineering, with special emphasis on Jurisprudence, Political Science, and History; and a second part for those seeking a broad preparation for life, that is, a General Course, or Division of Science, Literature, and the Arts in General."[8]

Students on the way back from class, Cornell University. Library with campanile in the background.

University Library (now Uris Library) with its iconic campanile. Boardman Hall (where Olin Library now stands) is at left.

In the spring of 1868 White traveled to Europe to purchase books and materials for teaching and research and to search for the most highly qualified instructors for the university. Colleges such as the College of Agriculture and the College of Arts and Sciences quickly became the backbone of the university and were supported by the enthusiasm of the founders. Cornell University also set much in store in the beginning to the effect that women would be afforded the opportunity to take courses, and in this initiative was in the first rank of institutions of higher education in the United States.

The university was inaugurated on 7 October 1868 and quickly was filled with eager students. Andrew D. White was first university president, and was a good friend of Fiske's who was later to stand with him through thick and thin.

Fiske arrived, an enthusiastic pioneer for the library, and with his enterprise succeeded in greatly increasing the choice of works in the collection. Early in 1874 the number of volumes had become forty thousand.[9] It also happened that he kept the library open longer every day—nine hours—than was the practice in many other universities in the United States at the time.

Fiske quickly earned the reputation of being a prescient and uncommonly energetic librarian, and his teaching also went well. He took pains with his students, untiringly steering them toward Scandinavian literary works that needed to be translated and made known to the English-speaking world. He acquired private collections for the library through purchase and bought worthy new works useful for instruction. Quickly in these first years the library became a thoroughfare for the university. In the library field and in bibliography Fiske's principal work was to endure, as he brought together precision and accumulated knowledge.

Many people were of assistance to the new university. A wealthy man by the name of John McGraw was enthusiastic about the founding of the school and truly a patron of it, contributing considerable funding toward its establishment. There were grandeur surrounding the university and considerable ceremony at its consecration. Great personages were in attendance and celebratory speeches made; everyone was in festive form.

At the inauguration of Cornell University a young woman, Jennie McGraw, gave bells in a unique carillon of generous range.[10] Jennie was the only daughter of John McGraw and had been an inherent well-wisher of this new cultural institution in which many hopes were bound up. The bells, nine in number, were installed in a high tower on campus.[11] Alfred Lord Tennyson's poem "In Memoriam" adorned their machinery. They were rung for the first time with ceremony at the inauguration, and still play today at set hours, reverberating over the town. They remind of Jennie and give the campus much of its rather special atmosphere.

The scene of Fiske's work was to be for many of the coming years at the university, where his knowledge came to good use.

Chapter 4

Jennie

Jennie McGraw and Willard Fiske first met in Ithaca in 1869. She was then twenty-nine and he thirty-eight, and she quickly made a deep impression on him. He had written poetry for a while, mostly for his own sake, and when he came home after their first meeting he wrote a poem to her, vivid and full of symbolism. The poem was dated November 1869 and, as far as is known, was the first he wrote to Jennie:

> My feet are climbing at last, at last,
> The snow-paved hill at mid-houred night:
> My soul is drifting so fast, so fast,
> From doubt and dark to love and light.
> The lake-blown breeze, so cold, so cold,
> Slow through the shadowed valley rolls,
> And the stars a-glare, so bold, so bold,
> Mock at my heart's presagèd doles.
> The cascade's murmur, so clear, so clear,
> Sounds in the gorge's gloomy deep,
> And flashing fancies, so dear, so dear,
> Across my dazèd vision sweep.[1]

The poems to Jennie were to become many, but remained concealed, as he did not show them until years later—lest her father know of them.

Jennie McGraw,
the woman who
completely changed
Fiske's life.

John McGraw, father of Jennie, had waxed wealthy through the sale of timber and had vast tracts throughout the United States.[2] Jennie was frail from childhood and when she was thirty-five it was evident she had fallen ill with tuberculosis, then a grave illness with no remedy at hand. Her mother had died of the same malady in 1847 when Jennie was seven. Her father then married Jennie's maternal aunt, who reared the girl, but she also died of tuberculosis in 1857. There was no wonder why the father should fear for his daughter. Yet Jennie had a good upbringing despite the loss of her mother. Her father facilitated her path to the utmost; nothing was spared. She learned everything considered desirable for young ladies to know at that time.

When Jennie was twenty-two she first took part in the diversions of Ithaca. She was intelligent, cheerful, and amusing, and enjoyed being among young people.[3] Her life was woven into the university's existence to a great extent, although she did not take courses there; as befitted a young woman in the upper strata of society, she attended lectures, musical recitals and meetings. She traveled more than was usual among young women at the time. Her father thought it beneficial to open her mind and he took her on business trips to the interior. In 1872 she went with him all the way to California. Thus she was better acquainted with the United States than would have been otherwise. She also traveled with Lettie, her cousin and friend, to Europe.[4] They were of the same age and got along well. Jennie had an easy time learning languages, and mastered French and German while abroad. She also frequented art museums in Europe and acquired considerable knowledge of art.

Jennie was radiant and attracted attention wherever she went, and there was never a dearth of interest in the young woman on the part of the men. She was clever, cooperative, and benevolent. When the Civil War broke out in 1861, she joined the nurses caring for the wounded soldiers.

Jennie McGraw was without doubt the most eligible young woman in Ithaca and beyond. She quickly awakened Fiske's admiration, and in little time his feelings transformed into an intense love he nonetheless considered hopeless because of the considerable class difference between them. They met each other in following years but he kept his feelings hidden. In her journals and letters Jennie wrote nothing directly about her thoughts of Fiske. Mention of him was neutral in tone only. They met often, however, in secret, and she emphasized keeping their relationship hidden.[5]

The years passed, and Fiske was occupied with his work. By 1875 Jennie's and his relationship had become steadfast, but remained strictly secret. The hopes of the penurious professor to marry a lady who was of such higher class were not likely to be fulfilled. Fiske was also cautious because of his position and was careful concerning everything he said and did. Few resources are available regarding this chapter in Fiske's life, but it is possible to conjecture that in private, he daydreamed and let his imagination roam. In his relations with Jennie he dared not be open, but he sat alone and composed poems that showed his state of mind. Among them was this one:

> Must I believe that these slow years
>   Have reached a fated goal at last?
> Must I believe that tears and tears
>   Shall wash away a tearless past?
> Must I believe in unseen spheres
>   Through-swept by passion's changeful blast,
> Where gladdening joys and saddening fears
>   On skies their sheen and shadow cast?

In the spring of 1875 Fiske arranged for his friend, the poet and translator Bayard Taylor, to come to Cornell to deliver several lectures open to the public. Jennie came to listen to all of them and wrote down what seemed to her noteworthy in order to relate to her female friends afterwards.[6] One of Taylor's lectures was on Goethe's poetry; he was thoroughly familiar with the topic, and his translation of *Faust* had awakened great interest in the English-speaking world.[7] The lecture was memorable and much affected Jennie; she stated later that Taylor had literally made Goethe a god.[8] Thus Fiske succeeded indirectly in bringing her into the world of poetry.

As time passed Jennie referred to Willard ever more often in her journal entries, but now as before in an impersonal tone; and it is not possible to discern any particular interest of hers for him from these writings. She was prudent and avoided doing anything that could offend her father. Jennie knew as it was that he was totally opposed to a union between her and Willard Fiske.

Chapter 5

The Women in Willard's Life

Two women had great influence on Fiske's life and his perspective on it. In the middle of the 1870s there was a close friendship between Jennie and Willard and also between her and his mother, Caroline Willard Fiske, a particularly colorful woman who attracted people to her; powerful and enchanting and unafraid to make her own way.

Caroline lived across two eras. She was born in 1804, five years after Washington's death, and lived during the administrations of twenty-three presidents. She died in 1897, ninety-three years old. Turning eighty, Caroline began learning Italian,[1] and when she was eighty-eight published a short-story collection, to the astonishment of all.[2]

Jennie McGraw was charmed by the energy of this remarkable woman, and the son did nothing to spoil the relationship. Caroline then lived with her son, and her pronounced opinions on men and matters had great influence on him. He later wrote her many detailed letters from Iceland. Caroline was not particularly enthusiastic about her son's intention to go to Iceland and believed it could turn out to be the most dangerous of trips. She undoubtedly gave him a good lecture when she believed he had gone astray.

Once when John McGraw was traveling among his timber businesses, Jennie invited the Fiskes, mother and son, to stay in the McGraw house for several days. The news of their visit reached her father, and when John McGraw realized that Fiske, whom he thought an unworthy prospect for a son-in-law, and his daughter were falling for each other, he tried all he could to keep them asunder. He laid out a great sum and sent her on a long trip to Europe. Jennie was always keen about Europe and left with Lettie, her friend and cousin, on 18 November 1875, not to return before July 1876. John McGraw had then been contending with bad health for a time and passed away on 4 May 1877. Jennie mourned his demise acutely, as father and daughter were close. Fiske comforted her in her sorrow and wrote poems about the loss of her father.[3] Jennie was now without immediate family and suffered formidable loneliness.

When Jennie's father died she was thirty-six years of age, heiress to an enormous fortune and still unmarried. In her father's will, which he had promulgated the year before, it was stipulated that if Jennie died before turning fifty and had not borne children, the children of John McGraw's brother would inherit the estate. This declaration was to be of consequence some years later, as the chapter on "The Great Will Case" will relate.

In association with her father, Jennie learned a great deal about timber, sawmills and everything pertaining to the lumber trade. She devoted considerable time attending to her business affairs after her father's death. Douglass Boardman,[4] a family friend who was in the Cornell administration, oversaw the execution of John McGraw's will and provided Jennie all the support she needed running the business. He had daily contact with Jennie because of business matters, which occupied her completely for a time, and thus became well acquainted with her enterprises and finances.

John McGraw was one of the Cornell trustees and supporters, and after his death Jennie moved largely among the intimate circle of the university and had a second home with the Sage family, good friends of father and daughter. She was also in contact with other influential figures in the university environment. She met Fiske ever more frequently in private, and their association and conversation revolved considerably around literature. He indicated to her here and there what he considered worthy reading, and from the evidence of her diaries he clearly had influence over her literary tastes. They were in New York City at the same time and met nearly daily.[5] Fiske accompanied her to noteworthy public art exhibitions and also to see art works in private hands. He was quite knowledgeable in the history of printing and conducted her through the mysteries of Asian editions they found on exhibition in the city. There he explained for her the imagery of illustrated manuscripts and books, and she marveled at his erudition.

Life, however, is inconstant: Jennie's health began to worsen, and friends and relations worried acutely about her. She was often exhausted and did not engage in various activities that before would have been easy for her. In March 1878 she returned to Europe to regain and refresh her constitution. Her father's friends, who knew of her relationship with Willard Fiske, urged her to travel. John McGraw's wish that they not come together must be honored. Fiske had yet no favor in his passion; though John McGraw was gone, his associates saw to it that the couple did not cement a relationship.

Despite poor health, Jennie still had the temptation to travel. On the European continent she enjoyed herself, rehearsing all Fiske had imparted to her concerning Scandinavia, and went on a journey to Norway, to Kristiania[6] and from there all the way to Lillehammer.[7] Jennie was completely enchanted by the landscape, which was different from most she had ever seen, and relished every detail. Her health continued nonetheless to deteriorate as she journeyed south, all the way to Italy. From Rome she wrote her friend Lettie a downcast letter in January 1879, recounting that she had been especially ill the past two weeks and had avoided all that might have had an ill effect on her back or chest. She scarcely had strength, she said, for much these days, spending most of the time resting, but she would have a good store of memories she would enjoy recollecting. Her existence was dreary, and broken health was the cause of this sophisticated woman's veritable setback.

The situation was to change, however, as Fiske determined to journey to Rome to meet her; and her life took on new purpose.

Chapter 6

Unforgotten Island to the North

The year 1874 marked a millennium from when Ingólfur Arnarson established a farmstead for himself at Reykjavík and Iceland became inhabited. As the anniversary approached, Willard Fiske conceived and put into motion at once the idea that America ought to send the Icelanders a splendid gift of books. He knew as it was that Icelanders were literarily inclined but isolated, and could not easily obtain the literatures of other nations. He organized the collecting and sent letters to authority figures in the United States, urging them to come to accord on a noble gift for the Icelanders. It is not known to how many Fiske sent this appeal, but they were likely very many, and he received an excellent response. Aiding him were Henry Wadsworth Longfellow, Bayard Taylor and Harvard University professor F. J. Child. He also wrote to Lord Dufferin, then Governor-General of Canada, known inter alia for his *Letters from High Latitudes*,[1] which compiled critically important observations on Iceland along with drawings, sketches, and etchings. Dufferin was later to play an important role in the story of Icelanders who migrated to Canada in the last decade of the nineteenth century,[2] and he was warmly receptive to Fiske's request.[3]

Fiske's book appeal was published in Icelandic in the newspaper *Norðanfari* 18 July 1874 under the heading "Advertisements," accompanied by the following letter to Björn Jónsson, who owned and bankrolled the paper, from Eiríkr Magnússon, a librarian who had corresponded with Fiske:

Benedikt Gröndal
designed a famous
commemorative
plaque in honor of
Iceland's milennium of
settlement (874–1874).

Dear Editor,

I have received from Mr. W. Fisk [sic], university librarian at Cornell
University, Ithaca, State of New York, U.S. of America, a letter of
request, which I kindly request you make known to Icelanders, as it
shows that a more powerful and freer nation considers the anniversary of our little nation something to be happy about.

> University Library, Cambridge, 12 May 1874
> Eiríkr Magnússon

The gift of books arrived in several consignments during the anniversary year. Fiske laid the greatest emphasis on the sending of the
books, but there were also pictures in the shipments. Afterward he
was to learn that the pictures were not least among the items that
pleased the Icelanders. The books Fiske succeeded in collecting were
distributed among several collections. If there was only one copy, it
would go to Reykjavík; a second would, as Fiske had arranged, go
to Akureyri.[4] There were also instances in which books would go
into private homes. There is no doubt that these books from overseas
widened Icelandic horizons.

Fiske was fairly known among Icelanders for his collecting, and in newspapers and periodicals there appeared quite a few words about his generosity. In *Þjóðólfur*, 14 September 1874, séra Matthías Jochumsson,[5] who was then editor and owner of the paper, wrote the following:

WORTHY GIFTS FROM THE WEST

The remarkable professor, Dr. [sic] W. Fiske (Cornell University, Ithaca, New York), who has been in the forefront among those encouraging the United States to send us the considerable book gift, as was earlier reported in this newspaper, and will later be better described—has sent hither in the summer as handsome gifts eleven large, excellently lithographed images of Mary, made after the world-renowned portrait by Raphael, the Madonna of San Sisto. To these the pictures are sent, one to each: the Bishop of Iceland, the surgeon-general, "to that poet who has translated Tegnér's *Friðþjófssaga*" (M.J.), and then to the priests at those historically noble spots in the south: Oddi, Skálholt, Þingvellir, Reykholt, Borg, Helgafell, Hvammur in Hvammssveit and the school library in Reykjavík.

The editor of *Þjóðólfur* (M.J.) this same excellent man has honored further with three excellent sun pictures; this production of images is a new-found art.[6]

Séra Matthías also wrote a bit later, on 20 October 1874, a letter to Fiske thanking him for the picture of Mary and many other images. He declared himself to be rendering thanks in Iceland's name as well as his own. He now promised Fiske to send him perpetually a subscription copy of *Þjóðólfur*. Matthías fulfilled the promise, and letters often accompanied the newspaper. The following verse was in a letter he wrote 29 November 1879, sent with the paper. Matthías had met Fiske in Reykjavík during the summer and thanked him inter alia for coming to Iceland and for his sojourn.

Happy Yule! Happy New Year!
No arthritis but sated soul
Give the one that pours the cabbage
Of this life in your drinking glass.
There is the poet's prophecy.

After the books came to Iceland, Fiske's name was for the first time on the lips of everyone on the island. Icelanders were persuaded of his benevolence from his own turf (the United States) and wished he himself had come with the gifts. Certainly Fiske longed to come to Iceland and take part in the festivities, but resources did not permit, and yet another five years passed before he came to the promised land.[7]

Fiske maintained correspondence with Icelanders after he returned to the United States from Scandinavia, especially those he had gotten to know in Copenhagen. Nonetheless he also corresponded with others, and not only scholars but also various leaders and politicians.

Jón Ólafsson, a poet and editor,[8] wrote Fiske often during his sojourn in America and in fact much longer after. He let Fiske know his ideas on Alaska; he had much on his mind and sometimes sent him recent and amusing poems, including one dated Christmas 1874. In this poem he made good-natured fun of contemporary epitaphs, calling the poem

"Epitaph over myself"

Jón Ólafsson
All in all and nothing in nothing.
Born 20 March 1850, died when he finished living.
He lived only to irritate death,
And died of irritation over life.

The last three stanzas are as follows:

Himself he said to be a poet,
But some folk had their doubts,
This the earth will judge
As soon as he is gone.

Life's hidden mysteries he pondered,
Wrought verse, moreover, and wrote,
So sunk himself in that stupidity
He clean forgot to live, at last.

Out on cold and icy Frón,
All, both men and ladies,
Oft tell of him have heard;
Jón was he, the son of Ólafur.

At the instigation of Jón Sigurðsson[9] along with several other people, Fiske was elected unanimously an honorary member of the Icelandic Literary Society at the plenary meeting of the Copenhagen chapter on 25 May 1875, with all the rights and responsibilities enumerated in the by-laws of the society. Jón Sigurðsson, society president, signed the honorary certificate. The goal of the Icelandic Literary Society at its founding was to strengthen and uphold Icelandic language and literature, furthering thereby the culture and esteem of the Icelandic nation. The appointment of Fiske was, in context, felicitous.

Although Fiske traveled to Europe several times during his working years in the United States, he never succeeded in synchronizing those voyages with his youthful dream of coming to Iceland. Nonetheless, the dream remained in his unconscious as he improved steadily his knowledge of land and nation.

In 1878 Fiske decided to seek a leave of absence from his duties at Cornell to organize a voyage to Iceland. He had served Cornell well through diligence and hard work, and readily obtained the leave. Jennie was then in Europe and Fiske had likely decided to use the time to travel himself while she was away. In the spring of 1879 he was ready to sail to Europe to take passage to Iceland.

Chapter 7

Travel to Iceland Is Not for All

From the middle of the nineteenth century steam vessels began to sail out to Iceland. At around the same time scheduled service began between Denmark and Iceland. In the 1858 reference work *A Handbook for Travellers*, considered a good and reliable travel guide, those who intended to go to Iceland were cautioned that journeys on the island could be difficult and unsuitable save for the hardiest travelers. Those who headed to Iceland would have to have a definite purpose to their journeys; otherwise they would likely encounter disappointment. There was no point going on a trip without purpose.[1] It would not be possible to travel around the country other than on horses or on foot, unlike in most neighboring countries where roads had been built and people traveled in horse-drawn conveyances or by train. Many foreign guests thought it a novelty to travel long distances astride diminutive but trusty and sure-footed Icelandic horses.[2] The horses were not only for carrying the travelers but also the baggage, all the equipment and food, often considerable and heavy, and therefore there was a need for many of the animals to carry people and baggage between places.

Though there were not especially many who undertook the tiring and difficult voyages to Iceland during the nineteenth century, it is possible to divide these into four basic categories: First, travelers with interest in exploration and mountain climbing. They were relatively many during the latter part of the century and sought especially the less-beaten paths. On the other hand there were the typical tourists. They came mostly on brief visits, went especially to known tourist destinations, and took in the natural marvels. Third were the scientists. They were rather frequent guests, given Iceland's uniqueness; especially geologists, zoologists, and botanists. Fourth and last were travelers with an interest in culture and history, and their stay was generally on the longer side.[3] Fiske belonged to this group.

Iceland, island in the uttermost ocean, aroused curiosity out in the wide world long before Willard Fiske planned his own trip, and various unusual stories existed about the country, likely because few foreigners had gotten to know the place on their own. The perceptions of foreigners who had come to the country were generally twofold: either they praised this unusual and enchanting land to the skies or they became disgusted with the primitive life of the island denizens and with the uncleanliness. For them, Iceland was either the heavenly kingdom or hell. The country was strange in the eyes of many, not least because it was difficult to come out to and subsequently to journey around it. It fascinated many foreigners that few people lived on the island and likewise that they lived a nearly primitive existence. Technology was close to nil and virtually no changes had taken place in agricultural practices since the era of the medieval commonwealth (the twelfth and thirteenth centuries). Here was a retreat from the coal dust of industrial zones (European and North American) that by and large lay remote from rustic nature.[4]

In the last part of the eighteenth century and in the nineteenth century the number of travelers enchanted by the land's stark contrasts multiplied and remarked how it was simultaneously fearsome and charming, magnificent and dreadful. Increasingly the awesome and often rough-hewn nature of the country became even beautiful in the eyes of those who came there. Certain natural phenomena received more attention than others, and some places likewise enjoyed more popularity. Natural wonders rare elsewhere incrementally became emblematic of the country and its nature, with pictures of them appearing one after another. All this Fiske found interesting, but he was nonetheless seeking out the culture and spiritual wealth of the islanders. Undeniably, he also took pleasure in seeing this unique nature from which the sagas derived.

Under the force of the Enlightenment, the narratives of Iceland and the Icelanders underwent a change. The older narratives were less in vogue in this new perspective on the world. The desire was for more that resonated with reality, with sagas and religion jettisoned. Several well-written works on Iceland and Norse culture were published from around the middle of the eighteenth century onward, and they had significant influence among people of culture. Just prior to the end of the century there was a new tone, with romantic influences becoming perceptible and then ubiquitous in the nineteenth century.

The enthusiasm of foreigners for the cultural heritage of the Icelanders grew much during the nineteenth century, and much had been written about the accomplishment of the island's people in the area of literature. The Icelanders were considered to have saved the Norse and Germanic cultural heritage through saga writing and a lengthy written tradition. Because of the isolation, much remained unchanged or little changed; and because of persistence in the old manners and customs, or a lack of imagination to pursue innovation, much stagnated compared with other nations. Some thus maintained that the ancient ways of the ancestors in Central and Northern Europe had been preserved intact in Iceland—speech, clothing, foodways and house customs—though assuredly much had worsened since the high tide of the Middle Ages.[5]

Fiske did not come alone to Iceland. His associate and student from Cornell, Arthur Middleton Reeves, went with him on the voyage and subsidized a portion of Fiske's fare, as he was from a wealthy background. Reeves had long had interest in Nordic languages and culture, and Fiske encouraged him to translate major Nordic literary works. At the university, Reeves had set himself to translating *Frithiofs saga*, by the Swedish bishop and poet Esaias Tegnér.[6] Reeves was an enthusiastic student and full of ambition. Graduating from Cornell in 1878, he was ready to journey with his teacher.

Reeves seemed to have made real progress in Icelandic during the trip, and many people in their letters to Fiske remarked what a pleasure it was that a foreign man of education exerted himself to learn the Icelandic language.[7] Reeves always had great interest in Icelandic literature and himself possessed a good collection of

Icelandic books. He later researched the Norse discovery of America and published his results in the book *The Finding of Wineland the Good*,[8] which aroused considerable attention in the English-speaking world. He died in a railway accident early in 1891. His mother desired to set on his grave a marker of Icelandic rock, and she received a beautiful natural stone, untouched by human hands, which Björn M. Ólsen arranged to ship.[9] On it was later carved in runes the celebrated verse from "Hávamál": "Flocks die, / kin die, / the same self dies, / yet word's renown / dies never / to whomsoever good remember."[10] It was thought quite fitting, as Reeves so loved Iceland; and he was in no way inferior to Fiske in his knowledge of Icelandic culture and literature.[11]

Chapter 8

Arrival in Iceland

The day arrived. The travelers left New York on 21 June 1879 and sailed to Liverpool. From there they went to Scotland to take passage with SS *Camoens*, which departed Leith for Iceland on Saturday, 9 July.[1] The ship, which sailed frequently between Scotland and Iceland, carried goods and people to Iceland and made the return trip with, among others, Icelanders westbound connecting with a ship that carried them to North America, as migration westward was then considerable.[2] *Camoens* was a large steamer with a spacious dining room on deck. The passenger accommodations were considered roomy and airy, and were completely separate from the dining room. Traveling in such a vessel was expensive.[3] The advertised fare for a first-class cabin cost was eight pounds Sterling, and for second class, five pounds. Board, excluding beverage, cost six shillings per diem.[4]

The ship sailed past the Faroes, and Fiske longed to go ashore there, but it could not be arranged. Therefore he had to content himself with gazing on the islands from afar.[5]

Fiske kept a journal during the voyage. The journal is an important source, and was found nearly by chance in an old portmanteau after his death.[6] The ship sailed east before the land and on 12 July, when Iceland was finally visible, off Höfn in Hornafirðir,[7] Fiske began to write in the little notebook, which he continued faithfully during the four-month journey around the country. This was not a conventional journal, written in daily about the day's events: he also wrote down titles of books, personal names,

„Camoens", *gufuskip Slimons í Leith,*
1054 smálestir, með 170 hesta afli, fer
frá *Granton* til *Reykjavíkur* um 24. júlí,
með góz og farþega (fer umhverf-
is Ísland, kemur við í Húsavík).
— *Granton* til *Akureyrar* um 8. ágúst,
með góz og farþega.
— *Granton* til *Reykjavíkur* beina leið
um 23. ágúst, með góz og farþega.
— *Granton* til *Borðeyrar* og *Akureyrar*
um 10. sept., með góz og farþ.
— *Liverpool* eða *Granton* til *Seyðisfj.*
beina leið um 28. sept., með góz
og farþega.
Fargjald: á 1. káetu £ 5 (90 kr.);
fram og aptur £ 8 (144 kr.).
á 2. káetu £ 3 (54 kr.);
fram og aptur £ 5 (90 kr.).
Fæði (að undanskildum ölföngum) 6 s.
(5 kr. 40 a.) á dag.

Advertisement in the newspaper Ísafold, 18 July 1879. SS *Camoens* arrived on her first Iceland journey 12 July and sailed for home the next day with 332 horses. She was called the Slimon Line's horse transport.

and Icelandic names of flowers along with their Latin names, to familiarize himself better with the plants. Likewise he wrote down expressions and sundry elements of the language that he wished to grasp in his memory. Evidently the "white nights" came upon him somewhat unexpectedly, and he could not admire enough the brightness that was equal night and day. They sailed along the eastern strand of Iceland, Fiske continuing to admire the land and light. He noted particularly in his carnet that it was possible to read a book in the middle of the night as if it were broad daylight.[8]

The clearness of the air and the azure of ocean and mountains captivated him,[9] and in the poem "Nearing Island," dated July 1879, he depicted his sentiments when he saw Iceland rising from the sea:

> Now rises fair above the swelling sea
> The far-sought land, of long and keen desire,
> Whose olden story and whose golden speech
> Have winged for me such dear and trancéd hours—

What time its poets' deftly-braided verse
I scanned, or conned the quaintly-woven tales
That paint its ancient heroes' deathless deeds.
O realm of blended frost and fire upbuilt;
Of seething fountains sprung from frozen fells;
Of god-enkindled torches flashing far
In blazing splendors over nocturn skies;
Of flame-red lava-cateracts that pour
Down slopes of blanchéd ice; of skies that smile
As dark-browed midnight kisses light-eyed noon—
A monarch grim in lonely state thou sitt'st
Thy wide and wild and wavy ocean throne,
Enrobed in wintry black and summer green,
And bearing high thy crown of snowy white!
Thou rul'st my mind as she o'ersways my heart.[10]

There was much to say about the people aboard. Fiske noted that Sigríður Einarsdóttir from Brekkubær in Grjótaþorp was especially lively and amusing. She was married to Eiríkr Magnússon, a librarian at Cambridge, and was going to Iceland on holiday.[11] Sigríður was splendidly gregarious and played guitar and sang, to the pleasure of other passengers. Her brother-in-law, Helgi Magnússon, was aboard with her, but he disembarked, as did Fiske and Reeves, at Húsavík on Sunday, 13 July.[12] Many passengers continued with the ship to Reykjavík.

A letter from Fiske to Charles Dudley Warner, his friend from youth, on 13 June 1879, shows that the plan for the trip remained incomplete:

Ho for Iceland! I expect to leave by the Britannia June 21st for Liverpool, thence to London and from there to Iceland by way of Edinburgh. From the latter place I sail July 11, spend 3 or 4 weeks in Reykjavik, make an excursion to the Geysers and Hekla, and then take a steamer around the island, touching at some 15 points, sailing in and out of the beautiful fjords—a trip of say 24 days—I reach Edinburgh again the last days of September. I go with a most agreeable graduate of the Univ. by the name of Reeves, who has the Icelandic craze, and who pays half my expenses.[13]

Fiske wrote many other letters in which he reiterated how satisfying it was getting to know the land and nation.

Fiske's letters to his mother are also an important source, and he wrote her often from Iceland.[14] As mentioned before, she was not especially taken with this adventurous side of her son. She did not understand his longing to travel, reproved him and thought this trip most dangerous. Therefore he did his utmost to describe his journey to her meticulously, assuring her everything was as well as could be desired.

Fiske benefited from his generosity and concern regarding the Icelanders when they celebrated the millennial of Iceland's settlement in 1874. The newspaper *Þjóðólfur* on 19 July 1879 remembered the gift of books and encouraged people to show him warmth and hospitality.

There was no need to urge the Icelanders to the extent Matthías Jochumsson, editor of *Þjóðólfur*, did. Most Icelanders knew of the gift books that had been brought in 1874 and looked forward to meeting the noble guest who had been so benevolent five years before.[15] Later Matthías wrote another announcement in his newspaper to this effect:

Foreign travelers: Professor W. Fiske came hither from the north the sixteenth of this month and intends to sojourn here into the autumn. With him is a young scholar, Mr. A.M. Reeves. . . .[16]

Icelanders were well prepared for Fiske's visit, as the newspapers saw to it that they kept up closely. In *Þjóðólfur*, 19 July 1879, it was reported:

Willard Fiske, friend of Iceland, doctor of philosophy,[17] professor of Nordic languages and history at Cornell University in the state of New York, came ashore off the "Camoens" in Húsavík, and expects to stay until next month. He wrote to us from Edinburgh among other things: "With great anticipation I am preparing myself to land in just a few days on the shore of this land where my best thoughts and beautiful dreams have long had their home."

We allow ourselves to urge our honored fellow-citizens to show our excellent guest all the honor that we may. In addition to the costly gifts of books at the national celebration [the 1874 millennium], the Icelandic nation has much to thank him for as both the keen and nationalistic interpreter of our language and literature in North America.

In contemporary newspapers it is evident that discussion of Fiske's Iceland trip had been substantial and that the islanders had even in droves welcomed his visit. Until his coming, few foreigners had shown the land and people such interest as he, and the inhabitants scarcely knew how to react to all the positive and unexpected attention Fiske showed Icelandic matters.

Chapter 9
Terra firma

The long sea passage was over, to the happiness of the travelers. There was a high sky over Húsavík as they disembarked. They were very well received here as just about everywhere they went. At Húsavík Fiske became acquainted with the merchant Þórður Guðjohnsen, among others, and he and Reeves stayed several days with him, enjoying his hospitality in every respect before they took to the trek and pressed onward toward Reykjavík. For the journey they rented horses, the rent being half a dollar per horse per diem and

From Húsavík, Fiske and Reeves, his travel companion, rode to Ásbyrgi, where natural wonders awaited.

The travelers came to Jökulsá in Axarfjörður. The Icelanders on the journey wanted to name the little cascade on the river Willardsfoss after their guest.

Fiske was impressed by the volume of falling water at Dettifoss and thought the cascade no less magnificent than Niagara Falls in the United States.

one dollar for a guide. All told, these came to the equivalent of four dollars per day.[1]

First it was necessary to see Ásbyrgi and Dettifoss, about which Fiske and Reeves had heard so much. Fiske was completely taken with Dettifoss, finding the waterfall marvelous. He compared the cascade with Niagara Falls, which he had seen, and was not less impressed by Dettifoss.

They came to a little falls on Jökulsá in Axarfjörður, also named Jökulsá á Fjöllum, directly south of Dettifoss. The companions wanted to name it Vínlandsfoss (Vínland Falls), but after the visit of Willard Fiske it was called Willarðsfoss by many people. It is now named Selfoss (Seal Falls). Fiske later obtained a photograph of the falls, which accompanied the collection to Ithaca and until recently hung there.[2]

From Dettifoss they rode to Mývatn and then to Goðafoss, and heard of the ancient tale wherein the gods were cast into the falls. Everywhere they found tangible traces of sagas and narratives. Fiske had always had an interest in plants and botany; the flora piqued his enthusiasm and he observed attentively the tender little plants such as the forget-me-not. In his poem "Across Iceland" he wrote:

Travel in Iceland was not easy in 1879. Often travelers had to ford rivers. William Carpenter, Fiske's other American companion, recounted unbridged rivers and a lack of roads after their trip to Iceland.

> These broad plains are carpeted:
> Mats of sylvan grace outspread—
> Blooms of white and blooms of red,
> Lemon yellow, azure blue,
> Blossoms blithe of every hue,
> Gem-decored with shining dew,
> Dot the far-encircling view.[3]

The diversity of plants in this unsparing land with its inhospitable weather had not occurred to him: it never ceased flashing an unending azure as far as the eye could see. The brilliance was far greater and more richly impressive then he had imagined. The peculiarly Nordic brightness of high summer captivated him. In the poem "An Epistle from the Arctic Sea" he says:

> I breathe the clear and crystal air,
> So limpid pure, so sweet, so rare,
> So quick with breath divine![4]

Fiske saw the land at its most beautiful when the sun was highest. The moor-bird did not cease trying to amuse them en route, and the symphony of nature had a strong effect on him. The untouched land, the purity, the brightness, and the hospitality of the people made the journey into an unbroken adventure, and he never tired of praising this in his letters, writing that the companions were enamored of the land.

Fiske and company lodged on farms on their way and were everywhere received with open arms. Icelanders wanted to show them hospitality and brought forth the finest in the house. That woke the attention of their compatriots, and far and wide the travelers were offered spirits and more often than not fine wine.

There was significant importation of alcohol into Iceland during these years, a fact unsparingly exposed in the newspapers. The same year the Alþingi took up whether it was not necessary again to hike customs and import duties, the so-called alcoholic beverage duty, on alcoholic drinks to decrease their consumption. Levies were suggested that would take up to six times the purchase price.[5] Agreement was reached on a levy on brandy and other alcoholic beverages, though it would not be as high as the discussion in parliament had indicated.

Fiske was amazed to
be offered excellent
wine everywhere.
Advertisements in the
papers for alcohol
were frequent.

Fiske, being well read concerning the island, had made a rather clear itinerary before arriving, and knew what he wanted to see and experience. Yet the journey was still more enjoyable than he had anticipated, and except in part, he did not hold to his itinerary, but extended his sojourn. A journey was now promised to Akureyri. Reeves gave a colorful picture of the first impressions, depicting their coming to Akureyri around sundown when the snow-thatched mountains were hued in the red of the evening sun, the sky was bathed in nuances of color, and the sunset cast a deep copper light on the fjord.[6]

The newspapers of the place—*Norðanfari*, which was edited by Björn Jónsson; and *Norðlingur*, of which Skapti Jósepsson was owner and guarantor—were quite preoccupied with the peregrinations of Fiske. His visit was made known in *Norðanfari* on 24 July:

> Travelers. On the 22nd of this month [July] came here to the city 2 travelers from North America named Willard Fiske, a professor from Cornell University in Ithaca, New York (who at the anniversary year of Iceland's settlement in 1874 sent collections of books to Reykjavík

Miðnætursólin séð frá Akureyri.

Reeves described their arrival in Akureyri around sunset. He was especially moved by the colors of the evening sun, which bathed the fjord with a dark red glow.

and Akureyri, several thousand good books. All Icelanders ought therefore to welcome such a guest and proffer him assistance, wherever he goes, and what is more, as both are the kindest of persons. The professor speaks and writes Icelandic; he is forty-six years old, and Mr. A. M. Reeves twenty-two; he [Reeves] is a printing-house director and printer who publishes a paper called *Daily Palladium*), and Mr. Arthur M. Reeves, from Richmond, Indiana.[7] These travelers had left New York the 21st of June for Liverpool, England and thence to Húsavík with the steamship *Camoens*. From Húsavík they went north to Ásbyrgi, then to Dettifoss on Jökulsá in Axarfjörður and to another falls somewhat beyond, which they named Vinland Falls; from there they traveled to Mývatn and then to Goðafoss in Skjálfandafljótur, and so hence. From here they intend westward to Hólar in Hjaltadalur and from there to Hvammur in Dálir by Hvammsfjörður, so on to Geysir and Reykjavík, from there with [the coastwise steamer] *Diana* from the south and east around the island and back to Reykjavík.

One might say the companions could scarcely have obtained a better reception among the Icelanders. They were impatiently awaited and all put themselves out to make their stay as enjoyable as possible. The majority of Icelanders thought they owed a debt of gratitude to Fiske. The arrival of these guests was written up afterward in greater detail in *Norðanfari* on 6 August:

As was reported in the 35th–36th number of this paper, the 22nd of last month Mr. Willard Fiske, doctor of philosophy[8] and professor of Nordic languages and history at Cornell University in the town of Ithaca, situated in New York State, not far from the great city of New York in North America, came to town [Akureyri]. The professor, along with his traveling companion Mr. A. M. Reeves, editor and owner of a printing press, sojourned here until the 30th when they commenced their trip to the south and west of Iceland. The town residents showed this excellent friend of Iceland and his honored guest [Reeves] the best of receptions, as far as means permitted. Twelve of the townspeople held a midday dinner on the 26th for the companions, several rode with them along Eyjafjörður to show them ancient saga steads, the women's school at Laugaland and the costly land improvements that have been going on in Staðarbyggðarmýrar; he [Fiske] thought much of this visit. Finally many residents accompanied them to Möðruvellir to see the new school building, which the professor thought a very great happening that it could be established; he will be greatly keen on supporting this institution in word and deed, especially by instructing people in effective pedagogy as it is now customary to teach it in schools in North America. One of the townsmen accompanied him all the way to Ytri-Bægisá; to that place he wanted by all means to come, especially because the national poet Jón Þorláksson had lived there, and there reposed his earthly remains.

Professor Fiske is a most kindly man, and speaks our historic language quite well; he is very learned in Icelandic sagas and the history of our land both ancient and modern; he is entertaining in conversation and has great enthusiasm to do all in his power to strengthen development of us Icelanders, both spiritual and practical culture, and to propagate our tongue; he also teaches [Old] Icelandic at Cornell University. While the companions were staying here in town, they looked carefully at the district library, both print shops, and the hospital. They found very beautiful the farmstead at Oddeyri and the building of the Grain Cooperative large in the domestic style; the hayfields of L. Jensen and Frb. Steinsson beautiful, but most remarkable the river Glerá, which could be put to inestimable use if the knowledge and means were available to harness its hydropower. They declared that the same went for the town of Ithaca; there a river[9] runs in a deep gorge, which could be used to drive ten industrial engines, among them two print shops. He declared his intention to support our idea to set up wool-processing factories, as possibilities were great that they would be able to thrive here since a great quantity of wool was in the country itself and sufficient hydropower to run the machines; he was given the available information on that matter. Mr. Reeves, who is accompanying the professor, is devoting himself considerably to Icelandic bibliography, and has thus become well-read in our sagas; he takes photographs of various important places and afterwards writes narratives in his newspaper, and we may rely on it that the story will bring us out well, as he has both an excellent friend of Iceland and a scholar such as Professor Fiske traveling with him. Doubtless the journey of these travelers around our land will be one of the most fortuitous for our future of those undertaken by foreigners. It is a true saying that "the eye of the guest sees clearly," and where good will and knowledge keep company, there is hope for great accomplishments. In conversations the professor gave much information about his homeland, the world-famous America, and to us Icelanders much guidance; thus he conveyed that it would be more necessary to apply the national treasure or those funds we set aside in our relief fund to improve our roads and to strengthen communications in the country, and above all to link Iceland together with the larger world via one telegraph, rather than accumulate money in reserve, as this is the life's strength of every nation, but each hour had to take care of itself. He was of the opinion it would be natural to lay the telegraph cable from Iceland to the Shetlands, and that the French or British government should provide half of the funding as each nation had a large fishery off Iceland; and the state and national treasuries of, respectively, the Danes and Iceland the other half, after which Iceland would fund one line across the island. These and other observations of his for the amelioration of Iceland he communicated to us with enthusiasm.

Fiske sojourned in Akureyri, observed the town carefully, and met local officials.

Fiske's prescience and progressive bent aroused Icelanders' daring, their optimism and faith in the future. Newspapers touched on this time and again. Never is a good line too often quoted, and what is set in print is strengthened in human cognizance. Fiske also described to people the potential of hydropower and predicted the Icelanders would not need coal for energy in the future, as they could rely on the power of water. He foresaw Iceland as having a great economic future ahead.

A brief but educational sojourn in Akureyri assured that Fiske understood better the needs of the people and without doubt provided him further motivation to be of material assistance. He had become acquainted with advances in technology and longed to inculcate Icelanders in modern industrial methods, fully aware doing so would improve their living standard. Telecommunications were always uppermost in his thoughts. *Norðlingur* stated:

> Professor Willard Fiske is not only an excellent scientist, but he is also thoroughly familiar with all the tremendous advances and discoveries of recent times, and it was most informative speaking with him about them. The professor is writing dispatches from here

to one of the largest newspapers in America, the *Tribune* in New York; and Mr. Reeves is doing essentially the same for his own paper: it will be a pleasure to see these reports. Mr. Reeves is a good poet, and he recited a beautiful poem on Iceland at the banquet.— We hope to be able later to gladden readers of *Norðlingur* with a summary of the travel narrative of these excellent men.[10]

One may see economic elements were high in Fiske's thinking, not less than literature and history, and he saw rapidly that Icelanders were behind in technical development. He nurtured several ideas and obviously had some experience regarding the state of science and technology away from home. *Norðanfari* held forth reporting on Fiske's ideas for the connection of Iceland with the wider world, and what technology he envisioned for moving Icelanders ahead in this area. On 25 August 1879, under "Innovations," one could read:

> The editor of *Norðlingur* understands that Mr. Willard Fiske has in mind to provide Akureyri a telephone from the celebrated genius Edison; that line will run from the *Norðlingur* office out on Oddeyrin. Professor Fiske is acquainted with Edison, and we think it would be novel if Icelanders received a telephone line ahead of other European nations. We do not know that Edison's talking wire has come into the hands of the Europeans, except that a cousin of Edison's alone showed this wire in London in the spring. The wire carries the words of people unspeakably long distances, and it may be deemed among the most useful inventions of the last centuries.[11]

Fiske thought the Icelanders isolated and wanted to assure that they received a news link from Europe that might bring them nearer to the inhabited world and provide them enlightenment regarding whatever happened out there.

The aim of the Iceland trip was to see as much of the land as possible and to get to know the nation as well as might be done in a brief time. Accordingly the companions went far and wide, having lengthy and profitable conversations with the people.

Fiske wrote to his mother on 24 July that things were quite well with him and Reeves in a large and comfortable hotel in Akureyri and that they had inspected the library there, where he had seen that special shelves had been crafted for the gift books sent to the collection in 1874.

On Sunday evening, 27 July, was held a banquet where most of Akureyri's leading citizens came together in honor of Fiske and Reeves. Toasts were drunk and speeches held; the gathering endured well into the night and the Americans thought the Icelanders had an unbelievable capacity for enjoyment.[12]

After a fine banquet at Akureyri Fiske wanted to visit several locations about which he had read. The hosts could not tear themselves from their guests and a total of twelve men rode with them to Möðruvellir in Hörgárdal to enjoy the camaraderie as long as possible. Fiske was much impressed by the place and thought it exceedingly beautiful, as Möðruvellir stands on level country and has much cultivated land down by the river Hörgá. There he saw possibilities for profitable cultivation. Before the eye rose majestic mountains that diminished not at all the beauty of the place.[13] The church, which had burned to the ground in 1865, had been rebuilt, and Fiske found it quite pretty in its simple manner.[14] Work was proceeding on establishment of the Möðruvellir school, and of course the educator in Fiske had the greatest enthusiasm for it and its course of study, and thought it well prepared. There was to be a school of two winter terms of theoretical coursework, with an intervening summer term to teach practical agriculture. In the school the intention was to offer multi-faceted education to lads aged fourteen to twenty-four years, teaching languages, natural science, history, and geography as well as the mother tongue; and precisely that year a bill, subsequently adopted, lay before the Alþingi to broaden a curriculum in the direction of agriculture.[15] Jón Hjáltason[16] was named first principal and the school began operating 1 October 1880. In the year 1902 the school building at Möðruvellir burned to ashes. The school then relocated to Akureyri and took the name Akureyri Secondary School (later the Akureyri Gymnasium).[17] Fiske never forgot this educational establishment and maintained ever after good correspondence with the principal and faculty. He endeavored to send the school a great many packages of books. Among them were dictionaries and grammars, books on agriculture, literature in various languages, natural science, history, and other material that might prove useful for teaching. The school lads were very thankful to him and together wrote him a hand-some letter of appreciation on 2 March 1882: "It is unfortunate we cannot reward you as ought to be, yet it is as good as done that we shall never forget your benevolence and your name. It lives in our thankful hearts, and there you have raised yourself a monument, high-heaped on a hill of praise"—and underneath they signed the letter "Disciples of Möðruvellir School."[18]

Fiske, who had made it his life's work to facilitate people's education and the increase of their knowledge, was quick to understand that the effort might be pressed to make school available to as many Icelanders as possible. He also had great interest in how the education of women was organized in Iceland, and devoted particular study to it. The Cornell outlook that men and women ought to have equal access to the classroom had been inculcated in him.

Much was discussed and written this year of 1879 in newspapers about the educational possibilities for girls in Iceland. Girls' schools matured, establishment of a school for females in Húnavatnssýsla was under way, and it was only the space of a year until the school at Laugaland began functioning: instruction commenced there 1 October 1880. It was decided the girls would receive would receive free tuition, paying 70 aurar per diem for heat, light, and meals.[19] The goal of the course was household management. The textbook courses included, among others, Icelandic, domestic accounting, geography, world history, botany, and health; but also there were lessons in cookery, wool-working, and laundry as well as the sewing of clothes and other needlework.[20] At this time the Girls' School in Reykjavík was also likewise operating, and there it was possible to have instruction in diverse modes ranging from full-time attendance to a single hour; the least expensive unit cost ten aurar per hour of instruction.[21] Thus went the effort to meet lower-income female students halfway.

Fiske attentively followed the plan for strengthening and ameliorating education in Iceland, advising variously based on his experience in the United States.

Chapter 10

Akureyri Sojourn

Fiske and Reeves had a good time in Akureyri. There they encountered men of influence—a district governor, editors, printers, merchants, and booksellers. Akureyri was then scarcely more than a cluster of houses that snuggled on the sandbank and on the beach under the slope.[1] The residents numbered under five hundred. The companions had a look around town and visited several homes. Fiske also came to the district library and rejoiced to see books there he himself had sent in 1874, certain the gift had come to good use.

There were various happenings in this growing urban nucleus. The Progressive Society of Akureyri (Framfarafélag á Akureyri) was founded in 1879. The instigators were Eggert Laxdal, a shop manager, and Friðbjörn Steinsson, a bookbinder. They commenced a Sunday school for apprentices and others and took the initiative to introduce public lectures and the teaching of gymnastics. The Progressive Society was a newcomer to the place and accomplished much that was useful, though the organization endured only briefly.[2]

Skapti Jósepsson, who was an entrepreneur there, got to know the companions well in Akureyri. He was quite taken up with the visit and described Fiske thus in his newspaper *Norðlingur* on 11 August 1879:

Willard Fiske, the noted scholar and passionate friend of us Icelanders and our literature, he who has greatly augmented our libraries with the most useful books, came here late last month. No such scholar and equally great friend of ours has come since Konrad Maurer[3] visited us. Professor Fiske is in his fifties, with dark hair, and a rather full beard; the face is "Greek," and the noblest, and from his eyes shines equally intelligence with benevolence, for it is true he charms whomever he speaks with, as he is in all manner most affectionate. Never could one find a more knowledgeable person in our literature than he, as he has nearly two thousand volumes of Icelandic books and books on Iceland. He teaches Icelandic, Nordic languages and German at Cornell University in the town of Ithaca in New York State, three hundred English miles from New York City; he has of all men most propagated and made famous Icelandic literature in America. He stepped ashore at Húsavík and then went to Ásbyrgi and Dettifoss, and farther up along the river Jökulsá, where another falls in the river is unnamed. He christened the waterfall Vínland Falls, but we have chosen rather to know it by our friend, and to call it Willard Falls, and thus must all concur who have somewhat known or seen or spoken with the professor. It is also a venerable Icelandic custom to name after one's friends. Into Mývatn district came the professor and thence straight to Akureyri. Here he was received as a dear friend and accompanied onward to Eyjafjörður. He came to Hrafnagil, Munkaþverá and Laugaland and was, as expected, everywhere most well received. He thought much of the visit to the library of Jón the farmer at Munkaþverá, and thought the farmer most wise. The professor was very happy about the girls' school at Laugaland, but they place more importance on schools for females in America, as one man has given a couple of million krónur to Cornell University alone for women's education.[4]

Fiske was keen on education out in the rural areas but had, as stated earlier, no less an interest in human productivity and profit. He wanted to journey more widely throughout the district and have a better look around. Citizens of Akureyri rode with him into flower-covered areas of Eyjafjörður. He quickly saw that the farmers were a tough lot but likewise discerned that modern technology had not made inroads into the country, and Icelandic farmers were worse equipped with tools and machinery than those at home in New York State. He pointed this out to the farmers and urged them to acquire machines and thereby increase their productivity. *Norðlingur* reported on this foray:

> Mr. Fiske found Eggert Gunnarsson's land improvements at Staðarbygð exceptional, declaring such work a handsome example for imitation, and called this the most significant human endeavor he had seen in Iceland, but he thought the comment of an adviser to Iceland in this matter bad and ridiculous, as it [the comment] would be an enduring monument to the intelligence and benevolence of the adviser to us Icelanders and the progress of the country.[5]

In the remoteness of these Icelandic regions a guest such as Fiske was a welcome diversion. It was considered an honor to receive him as a visitor in one's home wherever he went, and everywhere people desired to display him goodness. In the towns the best of food and drink available was proffered and in the municipalities of Akureyri and Reykjavík were held for him magnificent banquets. Where he stayed he had over him down covers.[6] He often remarked later that sleeping under eiderdown had been incomparable. At this time Fiske had begun suffering much from arthritis. Eiderdown covers, light and warm, were thus memorable to him. Again from *Norðlingur*:

> The 26th of last month [July] a banquet for our guest was held by the town residents at the house of the host, L. Jensen. The editor of *Norðlingur* spoke first in honor of Professor Willard Fiske; Mr. Fiske answered that speech in excellent Icelandic and with great amity toward us Icelanders and our literature. Then Eggert Laxdal the shop manager gave a speech honoring the United States and the bookbinder Friðbjörn Steinsson for the professor's traveling companion, Mr. Arthur M. Reeves; and both were spoken of well. Mr. Reeves is a university graduate and a student of Mr. Fiske's, the gentlest in manner, highly gifted and well read. He edits a newspaper called *Palladium*, in the town of Richmond, Indiana; he is owner of a printing press and around forty printers work with him daily. Mr. Reeves speaks Icelandic remarkably well after so brief a sojourn here in Iceland, and he is most well disposed toward our land. He is taking photographs of various places of note on his journey. The entire banquet went off excellently and was most enjoyable.[7]

Glerárgljúfrid

Fiske was brought to
Glerá and the Glerá
gorge. He saw multiple
possibilities for the
use of hydropower.

Fiske was brought around Akureyri and introduced to people.
He noted that the place carried with it a neatness, and moreover a
comeliness. The potato gardens extended up the slope and flowers
in the house gardens tilted their petals in the face of the sun.

Fiske and Reeves were brought among other places to Glerá, and
Fiske was of the opinion that the water power was suitable for factories, and might be employed with minimal cost, "and he showed us
here as elsewhere the best support and assistance," according to one
Akureyri resident. People placed great hopes in his sense of enterprise
and his good counsel, especially economic advice. It would seem a
misunderstanding was evident that Fiske was during those years a
wealthy man or, so to speak, it was wishful thinking that so benevolent a man of action had funding up his sleeve to bring projects to
realization. Fiske felt the isolation of Iceland to be a great misfortune,
hampering the nation's development, and it became often mentioned
that he wanted to bring it in contact with the wider world. After the
sojourn he wrote articles in foreign newspapers about telegraphic

Oddeyrin in Akureyri. Fiske wanted to establish a telegraph between Iceland and other countries, and thought the office of the newspaper *Norðlingur* here a desirable connection.

communication between Iceland and Scotland, and papers in Iceland reported on his desire to bring about such a connection:

> This chieftain and excellent benefactor of Iceland appears still to have in mind to provide Akureyri a telephone connection that will lie from the house of the editor of *Norðlingur* and out on Oddeyri to the warehouses of the Grána Company. He thought it the most magnificent commercial edifice on Oddeyri and a fine foundation for independent Icelandic commerce. With shop manager Jakob Havsteen the professor and Mr. Reeves had great enjoyment seeing his egg and bird collection, which is excellent and unusual in its type here in Iceland.[8]

As came out in one of the passages from *Norðanfari* above, Reeves took photographs of various places of note and subsequently wrote narratives of his journey in his newspaper.[9] He was likewise industrious in his study of the Icelandic language, applying himself deeply to assimilate it as correctly as possible. He asked the indigenous population about literature and read considerably from it during the journey; and laid plans for the translation of *Piltur og stúlka* (Lad and Lass) by Jón Thoroddsen—but in the event he accomplished this effort many years later.[10]

Reeves was the life of the party wherever he and Fiske met people, and among other things he played guitar and sang.[11] He was a mainstay to Fiske, being twenty-five years younger, and more easily weathered wearing travels.

Chapter 11

Amusement and Erudition, Blended

The journey continued, southward now. Willard Fiske knew the œuvre of Jón Þorláksson, former pastor at Bægisá, and wanted to stop there. Séra Arnljótur Ólafsson, the priest at the place, was then at Reykjavík, as parliamentary business was not yet concluded.[1] His wife, Hólmfríður Þorsteinsdóttir, nonetheless received Fiske and Reeves with open arms. The women on the farms were dressed in Icelandic costume and the men were greatly enraptured by their elegance and by how well they wore their attire.[2] Around this time women had increasingly adorned themselves in Icelandic costume, cut mainly after the drawings of the painter Sigurður Guðmundsson; many thought it foreign ornamentation that had then become too showy on Icelandic women.[3] Like many foreign travelers, a tourist by the name of Samuel Edmond Waller, who was in Iceland some years earlier than Fiske, paid attention to people's attire, especially that of women. He was most moved by the cap with silver socket and long silken tassel, which he described well. He remarked that most women in Reykjavík wore the cap at least in church.[4]

To his great happiness Fiske saw various books from the fine gift of the millennial year 1874 in the house library at Bægisá: he had especially intended the works of Milton for the pastor there in memory of séra Jón Þorláksson's translation.[5] On the other hand he thought the library of séra Arnljótur most remarkable and astonishing in how well appointed it was with the best books and notable manuscripts. He recalled the library often later in his letters. This visit was recounted in *Norðlingur*:

He went to the unmarked grave of séra Jón Þorláksson at Bægisá, then went to see the falls there, where it is said séra Jón Þorláksson had composed many of his poems and had sat there with his work of translating *Paradise Lost*. Mr. Fiske has the greatest respect for Jón, which is why he also sent to séra Arnljótur at Iceland's millennium a splendid edition of Milton's *Paradise Lost*, embellished with all workmanship. All the reception at Bægisá was most magnificent and expressed as customary with splendor. From Bægisá the professor and Mr. Reeves intended for Hólar and so westward to Dalur and Hvammur, thence to Reykholt and Þingvellir, then to Reykjavík and afterward to Geysir and so with [S.S.] *Diana* around the island from the north.[6]

From Bægisá they continued through Öxnadalur and took in the imposing view of the mountains.[7] They gained Skagafjörður, and the surging Norðurá flowed beneath them.[8] After a nineteen-hour ride they came at last to Flugumýri, considerably relieved to find rest. The day after, Fiske wanted to have a look at the church and the grave of Jón Espólín.[9] To Fiske the landscape appeared magnificent, especially Mælifellshnjúkur, which was in its most beautiful

Bordeyri.   Utg Slgf Eymundsson, Reykjavik.

Fiske encountered Thor Jensen, a working lad, at Borðeyri and admired his knowledge of languages.

nuances of color. They accepted refreshment at Hofstaðir, an old church stead, and came to Hólar in Hjaltadalur around evening. Fiske scrutinized the cathedral, seeing the gravestones of past bishops in the floor and a picture of Bishop Guðbrandur Þorláksson on the left side of the altar. In the cathedral he also saw one of the copper engravings of Auguste Mayer, the French artist who had journeyed around Iceland with the expedition of Paul Gaimard somewhat earlier. He had not anticipated seeing the artwork of a foreigner in the church and was surprised and moved.[10] While Reeves went to Drangey with an accompanying Icelander, Fiske sojourned at Hólar and rested himself.[11] They met up afterward at Hofstaðir and continued the journey. Fiske benefited from coming to a location as historic as Þingeyrar.[12] There he went into the stone church built fifteen years previously.

There is a story that when Fiske came to Borðeyri on the way south, he called out in English to a young man struggling under a burden of water. He answered promptly in English. Fiske then spoke to him in German, and he answered without thinking in the same language. The young water bearer appears to have been Thor Jensen. Fiske remembered him for many years for his knowledge of languages and frequently sent him greetings from Florence.[13]

He came into the country of *Vatnsdæla saga*, *Laxdæla saga*, and *Egils saga*, and recognized the territory, being well read in the Icelandic family sagas; and stayed in Reykholt, where he bathed in Snorralaug. At this time it was thought scarcely possible to come nearer to Icelandic historiography. Fiske and Reeves sailed from Höfn to Akranes. Fiske was greatly impressed by the settlement risen there and enjoyed the hospitality of the inhabitants of Akranes as of other Icelanders whom he visited. Then they sailed across the bay to the capital.

On the journey Icelandic books were conveyed to Fiske as gifts in numerous places, something he obviously appreciated, endeavoring to express his grateful sentiments. All the letters that Fiske wrote and that have been preserved bear witness to his enthusiasm, his favorable opinion toward what met his eyes, and, not least, his faith that in Iceland most elements for living a positive and redemptive life might be strengthened. This was truly encouraging for Icelanders, and they themselves began to believe

The growing settlement on Akranes surprised Fiske. From Akranes he sailed to Reykjavík.

in the future. The clear atmosphere and all the wonders of nature enchanted him, and no less the kindness and hospitality of the inhabitants; he was astonished how many farmers spoke with him in English. He was most captivated, though, by how many books and manuscripts there were on the farms, believing they testified to the elevated cultural level of the populace. In several places he saw books he himself was responsible for sending to Iceland in 1874, and it may be surmised he was glad to see them put to use.

In some locales reading societies had been founded or small libraries compiled, and it caught Fiske's attention that there were works in foreign languages—Danish, Norwegian, and Swedish; also English and German. Icelanders thus read great authors in the original languages. It was now generally considered that formal schooling was for the good and prepared one for the future. People had come to believe that an individual, be he farmer, merchant, seaman, or laborer, would be more capable having had an intellectual no less than a physical formation. For Icelanders it was vital to learn several languages, if only to be able to use foreign books in various branches of learning. World history, geography, and natural sciences were considered desirable subjects, and everyone had to know arithmetic. But of course Icelandic language and literature had to occupy the principal place in the education of young people.[14] Fiske, in turn, was able to convey to the Icelanders what every field of study in the United States consisted of, and to speak about academic subjects at various levels of education.

Chapter 12

Reykjavík

In Reykjavík Fiske, pampered by the people, was indeed well received. He came to like well Reykjavík, a pretty town or rather a village with low-rising houses and plots marked off with stone fences. He wrote in his notebook that cultivation was more than he had anticipated. In the environs ordinary brushwood, wood cranesbill, and stepmotherbloom would be harvested, and he found himself invited to houses richly laden with flowers. He saw vegetable gardens

The populated center of Reykjavík seen from Hólavallahæð in 1847, some years before Fiske's trip (1879). Little must have changed in the intervening years.

beside the cottages planted with potatoes, cabbage, lettuce, radishes, turnips, and more for domestic consumption. He took note of the flowers in the windows and on the tables of homes.[1] Hens and cows sauntered undisturbed in town. Water-bearers perspired beneath their burdens and children played with stick and ball in the muddy streets. In the twilight shone the lamps that had been installed three years previously.[2] The harbor, where lay French frigates and German cargo vessels, was lively.

Various descriptions from this time show the village on the bay to appear quite rustic. In *Þjóðólfur* of this year there was a reminder of a notice from the chief of police regarding the ban on riding at speed through the streets of the town:

> Riding hard on the streets or driving loose horses, especially around street corners, could easily, without warning, become an irredeemable loss and accident, particularly for the crowds of children that at all times and too often unsupervised fill the streets of the town . . . Still, there is one bad habit that needs subduing, and we have before directed people's attention to it, and that is that people come hither from far-lying districts down into the town with cattle tied to horses' tails. This is animal abuse, a scandal in the eyes of

A calf reacts unfavorably to direction in Reykjavík. The city fathers endeavored to prevent residents from having animals in the streets.

foreigners and is practiced nowhere except here. People have to drive cattle or lead them with their own hands, and never tie them behind other animals.[3]

The office of the mayor of Reykjavík, moreover, announced in *Þjóðólfur* on 6 October 1879 that herewith all town residents were banned from slaughtering sheep or large animals any place save in stiles or behind houses, and not in public or in open spaces that turned into town streets. The announcement was signed E. Th. Jónassen.

Yet despite the country culture Reykjavík had become the picture of an urban area that compared to no other in Iceland. Fiske found a surprisingly considerable grandeur and the atmosphere of a capital in the city. There were parliament, the secondary school, the cathedral, and other institutions that made it the centerpiece for Icelanders. If there was commotion anywhere, it would be here.

In Reykjavík they met another student of Fiske's from former years, William H. Carpenter, who was contemplating a long sojourn in Iceland, not least in order to improve his knowledge of Icelandic. Carpenter was one of those students at Cornell in whom Fiske had kindled an enthusiasm for Icelandic language and literature.[4]

Fiske and Reeves found shelter with Mrs. Karólína Sívertsen.[5] She welcomed travelers to her house at 22 Hafnarstræti and had a knack for making her guests feel welcome. In Iceland there were few guest houses, and the companions chose unpretentious lodging in a home that had them nearer to the people than would a larger guest house. In some homes the lodging was excellent; in others, reprehensible from disorder and airlessness, as it said in *A Handbook for Travellers*, previously cited. To be certain, this book came out in a first edition somewhat before Fiske's journey to Iceland, but little must have changed in the intervening years. For all that, it was most usual that foreign travelers coming to Iceland lodged in churches, but there were isolated guest houses in settled areas, for example at Kolviðarhóll.

It is noteworthy that in this summer of 1879, lodging in the Þingvellir church was discontinued because the behavior of guests there was thought bad. Conditions improved markedly,

Ferðamenn.

Travelers set off on a journey from Reykjavík with pack horses, which were a common sight in the city.

coincidentally, during the second half of the nineteenth century for traveling inland. The first bridges worthy of the name were built, and roads laid.[6] It was, for example, a great improvement for travelers when a drivable road was laid to Þingvellir, which nonetheless had been a sought-after location for its history and beauty.

Fiske was keen on Icelandic national life and observed it in a social context. He quickly discovered that Icelanders were in general rather conservative, set in their ways, and minimally resourceful; and the administration of the country little enterprising in improvements. He paid Icelandic customs, dwellings, and apparel much heed, and was considerably occupied with food and drink offered him in Reykjavík homes, describing these in detail. He was of contrary opinion with most foreigners, who considered the Icelandic condition not merely picturesque but rather wretched; and he lauded to the highest all the accommodation he received. Repeatedly he brought forth words of praise for the trout, lamb chops, eggs, and rolled pancakes served him, and never tired of saying such good coffee was in no man's cup in America:[7] but in those years much chicory was imported into Iceland. As a matter of course Fiske requested the bill for accommodation, but few anticipated that he should reimburse for lodging or hospitality. Such a welcome guest was Fiske, who enjoyed the journey to the utmost possible, given he was not entirely in health. The gout struck him, confining him to bed two days while he was in Reykjavík.

Fiske met nearly all the men of importance in the country during his journey and received many invitations in Reykjavík. Séra Matthías Jochumsson lived then in Reykjavík and between Fiske and him there developed a fine friendship, two men of same spirit who enjoyed each other's company and conversation. They wrote each other often after Fiske departed from Iceland. Fiske was forever thinking of history and bygone times, as without consciousness of them there was in his opinion no connection with the present, let alone the future. He thus urged that the country's ruins and historic sites be researched, and with séra Matthías, one of Icleand's foremost composers of hymns ever,[8] he had a part in founding an archaeological society in Iceland to conserve the monuments of the country. Matthías recounted thus in his autobiography, *Chapters of Myself*:

> When my wife and I were in Reykjavík, we lived the entire time in a little house in Austurstræti, where Rafn Sigurðsson the shoemaker later built a larger one and where Thorvaldsen's Bazaar is now. With us lodged for a long while the archaeologist Sigurður Vigfússon, and we became great friends, to which my poems bear witness. It was in my house that the so-called "Archaeological Society" was founded. That was mostly at the urging of Iceland's great friend, Professor Willard Fiske. I invited him to my house with other major figures of the city, and then the society was founded.[9]

The intention of the society members was to search for monuments of antiquity, preserve them and increase knowledge of history and customs in Iceland. They had to see to it that artifacts were neither damaged nor lost when they were sought or excavated, and to assure their safekeeping. It cost two krónur per year or twenty-five krónur life membership for all to be in the society. In exchange, members received publications of the society and admission to its lectures. Fiske later sent the collection of the society many fine objects that will be described more nearly in succeeding chapters, for example from Egypt, where he subsequently traveled

Séra Matthías með Willard Fiske og tveimur amerískum ferðamönnum öðrum,
A. Reeves og W. Carpenter, 1879.

At home with Matthías Jochumsson. Seated are Fiske (left) and Matthías.
Standing are Reeves (left) and Carpenter.

several times and collected various artifacts. Séra Matthías said in *Þjóðólfur* of 27 November the same year:

> The primary reason for this society appears to have been that when Professor Fiske was in Þingvellir in the summer, he met the archaeologist Sigurður Vigfússon there. They talked among other things about the new and very much regrettable uncertainty about where the most sacred spot of the entire parliament site,[10] Lögberg, had been before, whether in that place it is now called, or where Dr. Guðbrandur and Dr. Kaalund have it, up on the lower cleft rim itself, directly over the parliament slope and the booths, north and up from Snorri's booth. They both spoke of the greatest need to research the site, which may still be called rather little known, preferably with scientific excavation. "Who is to pay?" Séra Matthías Jochumsson put it forward that there would then be an attempt to found a society, and offered his own house as a meeting place. Thus the first meeting of three came together before the society was fully up and running. It is also not necessary to dwell on the fact that to this end people have afforded this matter good and expeditious attention. But it is also in truth worth it, and in truth the time has been long coming that not we, but rather equally all who speak Icelandic, enter a society and fraternal pact to the end of redeeming, if possible, from total ruin, the painful minimal remnants yet able to be available and to be found of the ancient and sacred relics of our brief but beautiful antiquity.
>
> We cannot but be glad in the certain hope that the society has not been founded at an inopportune time, at least that the general public will support it in word and deed, and contribute many members.

Matthías informed Fiske in his subsequent letters that Sigurður Vigfússon had dug up three ancient booths, but the location of Lögberg remained uncertain.[11]

Long before Fiske's sojourn in Iceland, great stories went abroad of fiery upheavals in Mount Hekla; people thought tormented souls suffered punishment there for sinful behavior. Reportedly it was more typical to heat them in Hekla's fire, which erupted unceasingly with considerable noise. Many other strange stories were told about the land of fire and ice, all based on ignorance and fear of the unknown. Electric lighting was still far off in those days, and it was not odd that fantastic stories should circulate on dim winter evenings. This topic Fiske knew, and he longed considerably to go to Hekla; in August he undertook his voyage to the famous volcano. Carpenter accompanied him and wrote later that the journey had been memorable. They went first to Geysir in Haukadalur and stared in wonder at the gushing hot springs. Geysir did not erupt, though, even a little for them, but Strokkur performed as expected and went off beautifully. From there they proceeded to Hlíðarendi, Gunnar's homstead, and stayed in Fljótshlíð. Carpenter remarked how easily they had followed in the footsteps of Gunnar when he gazed out over the land and turned back.[12] They came also to Bergþórshvoll and refreshed in their memory the burning of Njáll. The journey went forward to Hekla with a stay on a farm at Hekla's foot. The journey also came to the ancient cultural site of Oddi[13] with a stay there. The life of Sæmundur fróði was uppermost in their thoughts at the site.

When the companions returned to Reykjavík, Fiske continued familiarizing himself with the lives and opinions of people there. Perennially he saw better that there were various lacunae whose curing could enrich people's knowledge.

Chapter 13

Ancient Cultural Values

As Willard Fiske was quite culture-minded, he wanted to undertake various kinds of improvements, and did not shirk from this endeavor. He knew as it was that the fewest of Icelanders had the opportunity to contemplate ancient artifacts of world culture,[1] and in 1897 he sent the Archaeological Society in Reykjavík many fine items. In his will he specified still other objects that arrived in Iceland in 1909, five years after his death. Matthías Þórðarson was then curator of the national museum. He received the objects, compiling a register of them; a quite detailed description accompanies each and every item. All of them are now preserved in the National Museum of Iceland and constitute a special section, the Fiske Collection.[2]

These were objects whose like were not in Iceland. The custom among ancient Egyptians was to place goods in graves, and often there were multitudinous and remarkable objects in the same burial. Among items Fiske sent to Iceland were early Egyptian objects from long before the Christian era. They rival objects that can be seen widely in international collections. There are, for example, papyrus leaves with Greek and Egyptian writing; furthermore, useful implements such as pitchers and flasks; ceramic mugs, vessels, and plates decorated in ancient patterns along with early lamps, some of which are not unlike cod-liver oil lamps. There are also delicate and beautiful pieces of jewelry out of precious metals or glass beads such as neck chains, bracelets, brooches, earrings, and fastening pins. Many of the pieces are ancient Egyptian amulets and statues that people commonly possessed and believed in.

In Fiske's gift were also figurines of mummies out of wood, beautifully painted but variously embellished: some are decorated with hieroglyphs, among them clay figurines of deities and animals. Also thought captivating was the painted wooden statue of Ptat-Sokar-Osiris. He was the god of creation, death, and the world to come, an amalgam of three deities: Ptat, creation god in Memphis; Sokar, a graveyard god, also from Memphis; and Osiris, god of the underworld, who was also fertility and harvest god. There are cat statues, the cat being sacred to the Egyptians, a companion and symbol of the goddess Bastet, originally from the Nile Delta. Feline graves were ubiquitous in Egypt, and bronze statues of the species were often placed in cat cemeteries as they, no more than people, were not deprived of worldly goods in their final repose. All this aroused attention in Iceland and transported people in their thoughts toward distant paths that very few would tread, thus offering insight into a remote and ancient civilization. The wonders of exotic culture were now come into Icelandic hands for safekeeping.

Of the younger items Fiske gave to the Icelanders, one might mention a chessboard from the seventeenth century that is possible to fit together. Upon opening it one can play backgammon on the side that turns in, and from the outside, there is on one hand a chessboard and on the other a millboard.[3]

The gift was accompanied by numerous pictures. These are copies of famous art works, examples of world art such as Botticelli's "Primavera" in a massive frame, something new in Iceland. There were also plates with holy images and a calligraphy parchment sheet with the "Ave Maria" and the "Credo" beautifully illustrated with illuminated initials and portraits of Mary, along with various articles from the early settlement of America.[4]

On the register of the National Museum of Iceland are now 144 items from the Fiske gift; it was his intention that Icelanders would receive insight, from what was to be preserved, into an ancient culture, older than the settlement of Iceland. One can imagine Icelanders rejoiced receiving these objects into the country.

Chapter 14

Showing Friends Respect

On 24 August 1879 a banquet was held in honor of the governor of Iceland, Hilmar Finsen.[1] This banquet was magnificent in every way, with little spared. The second important guest was Willard Fiske, which showed somewhat people's attitude toward him that he should be the second of the guests of honor. *Þjóðólfur* on 27 August 1879 said thus about the celebration:

The 24th of this month the members of the Alþingi held a truly magnificent banquet in the upper section of the hall (the great sleeping loft of the school). They wanted, at the close of the first term of the legislature,[2] to affirm our thanks—of parliament and nation—for [the governor's] both energetic and conscientious achievement in this first, sufficiently problematic period of the new millennium. The member for Barðstrandir, Provost E. Kúld,[3] who spoke in praise of him, emphasized especially the vigilance and application to duty of this governor, simultaneously with adroitness and dexterity, equally toward our parliament as toward king and administration. In his own reply the governor declared reciprocally his complete faith in the parliament. He recalled his arrival hence fourteen years previously; he had of course come unknown, and though not as a foreigner but as an Icelander and a native son. A significant chapter in our history had subsequently unfurled, not without conflict, but, he hoped, with great and good results, for which he wanted to thank, next to God, the parliament. "And what has passed," said the governor, "I turn hence from with glad faith in the future, not less in my work together with Parliament, if it is to be longer, but in the future of parliament and nation. In daily experience no one can forget that only through opposition and conflict will the truth be found and accepted."

The other guest of honor of this party was our new guest from North America, Professor Willard Fiske. After Dr. Gr[ímur] Thomsen[4] had spoken his praise, he answered in our language with a lengthy and brilliant discourse.

Fiske was rather a reserved fellow and not much for being in the spotlight. All the same he thought there was reason now to stand up and speak. He was better off for his experience and had seen his dream come true. For that he was thankful. Fiske believed the voyage had occasioned much good knowledge and wanted to make that understood. He was well-spoken, the discourse was impressive, and people listened attentively. The speech also appeared in *Þjóðólfur*:

> I have read nearly all the travel books that speak of Iceland; it was not a long time after I landed in Húsavík before I realized I was altogether unfamiliar with the country. Garðar Svavarsson[5] was not similarly unwitting as I when he came to Húsavík, as he had sailed "round about Iceland," as *Landnámabók* narrates, and as he had never read any travel books in English.
>
> Everything was new to me, because everything was other than I had imagined it, and much better than the wise traveling gentlemen had found it. Yet for me everything was also old; thus I found it not so unlike my native land. Sky and mountains, valleys and meadows, streams and flowers: all this was the same as in the New World. And when I went into the booths in Húsavík I saw farmers who were trading—the first Icelandic farmers I had seen—and it was impossible for me to imagine I was elsewhere than upcountry in America, among American farmers. It seemed to me I was seeing our old settlers, who journeyed from the old England to the new, and built there a mighty nation on the loam-free crags of this part of the country, which they called New England—where the same Gothic [sic] type, the same Norse nation is still to be found. It is often said Iceland is in reality part of the New World, and he speaks truer who calls Icelanders men of the New World, because they are that in nature and build. To my eyes Iceland can never, at least, be or become a foreign country.

As it seems to me I am a fellow countryman of yours, I have enjoyed seeing how much this part of America has progressed since the close of what a good friend of mine called "a waste of four hundred years." Everywhere the attentive traveler can discern signs of great progress—new schoolhouses, national highways, better dwellings, land improvements, more municipalities, faster communications among people and among regions of the country, and a new capability among the people. It is evident that a new era has begun here in Iceland, and it is notable how all is faring nicely when the nation is becoming totally free. He who is a little familiar with the matter knows the spiritual is moving forward just as the physical. Useful periodicals and useful books are multiplying year after year, and Icelandic literature is now in full flower. I do not think that in the history of Iceland or in the history of many larger countries there have been simultaneously four writers as good as these four, who "strike the silver string of splendored harp" on either side of Skerjafjörður;[6] and there have not been in the Saga Age, when many a fine skáld and many a storyteller went overseas, three Icelanders who have been more honored in foreign countries for Icelandic literature than those who are now acquiring for themselves honor and distinction in the three greatest universities of Britain. Rather I do not think, that in the Alþingi in the days when

> "there came Gissur and Geir,
> Gunnar and Heðinn and Njáll,"

have the addresses of these heroes been as manfully spoken—as it says in the sagas—as those I have heard with such pleasure in this house.

Yet there is something else that is eternally the same in Iceland, that does not alter with revolutions in government—that is the same in our day, long removed from the times when Ólafur pá dwelled in Laxardalur and Geirríður sat in his banquet hall and "spared not meat with men"—and that is Icelandic hospitality. From the day I stepped ashore, the fullest friendship has been shown me everywhere.—I cannot reciprocate kindness for kindness until all Icelanders dwelling between Húsavík and Reykjavík travel to America; for now I cannot otherwise but bid you and all my Icelandic friends to accept heartfelt thanks for everything. We travelers wish now that all should drink to Iceland's health, and we desire that the bond of friendship of the saga-rich island of the Western Hemisphere and the young continent thereof may always become stronger and stronger.[7]

Fiske's benevolence and positive outlook bore fruit, and Icelanders took on another, better perspective on life and the future. This land, which in the minds of many was unsparing and unlikely to afford people a decent life, took on a new feeling. A cultured man from abroad saw numerous possibilities for an amelioration of life; "clear is the eye of the guest."[8] Instinctively, men straightened up and raised their heads high.

Chapter 15

Circumnavigation

After a brief sojourn in Reykjavík, Fiske and Reeves wanted to see the sea villages, now that they had seen something of the interior districts and gotten to know the farmers, life in the populated areas of Reykjavík and Akureyri, and various natural phenomena.[1] They took passage with the coastwise steamer *Diana* when she left Reykjavík 27 August 1879 and sailed around the island, along the southern strands and eastward afterward along the coast. The journey took ten days, and for most of it the heavens were a vault of cloudless blue over the travelers' heads. The companions were most gratified.

Autumn was approaching, and many people had business in Reykjavík. Schoolboys congregated aboard to tread the thorn-strewn path of education in the Learned School,[2] then the sole school for Icelanders that offered higher education aside from the seminary and the medical school, which had their specialized training. Also aboard were several members of the Alþingi; and moreover travelers between specific locations, some of whom were going to Reykjavík.

Fiske gave his mother a good account of the journey in a letter dated 10 September. Along the way he had occasion to get to know people from many corners of the country and from many occupations. He made a special effort in this, and that he could speak some Icelandic facilitated exchanges. The people on board were attentive and wanted to hear his perspectives on one matter or another. Schoolboys admired him and wanted to be in his

On Fiske's journey with SS *Diana* there was a tailor aboard offering services in every port. Advertisement from the clothing shop of F. A. Löve.

vicinity on the ship and make their acquaintance. Fiske, who was pleased and kind, utilized the occasion to tell them of schools and student life in America, and equally manifested curiosity regarding student society in Iceland. He had great faith in the possibilities in Iceland, not least in cultural matters, and unsparingly encouraged the school lads. The boys, humble, listened and were moved. Here spoke a new voice; they were more accustomed to hearing of the wretchedness and hopelessness of this land. Fiske paid no mind to status and spoke equally with high and low. There was the commencement of his devotion to the Learned School in Reykjavík and his acquaintance with the students. Correspondence between many of them and Fiske continued as long as he lived. Some of them proved of consequence later in assisting him with collecting Icelandic books.

Veils of fog were on the mountain slopes along the eastern strand, making the landscape still more mysterious. At Eskifjörður Fiske went ashore and met an old friend, Jón Ólafsson, who had visited his mother and him in Ithaca.[3] They had corresponded somewhat over time. Jón was now editor of *Skuld*, a newspaper published in Eskifjörður. Their reunion was felicitous, with much to recollect. That Jón and his wife had just lost their young child overshadowed the gladness. The sorrow was heavy, but the men nonetheless had a good time together.[4]

S.S. *Diana* sailed north along the coast and onward past Grímsey. The companions longed to land, but the opportunity was not availing. They had to content themselves with gazing at the island, but Fiske inquired much about human habitation there.[5] Then a spark quickened that lived in him thereafter. He was filled with wonder and moved when he heard of the inhabitants' energy and enterprise, and not least did it stay in his memory that the Grímsey islanders were said to be good chess players. Fiske was determined to acquire more knowledge of Grímsey and those who dwelt on the island. In his letter of 3 September to his mother he states:

> We had splendid views of Hecla and the great glacial mountains on the southern coast and of all the Eastern fjords, and hope that we shall enjoy the scenery and the N.W. and W. as much. We have also seen some fine waterfalls along the shore. The weather was so good that the Captain sailed between the Vestmanna islands and the coast so that we saw the beautiful insular group with great distinctness—a rare sight as fogs so generally prevail in this quarter.[6]

SS *Diana* sailed past Grímsey. Fiske longed to come ashore there, which proved impossible. He later took the island under his wing.

Fiske was interested in knowing the names of the school lads on the same journey as he and Reeves were. He asked one of the passengers, Jón Finnsson, to write down their names. According to Jón, himself a student on his way to Reykjavík, the following schoolboys and students beside himself were aboard S.S. *Diana* on this coastwise journey:

> From Seyðisfjörður were: Jón Magnússon from Skorrastaður, Halldór Bjarnarson from Eyjólfsstaðir, Þorsteinn Bergsson from Vallanes.
>
> From Vopnafjörður were: Þorsteinn Halldórsson from Hof and Arnór Þorláksson from the same place.
>
> From Húsavík was Hannes Þorsteinsson out of Þistilfjörður.
>
> From Akureyri: Jóhannes Sigfússon from Gnúpufell and Einar Benediktsson from Hjeðinshöfði.
>
> From Sauðárkrókur were: Jón Jakobsson from Miklabær, Björn Ólafsson from Ás in Hegranes and Stefán Stefánsson from Heiður in Skagafjörður.
>
> From Skagaströnd: Arnór Árnason from Hafnir, Sigurður Árnason said to be from the same place and Árni Bjarnason from the same town.
>
> From Ísafjörður: Ólafur Einarsson from Hvítanes, Magnús Ásgeirsson from Kleyfar, Kristján Riis of Ísafjörður, Adolph Nicolaisen from Ísafjörður, Jón Arason out of Reykhólasveit, Magnús Magnússon of Ísafjörður and Sigurður Jónsson of Ísafjörður.
>
> From Flateyri: Páll Stephansen from the same place, Halldór Torfason of Flatey and Ólafur Stephensen from Holt.
>
> From Vatney was Rútur Magnússon.
>
> From Stykkishólmur were: Jón Stefánsson of Grundarfjörður and Brynjólfur Kúld of Stykkishólmur.[7]

All told there were twenty-eight strong and happy men who intended for themselves a large role in life.

A young man, Jón Egilsen from Kornsá, was likewise on board, and stood at a distance, listening. He disembarked at Skagaströnd and preserved memories of the cosmopolitan Willard Fiske. Jón received pictures sent by Fiske during autumn and thanked him

They sailed past Drangey in Skagafjörður. Reeves had earlier visited Drangey while Fiske waited at Hólar, the former northern episcopal seat in Hjaltadalur.

kindly for them.[8] It is notable that much later, in 1898, Jón sent Fiske a detailed letter about his life's course. He resided then at Blönduós. It was his sad fate that he was not allowed to pursue his education, the only thing he had truly longed for.[9]

In the letter Fiske wrote to his mother from Akureyri on 3 September he says:

> Here we are back at our old Akureyri again, on our trip around the island, and are being warmly greeted by the friends we made at our former visit a month ago. We have thus far had delightful sunny weather on the south and east coasts, but to-day it is a little colder, and the mountain tops are covered with new-fallen snow. The Diana, on board which we are, is a very comfortable little boat, with excellent fare, but is inclined to roll a good deal in a heavy sea.[10]

And again he wrote to her, after the memorable journey, in a letter dated 10 September:

> This morning we came back safe and sound from our trip around the island, after a most delightful voyage. We had uniformly pleasant

weather down to the last two days, when mist and rain set in. This deprived us of a view of the Snæfellsjökull, one of the finest mountains of the world [. . .] The table on the steamer is good and we had seats at the Captain's table. We got fresh vegetables, salads etc. at each port, and at every two or three ports a fresh beef was slaughtered for us. Besides this we had turbot—a most delicious fish caught everywhere here in Iceland—halibut, eels, sole, and a kind of clam, which is better, I think, than ours.[11]

The newspaper *Ísafold* said of the journey on 26 September 1879:

S.S. *Diana* came here [to Reykjavík] on her latest coastwise sailing the eleventh of this month. With her came many school lads, the North Americans university instructor Fiske and Reeves, and various others. [*Diana*] left again the twentieth of this month for

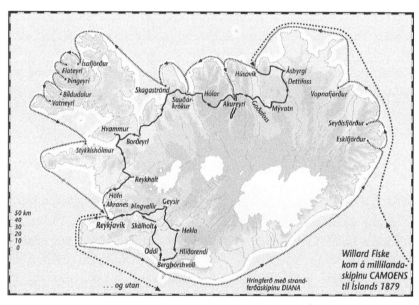

Fiske's routes by land and sea. Map by Guðmundur Ó. Ingvarsson. The map indicates the approach of S.S. *Camoens*, coming from Scotland, off the southeast coast of Iceland, and thence north and northwest to Húsavík, the intended port of call. The map also marks Fiske's subsequent counterclockwise circumnavigation of the island in the coastwise passenger vessel S.S. *Diana*, commencing and terminating in Reykjavík.

Seyðisfjörður and from there to Denmark. The skipper himself acknowledges the ship is too small for coastwise sailing, seeing she has too little berth space for second-class passengers.

The circumnavigation terminated in Reykjavík; it may be said the traveling companions had managed to see much of land and strand in their Icelandic summer journey.

Chapter 16

Education

Upon arriving in Reykjavík they stepped ashore on Fischer's Wharf and were conveyed into town. Many sought to give shelter to the companions, and they accepted lodging with Páll Melsteð in the building of the Women's School. Þóra, Páll's wife, had through unstinting perseverance established a women's school on the Danish model in Reykjavík a few years previously. It was to Þóra Melsteð's great advantage to receive Fiske in her house and be able to discuss with him education and girls' attendance at school, her great passion. She had a difficult time with her school, and many believed there to be no reason to educate women in word and deed. Hitherto there had not been reason women should have access to formal schooling, and why ought there to be a change in that?

Þóra and Fiske sat long hours together and discussed the position of girls in the educational system. Þóra was amazed how advanced Cornell University was in this respect, and this became an incentive for her for the running of her own school. When Fiske had left his lodging and quit the country, the students Bogi Melsteð (brother of Páll) and Ólafur Davíðsson, later a folklorist, were permitted to live in the room, and considered it an honor.[1]

As stated earlier, Fiske "adopted" the Learned School in Reykjavík, and quickly took action to broaden the students' opportunities to acquire knowledge by sending books. In his letter collection are many missives from two rectors of the school, Jón Þorkelsson (1822–1904) and Björn M. Ólsen; and also from many students. The first letter came in the autumn of 1879; instructors and instructed wrote him a collective word of thanks dated 28 November 1879 that read:

Dear Professor Willard Fiske. With the mail ship just arrived we have received the books and newspapers you have sent to our library and reading room, and we therefore take the occasion with this letter to bring before you our most respectful appreciation.

This gift of yours will ever be for us a precious sign how much you, a foreigner, esteem us; and not only us, but also our native land and nation. We believe we shall not be better able to signify to you our gratitude than to assure you we shall to the best of our ability utilize your gift to the utmost to familiarize ourselves with the culture and customs of your great native land and of the other civilized nations of the world.

We know of a certainty that it will gladden you to hear we have certain hope this generous gift will lead to the establishment of a reading room here in the school.

Dear Professor!

Wherever you are and wherever you travel, may you be completely assured that the best wishes of Icelandic hearts accompany you.[2]

Under the letter appeared 105 names. It was especially beautifully copied and delicately embellished. The letter pleased Fiske, and he knew then his gifts had found their mark. He was persuaded they would bear fruit in the long run. It can be imagined that Fiske's gift books must have been a pure windfall for impoverished school lads, and they wrote him another letter on 27 June 1893:

In March 1880 Ithaca, our school's reading society, was established and dedicated to you, a foreigner, the initiator of this. Since then you have shown our society more good will than any other person through sending it a great quantity of gifts, both funds and books, journals and newspapers; and most to thank you for is that the society has flourished and thrived.[3]

The gifts from Fiske were crucial for the library and soon made for a handsome and popular collection in the school. In the reading room hung a framed portrait of Fiske, reminding students daily of the society's generous benefactor. Other pictures from abroad, which Fiske sent to the school, adorned the walls and whetted the longing of the school lads to go abroad and see the world. Letters of appreciation from the school were many, with many signatories. Long afterward he received reports on how the reading room was faring. Thus in a letter of 13 May 1895:

> The undersigned executive committee of the reading society "Ithaca" finds itself called upon to address you and attest to you in the name and authority of the society our innermost and most respectful thanks for all the great benevolence you have shown our society both formerly and latterly and continued to show perpetually through gifts of instructive and entertaining books and newspapers.
>
> We can say in truth that your newspaper and book gifts have opened for us a new world, brought us news and knowledge from the great nations of the world, provided us with opportunities to become acquainted with their life and cultures; and that is therefore more precious to us, who live here on a remote island, far from the educated world, and thus have, as is natural, a restricted horizon.
>
> As we know how much importance you attach to our collection, we would like briefly to report to you on its state. It now has around 1500 volumes and therein numerous and good books unavailable in other libraries here, especially fine-art material. The collection holds most of the newspapers and periodicals published here in Iceland, and in addition several Danish weeklies and periodicals. Newspapers and periodicals are always on display on vacation days in the reading room we have in the library of the Latin School. The reading room is generally very well visited, and especially quite crowded the days after arrival of the mail packet, with newspapers and books from you. Books of the society that are not for use in the reading room are kept in another room in the library and lent out to society members. In all during the past year there have been 1876 circulations. Society finances are overall in good shape, and entirely debt-free. Contributions from Society members—instructors and students—totaled 172 krónur in the past year; income 221.80 krónur. Annual income is reserved both for purchase of books and

newspapers and for binding. For purchasing books and papers was set aside 142.37 krónur, and for bookbinding 63.60 krónur.

As a sign of our affection, respect and gratitude we would like to send herewith to you a picture of the Society members. We have neither gold nor treasure to offer, and know likewise you would not desire such. We cannot offer you other than our most amicable thanks, which we convey to you from pure and unalloyed hearts.[4]

The final letter from the school to Fiske was from 29 May 1904, four months before he died. Twenty-five years had passed since he had aroused the enthusiasm of the school community with beneficence toward the school and concern for the state of education in Iceland. It is clear that people aligned themselves well to how Fiske's generosity and good will had positive influence in a progressive direction, and how this had supported the establishment of schools on a broad basis. In the letter it further stated, among other matters:

It was not enough that your encouragement, dear Professor, came to launch our Ithaca society; you have during this past time shown it the greatest support with valuable gifts of books, periodicals and newspapers every year, and it has been no small reinforcement for the society to acquire so many good books and have the choice of periodicals and papers to keep up with events much better than before, when there was much less regarding this and it was scarcely so significant.

This measure of your consideration, which has never ceased, is a telling witness of how much you care for our society and had it always in mind. And to remember this and pronounce before you our heartfelt thanks it is for us all the more poignant as we also feel and appreciate fully well that you have in another so great way shown that you are in every respect a true friend of our land and nation, that you love Iceland, have with passion fostered its literature, and with each and every opportunity have upheld the country's honor and written so many warm words of generosity on our behalf. We convey our thanks to you with full knowledge that there are many more than we who bless the hour you set foot on this land.

Gratitude and a grateful disposition are all we can convey for your generosity, dear Professor. That we have confirmed to you here, as we bid the Lord from the heart to render successful all the days of your life yet to come.[5]

With young but well-formed hands, Guðbrandur Jónsson, president of the reading society, and Pétur Halldórsson, secretary, signed. The background of the reading society is that when the school moved from Bessastaðir to Reykjavík in 1846, the students and several instructors founded a reading society there, but apathy and lack of interest had afflicted the school's students and faculty, and it appeared the society would fold. The society declined precipitously before 1880 and in that year only a third of the students were members.[6] This Willard Fiske had heard when he sojourned in Iceland. He strenuously urged the school's teachers to remedy the matter, and it was done. All the instructors were agreed it would be necessary to set the society on its feet, and it was determined that all permanent teachers and all students should be members. The instructor Björn Ólsen compiled a draft of by-laws based on instructions from Fiske, and in the second paragraph it states: "The goal of the society is to strengthen the culture and knowledge of members, especially to increase their familiarity with the cultural circumstances of other living nations."[7] In the report of the school it is stipulated the name of the society be changed, and the new name set in honor of Professor Fiske, who has a home in Ithaca in the United States in North America. He might be called the society's founder in this new light as he had also supported it by donating a considerable number of books and newspapers. Halldór Hermannsson comments:

> One may find in the school reports, after Bjarni[8] became headmaster, lists of the books this reading society, or students' library, as it was usually called, purchased yearly. It was chiefly modern literature suitable for schoolboys and educators. But with time the society slackened, and in 1879 there were only thirty-four members out of one hundred boys who then were in school, and it came to the point that it would be abolished. Precisely that summer a good guest came to Iceland, Willard Fiske from Cornell University in Ithaca. He knew how to deal with the situation, and based on his contributions a new reading society was established. All schoolboys would be

members; also all the instructors and likewise adjunct instructors, if they wished. Thus the Ithaca Reading Society, which all know and it is not necessary to describe here, came under way. . . . Here is an institution that has been for the use and happiness of all the youthful scholars of the school these many decades it has existed. Fiske was the man most supportive of this society while he lived, yearly sending books, papers and periodicals; and we thus could follow what was happening out in the world. A board of students managed the direction of the society, and I remember that I had been its chairman the last year I was in school.[9]

Acquisitions varied considerably in the students' book society, from five to fifty books per year.

In the Reykjavík School there was a school library, Bibliotheca Scholae Reykjavicensis (BSR). Beneath that collection was raised in 1866 a building through a gift from an Englishman, Kelsall by name.[10] The reading society went into that building and gradually the society library assumed the name Ithaca, and then the building, which had long housed the books of both the school library and the society. Vilhjálmur Þ. Gíslason stated about Ithaca in an anniversary article that common usage in the school had identified the entire school library with the Ithaca name, or rather everything in the library building, although in reality it was only the library and the students' reading society that were named Ithaca after being resurrected in 1880 through the instigation of Fiske. The name Ithaca was then chosen in recognition of the new society's benefactor. A five-member board directed affairs of the reading society—four students and one instructor.[11]

In Fiske's book gifts during the years 1880–1904 were all told 534 books, 505 periodicals and papers—i.e. unbroken annual volumes—and 1063 individual issues. He sent good and useful books, and his gifts of journals were no less in value. Among them were French, German, English, and Italian papers and periodicals. When Fiske passed on the society lacked the resources to sustain purchases of foreign periodicals at such a level.

Fiske was quite satisfied with the progress of matters and proposed that the collection also be open to foreign travelers over the summer, as many of the books were in foreign languages and could assist them in getting to know the Icelandic land and nation.[12] Little was thought at this time about educating foreign visitors regarding Icelandic circumstances, so the idea was not so bad. In the spirit of education Fiske also sent numerous copies of famous pictures, which he knew would be well received.[13] These were pictures from Greco-Roman antiquity, likenesses of deities from foreign civilizations, and renowned leading figures in world history. In his last years Fiske also sent many chessboards and pieces, with the result that a chess club was set up in the school. His gifts amounted to 2200–2300 in number and were an important component of the reading society's holdings at the time the gifts were arriving.

The students did not, however, sit perpetually at their books, and the teachers complained bitterly over the boys' conduct in letters to Fiske. Björn M. Ólsen wanted to institute order, punctuality, and industriousness, but the schoolboys were sorely dissatisfied and rejected this punitive regimen over them. They especially endeavored to retaliate against Björn because it was easy to stir him to anger, and that incited them. Often there were quarrels and disturbances in the school, and so things went for several years. After Björn was appointed principal of the Learned School he wrote Fiske in 1904:

> As you may have heard or seen in Icelandic newspapers, this winter has not been good for the school. Certain agitators among the schoolboys have caused various disturbances, and as a consequence a great many have been expelled from school or have quit. This has been very uncomfortable for me and caused me many worries.[14]

One of the greatest troublemakers was Jón Þorkelsson (1859–1924), later a scholar in Icelandic literature and national archivist, who had been sent to school because he was lame and thought not likely to take on physical labor that might be useful.[15] Jón later made a significant contribution to the acquisitions in Fiske's Icelandic collection. Einar Benediktsson was also a participant in the mischief. So great a trial Björn had of the boys' aggressive demeanor that he blamed them for his worsening health and was driven from the post in 1904.[16]

Fiske thought much of it that many poets in the school had started writing and worked with zeal. The most prominent school poets were Þorsteinn Erlingsson, Ólafur Davíðsson, Jón Þorkelsson, Valtýr Guðmundsson, Einar Hjörleifsson, and Einar Benediktsson, who was already determined to become a great poet. All were subsequently to venture abroad and win fame. Fiske followed their development as poets carefully. He also had the opportunity to get to know some of the established Icelandic poets, such as Steingrímur Thorsteinsson and Benedikt Gröndal, quite well.

The autumn Fiske was in Iceland and became acquainted somewhat with school lads there were over one hundred studying in the Learned School, divided into six grades. Björn M. Ólsen had general supervision of the boys outside class hours; the teacher Sigurður Sigurðsson[17] was detailed to assist him and took part in the supervision with him. This was thought substantial work as the boys were unruly and scheming and respected neither rules nor rod. Things improved with a supervisor from the ranks of the disciples; he was named "inspector scholae." First to discharge that office was Hannes Þórður Hafstein, son of Pétur Havstein, deputy governor at Möðruvellir in Hörgárdalur. Hannes, later a poet and the country's first prime minister, was then in the sixth form.[18] Many of those who graduated from the school sailed to Copenhagen for further study. Some attained their objectives; others did not and retreated from study.

When Fiske came to Iceland school issues were being pursued in the country, and much written about them in the papers. Out of the Women's School in Reykjavík issued girls who were very accomplished in both word and deed, and in the winter of 1879–80 there were twenty-three young women students there. Women were very energetic around these times: as they likewise had the location for the wool-working school in Reykjavík, they joined it with the Sunday school where writing, arithmetic, Danish and other useful subjects were taught. They had received a four-pound stipend from supporters in London,[19] and the school was especially intended for poor girls. In the seminary there were in this year (1879–80) twelve students of theology, and six students in the medical school, according to the newspaper *Ísafold*.[20]

Sunset in Reykjavík. Fiske came to Iceland in high summer, making especially good use of the added daylight.

It was not without purpose for those who stood behind education in Iceland to receive an optimistic and enthusiastic man from out in the world on a visit, and it strengthened the general belief that book learning would be, despite everything, in the picture. The educator from Ithaca encouraged people in various ways and impressed upon people that education would be a foundation of progress and well-being. Fiske had an absolute faith that education of young people, not least women, might set Iceland on a successful course.

Chapter 17
Departure

That second of August was a national holiday in recognition of the fifth anniversary of the constitution, giving the traveling companions an opportunity to take part in the celebrations in Reykjavík. Most members of the Alþingi and a large number of city residents came, along with people from surrounding districts. A poem by Steingrímur Thorsteinsson, which he had composed and had had printed for the day, was sung. Steingrímur spoke as well on behalf of Jón Sigurðsson in Copenhagen,[1] and the speech was well received. The work and policy of the Alþingi were also noted and the health of the assembly toasted with special appreciation for its undertakings in cultural empowerment and national employment.[2] Matthías Jochumsson spoke on behalf of Iceland, exposing a wish that it would become a custom in the country to celebrate the national holiday (of constitutional reform) on the second of August 1874 with meetings or festivities, at least every other summer or every session year.[3] Fiske thought this a notable event and interesting to be present. He utilized the time in Reykjavík to meet people of interest and was often invited to afternoon coffee or supper with denizens of the city.[4]

Yet soon it came about that the companions would be leaving the country, and on 11 October 1879, just before the departure, a farewell banquet in honor of Fiske and his companions was held in "Glasgow," the finest house in the city (although it was to burn in 1903).[5] Nothing was spared to make the celebration the most magnificent and memorable. The banquet hall was handsomely

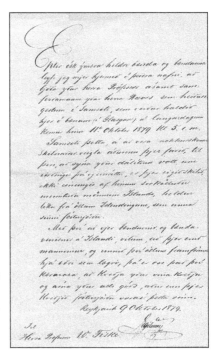

Prospectus for the
dinner in honor of
Fiske and Reeves
held in Glasgow
House, Reykjavík,
11 October 1879.

decorated and candles placed throughout, so the space was amply
bright. Egill Egilsson was responsible for the banquet, which was
well prepared, and fewer than wanted were able to attend. It was
evident that people from most social strata were able to see and
greet this cherished guest, though farmers especially, whom Fiske
got to know on his journeys, were numerous at the banquet. Food
and drink were of the finer sort and the tables groaned under the
delicacies. The banquet was thought quite a success as much was
done by way of entertainment—for example, songs, a brass fanfare,
toasts and conversation. In *Þjóðólfur* of 15 October 1879 appeared
the following description of the event:

> Farewell dinner. Mr. Egilsson was responsible for a farewell banquet
> held the eleventh of this month for Professor W. Fiske and his associ-
> ates, though but a few of those who had wanted found a place there.
> Egilsson had, with the brilliance for which he is known, prepared
> everything and seen to it that men of most classes, but especially
> farmers, were able there to see and greet our cherished and renowned

guest and object of affection, the American professor. The party went forward superlatively, as people were entertained variously with songs from the harp society, a brass fanfare or toasts and talk. "Glasgow" [the hall] was festively illuminated for the evening with eighty to ninety lights.On behalf of the guests Árni the national treasurer spoke a handsome address, and Professor Fiske replied with some cordial salutory and intercessory words for land and nation. Various other toasts were drunk; on behalf of Mr. Paterson Dr. Hjaltalín spoke with recognition for his energy and cordiality with his pressing work with sulphur, and he, speaking in Icelandic, drank to the health of Iceland. Egilsson spoke on behalf of the farmers, Þorl[ákur] Ó. Johnson on behalf of America, Páll Melsteð to the health of the ladies, síra Matthías Jochumsson on behalf of the ladies of America, and so forth. Reeves and Carpenter, the professor's companions, also entertained well in their turn with American student songs. But as the gist of what was said during the event, we produce here the poem that was sung on behalf of the guests:

> Now gone is the far-faring fowl from ground autumnal,
> Only as devoted friends soon part with us;
> Welcome thus hither on a visit to Icelanders,
> Here you encounter cordiality's intent.
> Hail, our dear Fiske! With companions twain,
> Felicitous guests from the New-West World.
>
> You came and sojourned in our snow-crowned land
> In the gold-chased décor of comely sky,
> When high summer rejoices in clearest light,
> Thus you encountered the ice-floe bride.
> You saw most imposing sights of our fatherland.
> You saw of the people the worst and the best.
>
> By you is the nation's life as fulsome oak
> With thousands of branches in blossom,
> By us a dwarf birch weak in waxing,
> Thus hindrances harm its advancement;
> Otherwise is earth's hollow, than heaven's reach,
> Though it have a small stretch of green.

Distress, nonetheless, never defeats the mind when lofty,
We seek to live, never merely subsist;
He thus may opt, diminished in destitution,
To love the noble and great;
To free men from a free land
We pronounce our gratitude and affection.

To a land where, honor-rich, the light of freedom shines,
There neither king nor thrall is found,
There achievement is nobility and enterprise praise,
That uniquely make the nations strong,
Bear you now greeting across a swelling sea,
Oh send us back much living seed!

As Leifur the Lucky we were happy this evening,
Then came he from Vínland of old;
Now sings and toasts the welcoming host,
For found is the disappeared land:
"The Vínland of old is a new land of friendship"
From Icelandic lips shall often resound.[6]

Thus wrote Steingrímur Thorsteinsson, and his poem was praised as were most he composed in those days.

Fiske expressed his thanks with well-crafted praise of the inhabitants and, not least, of the significance of the friendship. In the discourse could be discerned the sorrow of parting. Professor Fiske's talk appeared in the same issue of *Þjóðólfur*, and went thus:

Good gentlemen and friends!

"Oft sorrowful breast under sightly raiment," says the Icelandic proverb, and this evening we know, my fellow countryman[7] and I, that this saying is the truth. In Egypt in ancient times—everyone has read the story—it was a custom, when a banquet or other pleasant gathering was held, to have a skeleton sit at table to remind that life is not just pleasure, that man is mortal, that finally there comes the hour of departure, which is quite other than happy. It is not necessary to show us, your guests, this skeleton of the ancient Egyptians this evening. Unfortunately, we are fully cognizant that the unpleasant hour of leaving is quickly arriving. We know well we have to leave this saga-rich, this instructive land, where we have found—in the north and east no less than the south and west—so many good friends, where we have seen so many surpassingly beautiful days.

I have hitherto never comprehended the words *Njála* and the poet have the champion say when he stands ready by the sea for journey. Yet now, were it possible, I would turn back, as he turned back, and say, as he said:

"Here I would stay all the days of my life that God sends me."

There is something, though little it be, that an individual can accomplish, and if God grant me health and strength, I intend to work from now on for the progress of Iceland in as large a manner as in my power. From my memory will never pass Iceland and the Icelandic nation.

And now we proclaim a fond farewell. You have our thanks for all your and your countrymen's hospitality and kindness! May the God of your fathers, the God of the nations, bless you and Iceland always!

It is safe to assert that Fiske moved the feelings of those present, and these words doubtless dwelled long in people's minds afterward. It is likely that all the letters he received later from Icelanders, letters from friends but also those with requests for all kinds of aid and assistance, had their roots in this address. The speech was also published in *Norð-lingur* on 12 December 1879, as the people of the Northern Quarter had somewhat to do with Fiske. Skapti Jósepsson, the editor, also wrote him a letter on 7 November, saying:

Unforgettable to all of us who met you are the hours together, and it is therefore natural we envy our brothers to the south for having been able to enjoy your company so long; and we thus nurture the hope that we have had some small part of your beautiful, affec-tionate parting address, dear sir! And that you have promised never to forget Iceland, distance notwithstanding. People have full and firm faith in you, at least in your promise, and hardly could *any Icelander* be as popular as you, though a foreigner.

Precisely the same sentiment as appeared in the address was to be found in Fiske's letter to Jón Sigurðsson many years before, when he wrote: "Believe me, that at all times and in every way I am ready to

Letter from Fiske to Jón Sigurðsson forseti on 25 August 1852, in which he writes: "Believe me, that at all times and in every way I am ready to help the island in any manner which may lay [sic] within the reach of my ability or influence. God bless and prosper it."

help the island in any manner which may lay [*sic*] within the reach of my ability or influence. God bless and prosper it."[8]

Fiske received more poems of praise on his departure. Matthías Jochumsson, editor of *Þjóðólfur*, published his poem on the departure of Fiske on 31 October 1879, calling the poem "On the Leavetaking from Iceland of Professor W. Fiske, 18 October 1879":

> Nymphs of land and lake,
> Lead the honored guest!
> Many-versed spirits,
> Of weather give the best!
> Snowland's Athena, Saga wise,
> Lead thine Odysseus
> Back to Ithaca!
>
> Odysseus laid waste
> Ilion's holy burg
> Over the ages led
> Misfortune, evil, sorrow,
> Fire at last stuck in the land,
> Triumphant later vowed on a god
> And commenced his tremendous wandering!
>
> Odysseus the Second!
> No city you conquered,
> Still from the snow-driven land
> Sorrow now accompanies you:
> Thou hast lit a Trojan pyre,
> Gladdened the genial cardiac fire
> In every soul of the land!
>
> Noble, kind guest,
> God lead thee home!
> May the warm companions twain
> Enchant hence westward!
> On thee, Willard! our wish cries:
> Where a man is mentioned for good,
> It will be mention of thee!

Sigríður Jósepsson, wife of Skapti, the editor of *Norðlingur*, later composed a melody for Matthías' poem, and Skapti sent it to Fiske on 10 May 1880 and wrote: "Herewith my wife has decided to send to you, dear sir, a melody she has composed for the poem about you by Matthías. We hope it will become a *popular* hymn."

Eiríkr Magnússon, librarian at Cambridge, also wrote a poem about Fiske, and he and his wife Sigríður were good friends with him. The poem is quite a lengthy one; Eiríkr called it "To Professor W. Fiske." *Norðlingur* received the honor of printing the poem; only the first stanza appears here:

> Now you have endured the land of frost,
> Beneath the northern latitude's light,
> Where blue heath mingles
> With moorland gray and glacial,
> Yet high among the crag-borne whitethorn
> > Occupies a frozen throne
> > And glistens billowing clouds on high
> > In the sun of a brighter heaven . . . .[9]

Fiske and Reeves were truly moved and grateful. The entire journey was a pleasure for them, and Fiske achieved fulfillment of his longstanding wish. The board of directors of the national library in Reykjavík[10] decided to offer him a gift of books at his departure. In the gift were among others the following: *Ágætar fornmannasögur*, printed at Hólar in 1756; *Landnáma*, printed in Skálholt in 1688; *Vatnsdæla saga*, from Akureyri, 1858; Snorri Sturluson's *Heimskringla*, printed at Leirárgarðar in 1804; and others that enhanced his collection.[11]

It was time. The ship beckoned and soon would stand out of Reykjavík harbor. The companions Fiske and Reeves left Iceland 18 October 1879. In *Þjóðólfur* of 31 October the following notice appeared:

With the mail packet of the 18th of this month sailed for Copenhagen Professor W. Fiske and his companion, Mr. A. Reeves. The professor intended to stay for a time in Berlin with his friend [Andrew D. White], the American ambassador.[12] The sincere best wishes of all who made their acquaintance accompany our guests. They were

Departure of Fiske and Reeves from Iceland: A photograph of part of Reykjavík harbor.

enthusiastic about getting to know our land—nation and literature—while they sojourned here. Mr. Carpenter is staying on until spring to learn thoroughly our tongue and literary history. At the urging of Professor Fiske the respect for our language and the enthusiasm for our book history would seem to be rapidly increasing these years among the most cultured people in America.

Before the undersigned say farewell to Iceland, they would like to attest their heartfelt thanks to all with whom they have met and become acquainted on their journeys throughout the land for the fine reception they have encountered.

Professor W. Fiske	Arthur M. Reeves
Ithaca, New York	Richmond, Indiana,
U.S.	U.S.

According to *Þjóðólfur* the fall climate was unsettled, with volatile weather and sudden squalls of hail. The shadows of autumn had become long and nuanced with it. Esja stood as a queen in a blue-violet gown, looking out over Faxaflói toward Reykjavík. Gray cloud wisps hovered at mid-slope. They stood out from Reykjavík on a surly autumn sea. Atlantic sailing lay ahead.

Chapter 18

Lasting Links

Fiske long enjoyed his acquaintances with Icelanders. He succeeded in winning the trust of people at all levels of society, forging ties of friendship with many with whom he later corresponded. Many of the letters to him dwelled on societal reforms of various types, but the spirit also took wing, alighting on a higher plane in his correspondence with some of the foremost poets of Iceland at this time, Matthías Jochumsson, Steingrímur Thorsteinsson, and Benedikt Gröndal. The poets were quite diligent acquainting Fiske with contemporary Icelandic poetry, their own and others', sending him books of verse and other works that might please him. And they wrote to him as well on daily happenings while teaching at the Learned School, telling him of its activities and of the school lads.

Some Icelanders appeared to write exclusively to maintain contact with Fiske, and it was common that people bade God to bless him; many were concerned about his health. As mentioned earlier, Fiske suffered from arthritis, which increased with the years and explains why Fiske never returned to Iceland. In many letters of encouragement from Iceland, he received invitations, and people offered him good lodging and eiderdown covers. It is clear many desired to meet him again, and there was similarly no lack of longing on his part, but he did not trust the state of his health. The warmth of southern lands suited him better. There it was easier to receive medical attention and take respites at health resorts. People also gladly anticipated receiving a picture of him to

remember better his appearance. Many longed for greater association with him, desiring to find work with him and assist with the
Icelandic collection.

In Fiske's correspondence can also be found a swarm of letters
with stories of chess matches and chess problems. In the wake of
this great enthusiasm, chess societies sprang up throughout the
land, and the Chess Society of Reykjavík came into its strength.

Chapter 19

Devotion to Icelanders

As described above, Fiske wrote energetically about Iceland and Icelanders in foreign papers before he came to Iceland. After his Iceland journey he carried on, and now was richer in experience, having seen things with his own eyes. His knowledge of the land was all the more acute, and there was little he could credit himself with not having expertise in. *Þjóðólfur* was able to report on its front page of 11 December 1879:

> Professor Fiske and *The Times* [of London]. In *The Times* of 1 October is an article by Professor Fiske (who was then here), well composed, as was to be anticipated, and to the honor of our land and parliament. Immediately after, the same (general) newspaper brought out a lengthy article on Iceland, by one of the directors; it intrepidly discusses our history and the connection with the Danes and their government in the days of old bent on the unequal treatment of us. *The Times* predicts for us a rapid and beautiful maturity and wishes us all the best. The professor has the best of things to say about our parliament. At one place he states: "There can be no question that the substitution of a lawmaking body for the old advisory Assembly has been of vast benefit to the island. The Houses have been composed of able men; the discussions have been of a dignified character; the public business has been despatched with reasonable celerity. . . ." He praises the generosity of parliament and nation in contributing funds and considers the biennial residuals (fifty to

one hundred thousand krónur) more than hoped for. He praises our progress since 1874 in communications and employment and then goes on to consider the most important matters before our parliament in the summer. "Over the Upper House . . . presided the venerable Bishop of Iceland, Dr. Pjetur Pjetursson. The Speaker of the Lower House has hitherto been Mr. Jón Sigurðsson, the patriotic statesman, to whose wise direction of its public sentiment the country largely owes its new political privileges." (. . .) "The casual traveler, unless he passes a longer time in the country than tourists are wont to do, can hardly estimate the progress now making [sic] by the people of Iceland. Many causes are contributing to this advancement besides the new constitutional government." Then he enumerates: sale of horses to the Scots [Fiske actually specifies "the English market"], the increase in decked vessels [the reference is to "boats engaged in the coastal fisheries"], progress in agriculture, especially the treatment of sheep, salmon-fishing, etc.; our construction, conditions, and health, he says, are becoming continually better, and that towns are coming into being here and there (he names Akranes especially as such a town): "What Iceland most needs, perhaps," he says finally, "is the abolition of the credit and barter system, which has been fostered by the Danish merchants greatly to their own advantage and to the injury of their customers. This is the same system which formerly prevailed on the Scottish islands, and which a wise legislation only recently abrogated. Next to this reform the principal want of the island is an extension of its new system of national roadways and the introduction into all parts of the country of wheeled vehicles. It is one of the misfortunes of the land that the means of communication which should have been provided, as elsewhere in Europe, during the latter half of the last century, and the earlier part of this, under a good government, must now be wholly created."[1]

After the death of Jón Sigurðsson on 7 December 1879, Fiske wrote much in praise of him in American and German papers, emphasizing that without him the situation of the Icelanders would have been considerably worse and that because of him various national rights would not be far away.[2] He seized the opportunity to promote Iceland, its political situation, and Icelandic circumstances with regard to land and sea. Fiske also compiled letters in English that described Icelandic literature, sending them to different newspapers to promote the land and nation of Iceland overseas.[3] They were informative and keenly written, and intended for those who likely desired to travel to Iceland.

Icelandic newspapers reminded now and then about the nationally known well-wisher by publishing his writings for foreign papers. After the Icelandic journey Fiske stayed in Berlin the first part of the winter and was to head for America in the spring; in *Þjóðólfur* of 22 March 1880 the editor, Matthías Jochumsson, reported on Fiske's writings of the past month. Fiske's intention to return to America had, however, to change, as passion intervened. Jennie McGraw was staying in Italy and Fiske decided to journey south to meet her.

Fiske's writings in foreign papers had a positive influence in Iceland; people believed him to be working toward economic improvements for Iceland from a distance, and this they esteemed. Icelandic papers quoted frequently from his articles, which met with universal satisfaction. *Þjóðólfur* thus reported on 22 March 1880:

Professor W. Fiske, who has been resident in Berlin during the winter, was ready to head westward home at the end of last month. In addition to many books and newspapers, various of which he sent here, especially to the new reading society of the Learned School, which he himself founded before leaving, he sent printed loose-leaf reports (compiled in English) describing our literature and other topics that foreigners who wish to become acquainted with our land and nation, or to journey here, need to know. These reports are so knowledgeably and keenly compiled that they may be called small-scale chefs d'œuvre. Concerning our compatriot, the late Jón Sigurðsson, he has written articles excellently put together in various of the most noted newspapers in America and Europe, and we shall point out that the biographies of our regretted, great countryman, especially those by Fiske and Maurer, will doubtless strengthen knowledge of and interest in Iceland among foreigners. "The great men of this century," says an intellectual, "are the fewest poets, soldiers and philosophers, even fewer clergy; rather they are the outstanding people of the fatherland and men of science."

Professor Fiske has moreover during the winter invoked the greatest enthusiasm in awakening attention in Europe and America regarding the necessity that there should be laid first of all a communications cable to Iceland.

Fiske also kept up closely with everything concerning Icelandic language and literature and gave an account of them to foreigners who pursued those interests. He had wide connections and constantly acquired information and reported on scholars who were writing books on Iceland or Icelandic literature. It was also a positive influence on Icelanders to see that Icelandic literature was sought after out in the world and appealed to foreigners. Often mentioned were known scholarly names such as Albert Ulrik Bååth, Konrad Maurer, Friedrich Wilhelm Bergmann, and Theodor Möbius. Fiske kept up closely with writings in German periodicals of the caliber of *Germania*, *Zeitschrift für deutsche Philologie*, *Beiträge zur Geschichte der deutschen Sprache*, and *Literarisches Centralblatt*; and was pleased that teaching in Old Norse-Icelandic Studies had increased in Germany in a few years' time, and found Icelandic language and literature to receive honest discussion from fine scholars. Accordingly Fiske predicted that Old Norse-Icelandic language and literature would receive greater attention in universities in many countries where the language would be the venerable Old Norse that so many wanted to learn, and the literature likewise in no time. He related what he knew about the teaching of Icelandic and was gratified that another American, Charles Smith of Boston, had gone to pursue Old Norse-Icelandic literature, studying then with Guðbrandur Vigfússon at Oxford. Fiske also noted editions of Icelandic works overseas, and that Lund in Sweden was becoming a center for Icelandic studies, among other places. Then he gave accounts in open lectures on cultural matters that he reported on. His articles on Icelandic topics he sent to Iceland, where they were immediately translated and recapitulated to appear, for information and enjoyment of the population, in Icelandic newspapers.

During the autumn Fiske began, when means permitted, to obtain for Icelanders various items they were in need of, and in his opinion they were many. Very many of the consignments of one kind or another were to be carried to Iceland until he died in September 1904, and it was far from only the largest locales that enjoyed his gifts. He posted parcels through Leith (in Scotland) to at least twelve post offices in Iceland, and from these places they were distributed in various directions. Residents of Grímsey, for example, received their shipments variously through Akureyri or Húsavík. Yet other shipments of his left from the Copenhagen vicinity.

Yet it was not exclusively in cultural aspects that Fiske employed himself helping Icelanders. The Southern District tremor broke in the year 1896, and news of it was carried to Uppsala, where Fiske was on a brief visit. Tryggvi Gunnarsson[4] wrote in a letter of 5 February 1897 that in Sweden Fiske had been the greatest instigator toward collection of contributions on behalf of those who suffered damage from the temblor. His influence reached out beyond the Uppland district into the Västmanland district, and farther in Sweden people collected funds to send to Iceland at the urging of Fiske. It seemed to Tryggvi that Fiske had for years thoroughly adored Iceland and wanted to have a picture of him and to write about him in the Almanac of the Patriotic Society of Iceland, asking Fiske to send him his biographical sketch for that purpose.[5] In the event he never received the sketch, as Fiske was not one to focus attention on himself. Tryggvi, who had become a bank director and simultaneously president of the Society of the Friends of the Nation, did not let that hinder him, and he published a lengthy letter on Fiske's life.[6] Fiske had mastered Icelandic so well that in the autumn he undertook to translate from the Icelandic two poems by his close friends. Prosody suited him well; he was himself a lover of poetry and had written poems for stashing away. The poems he translated were "Við hafið," by Steingrímur Thorsteinsson, which Fiske called "By the Sea" and published in the *Cornell Era*,[7] signing with his initials as translator; and "Leiðsla," by Matthías Jochumsson, which he titled "A Mystical Vision" and published in the same magazine. Fiske greatly enjoyed wrestling with translations: they strengthened his linguistic ability and refreshed his acquaintances with old friends. He maintained entertaining and fruitful correspondence with Steingrímur Thorsteinsson, whose spirit transcended the quotidian in old and new poetry and in reflections on Norse mythology.[8]

67 Behrenstrasse.
Berlin.

Jan. 12, 1880.

My dear Sir,

Do you poets not hear the pipes of Pan dying mournfully away in the distance? Do you not see the light of Valhöll glimmering fainter and fainter afar off? Do you not feel the rustling garments of the old deities, as they rush past and vanish forever, like frightened ghosts, into the gloomy recesses of oblivion?

For that is what it all means — these discoveries of Dr. Bang and Dr. Bugge. The ancient gods are dethroned, as Saturn by his sons, and the realm of poesy shall know them no longer. Out of the Edda they march. They ruled us all, but they now prove to have been only the disguised divinities and heroes of the South, who fled to the regions of the North, when they were driven out of their tropical home.

"Balder the beautiful is dead", said Longfellow, and it turns out to be true. The white Balder was only the mythic shadow of the white Christ, projected through a pagan camera. Höðr the blind was a masked Paris. Nanna, the tenderly-loved of Balder, is only Oinone. Loki is Lucifer. The jarl Angantyr is only Kentaur, with a Keltic article prefixed to his name. Loðyn, Thor's mother, is nothing but Latona. And how long is this to go on? When Völva proves to be merely Sibylla, with the first syllable of her name cut off. What certainty is there that we shall be able to keep Thor and Oðinn and Freyr? Will not some philologist soon find out that they, too, are false gods, who belong not to the old North, but to India or some other remote clime?

Seriously I feel a sort of tender compassion for you poets. For, whom will you sing now? Whose deeds will you chant? When Balder is gone, who is there left to praise? and the prose-writers, too, are shorn of half their glory. Here are the great volumes of Keyser, and Grimm and Simrock and Finnur Magnússon on the Old Northern or Teutonic Mythology. Many of their leaves must be torn out. Well may Dr. Maurer speak of these new results of Eddic study as an "überraschende Entdeckung" and as "wahrhaft verblüffend".

I wish that I could see you once more, and talk all these things over with you. But I can't, and so I can only sigh with you over the tarnished splendor of the ancient myths.

Good Bye!

ever faithfully yours,

Willard Fiske —

Mr. Steingrímur Thorsteinsson —

Letter from Fiske to Steingrímur Thorteinsson. Poetics and Norse mythology were mental preoccupations for Fiske, and he hoped to meet Steingrímur to discuss such topics.

Chapter 20

Lifelong Correspondence

The correspondence to Willard Fiske in the Fiske Icelandic Collection at Cornell University preserves a considerable quantity of letters from various writers.[1] Unfortunately, not as many letters from Fiske to Icelanders have been kept. The letters from Icelanders (among other writers) are multifarious but all manifest gratitude for Fiske's generosity. Some wrote to request some measure of assistance; others asked him to facilitate entrance to an American university or to an occupation in America. The pastor for the parish of Stokkseyri and Eyrarbakki, séra Jón Björnsson, requested financial support to build a church in Eyrarbakki. The pastor, then staying in Copenhagen, wrote on 11 November 1891:

> My countrymen are unable to help me further, as they are mostly so poor, and thus I had to seek help from foreign friends of Iceland. Professor Konrad Maurer in Munich is the only one yet who has helped me; in addition, the Queen of Denmark has given me an altar panel for the church, done by herself, and one man of substance here, who has a store in Eyrarbakki, a harmonium for it. The current debt the church is in is around three thousand krónur apart from the fact that it lacks instruments, which I am now purchasing here in Copenhagen second-hand and sending via postal steamship, though most of it will need to be on loan for the time being.[2]

Altar tableau Queen
Louisa of Denmark
painted and donated
to Eyrarbakki
Church, where it
remains an attractive
presence. Works by the
artistically talented
Louisa also appear
in Danish churches.

Of course Fiske sent money, as Jón Þorkelsson (rector of the
school) and séra Matthías Jochumsson had written a letter of
recommendation for the clergyman and guaranteed he was honor-
able and scrupulous in all matters. The altar screen the Danish
queen gave has long since looked attractive in the Eyrarbakki
church. It shows Jesus in conversation with the Samaritan woman
at Jacob's Well.[3]

Exchanges of letters with Icelanders endured all Fiske's life.
Letters other than those on book collecting and chess are from ordinary folk and officials, young and old, women and men. The letters
show people wrote about their interests, their joys and sorrows.
Most were letters of thanks, and Icelanders scarcely had words to
express how thankful they were for the gifts that steadily streamed
from him and were distributed throughout nearly the entire island.

Fiske's faith in progress resonated with many. It was now clear
that trade to and from Iceland was coming into strength, and
evidently in directions other than Denmark regarding commercial

transactions. Fiske was of the opinion that Icelanders could profit from importing timber and all kinds of machinery from the United States, exporting in exchange, for example, wool, eiderdown, salt fish, and cod liver oil.

A young student at the Learned School, Jóhn Jóhannessen, declared himself in a letter to be an excellent student except in mathematics. There he was mediocre and asked Fiske to send him textbooks in the subject. The lad closed the letter with these words: "I have heard that you are very gifted in Icelandic; perhaps it would be enjoyable to have a seventeen-year-old youth with you."[4] This was not the only example of Icelanders wanting to sojourn with Fiske for a longer or shorter time. Many other instances are in the correspondence in which people tried to approach Fiske, especially for work in his library, or sought to visit him or meet him where he was situated, for Fiske traveled widely, especially after 1883.

Einar Benediktsson wrote Fiske immediately in November 1879 (just after Fiske's departure) and several letters after that. The letters were lively and, among other matters, he discussed the pranks of school boys. But Einar also wrote about his anxieties, as in the summer of 1891 it was clear that he had not received a scholarship for law studies, which he had commenced at the University of Copenhagen, and he needed to stay a year longer in school than he had planned. He was upset by this prospect and said his father, the sheriff Benedikt Sveinsson, was not prosperous and that it would be difficult for him to support his son further in studies. Thus he sought from Fiske's kindness a loan of three hundred krónur he stated was necessary for an additional year in university.[5]

Benedikt Gröndal asked Fiske to obtain a microscope with a magnification of three to four hundred times.[6] Benedikt explained that he had made many attempts to obtain a microscope, but they had been inferior for his purposes. When Fiske was in Iceland he had urged him to let him get something for him overseas, and Benedikt had taken him at his word. Benedikt described his reaction when he received the instrument:

> That day—we were then in Þorlákur's house—Þorvaldur Thoroddsen was staying with us (6 September 1881), a girl came from the Rector[7] in mortal agony and asked me to come quickly; something arrived

that I had to take. I reacted quickly—I suspected something and went to the Rector's house—there lay the microscope on the floor, all in pieces and various things laid out around . . . I was pleased to be able to use this instrument, as I did not hesitate to use it; I found with it many small living creatures, in streams, seas and peat bogs; and immediately sketched them.[8]

The naturalist was clearly overjoyed with his apparatus, and its aid resulted in many of his drawings from nature.

Earlier Fiske had had great interest in geography and related fields. Now he renewed his old enthusiasm and benefited from the support of the explorer and scientist Þorvaldur Thoroddsen; they corresponded from 1880 until Fiske died. Fiske was quite curious and inquisitive about the natural world of Iceland, having worked for the American Geographical and Statistical Society in younger years (as noted in chapter 3).

The letters of Þorvaldur were tightly compressed knowledge as well as well-compiled teaching material. There he noted his intuitions regarding geography, meteorology, hydrography, and botany. He also sent Fiske all the articles and essays he had published on the natural sciences of the country and thought foreign naturalists paid far too little attention to Iceland:

In few countries is there as much for natural scientists to do as in Iceland. The practical instruction supported by research in the field is scarcely under way, and the general public ought thus to receive instruction in natural sciences. This could accomplish great good with time. Above all, Iceland will try to develop its industries, for when prosperity has become durable, I am certain Iceland will be able to develop education and science more than many think. And now all is coming together, and is improving little by little.

As far as scientific research of Icelandic nature is concerned, it has become far less than it should be, although Iceland is perhaps the most remarkable country for naturalists that can be imagined. For geologists it is a pure Eldorado, as it is the center of one of the longest volcanic lines in the world, faring from the north, from Franz-Joseph Land, south over the equator, and nonetheless geologists in Europe and America have not come so far as to know how many volcanoes there are or how often they have erupted; though some are known by name, people do not know where they are; nothing is researched... Greenland and Spitzbergen are in some measure better known than Iceland, where nature is concerned, for expeditions go there annually.[9]

Many of Þorvaldur's letters were written after he was appointed teacher at Möðruvellir. From there it is evident he was not at all satisfied with the circumstances of the country nor with the educational situation, and complained about the poor conditions for his research:

> It is worst for me here, that I am so unfree, but I shall never cease importuning the government until it takes a proper look at Iceland. Perhaps it will be after my time, but I am able to do some of the preparatory hard labor. My countrymen are so set in their ways that it is not possible to motivate them; the lethargy of the young is very much to the fore. We are so few and so isolated that competition cannot establish an authentic life in us.[10]

In other letters Þorvaldur described exceedingly well his trips throughout the country and individual researches, whether in the highlands or in the low country. Some areas no one had journeyed to before to explore them. For Fiske these letters offered a wealth of knowledge.

Þorvaldur found it most difficult to sit quietly the entire winter at Möðruvellir, far from every laboratory and museum, and that microscopic and chemical studies should be totally impossible for him, as nothing was there to aid his research. Yet despite all the drawbacks Þorvaldur reported on in letters to Fiske, researches were quite his forte and he published many of them. His maps of Iceland are today still thought exceptionally good. For many years he was compiling materials for his magnum opus, *Landfræðisaga Íslands* (The Geography of Iceland), which came out in four volumes in the years 1892–1904, considered a watershed as it dealt with the history of all research on Iceland from the earliest centuries to 1880. This book is exceedingly informative regarding any aspect of Icelandic earth sciences, compiled by a vastly informed man of science.

Many people sent Fiske manuscripts of books, articles, and other works, products of their research and writing, hoping he would read over them and offer guidance or comment. The widely known explorer Vilhjálmur Stefánsson, then a grant recipient at Harvard University, stated to Fiske in a letter that he longed to write a book on Iceland and Icelandic literature, thinking both needed to be introduced to civilized nations. He bade Fiske read over the manuscript and offer his good advice, as Fiske knew so much about the topic.[11]

Jón Þorkelsson, rector of Menntaskólinn í Reykjavík, wrote Fiske many letters to thank his sending of books to the school and also to himself. He wrote about social conditions in Iceland and about how people were faring. His letters offer insight into life on land and sea. On 15 September 1882 he wrote on circumstances in Iceland:

Here things are generally rather bad than good to report. This year has been doubtless one of the most difficult years to have come over Iceland this century. Much of the livestock has died in many of the shires, especially Borgarfjarðar-, Mýra-, Snæfellsness- and Dalasýslur. The Greenlandic sea ice has encircled the entire northern part of the country all summer, so that no steamship has been able to make harbor in the north or around the country before the end of August. The haymaking has gone extremely badly in the north. In August in Skagafjarðarsýsla the temperature was never more than two degrees [Celsius, i.e. 36 Fahrenheit]. Neither worm nor maggot nor fly survived. At times snowstorms were so large that cattle were not let out, yet no hay was on hand for them but that which was taken from under the snow in the fields.

That which has happened since September has here in the south been the most considerable spell of foul weather, continual cold spells and storms from the north with rain and sometimes with snow. –No energy or drive to be had. Nature and climate undo all the aspirations of men![12]

Matthías Jochumsson wrote often and was thankful his entire life for the books, pictures, and other gifts, and above all for the friendship. He wrote animated letters recounting much that was happening in Icelandic life, and firmly encouraged Fiske to continue his advocacy for a telegraph cable to Iceland. He also discussed his poetry and on occasion requested information from abroad to enhance his own knowledge. On 3 November 1882 he wrote, having by then moved to Oddi in Rangárvellir:

> Which cultural-historical book do you think best to educate me about the century of Sæmundur fróði? I have compiled a few motives in my mind about him and his time, yet—how can one describe the "black school?" There I am stranded. Jón helgi (the Saintly), his foster brother, became glorious in the national faith but Sæmundur a sorcerer. After I began writing this letter, everything outside the window at Oddi became angel white. Oh that for me as a pastor it should go as well to color white the black raiments of sin of the parish: When culture and "freedom" come down in ruin and distress, then "bound" cold weather loosed in the souls, and faith, are totally confused, and friendship diminished—yet but for a moment.[13]

Poetry, probably composed extemporaneously, often accompanied the correspondence. On 16 June 1885 this verse concluded a letter from Matthías:

> Felicitous Florence yours,
> Accompany you all that fortify,
> Happiness, health, and peace.
>   Your friend,
>   Matth. Jochumsson[14]

The goldsmith Páll Þorkelsson sought funding to publish an Icelandic-French dictionary.[15] Páll had also invented a sign language, and Professor Finnur Jónsson wrote Fiske about it in order to underscore Páll's ability.[16] Some wrote simply to have contact with Fiske, to which he truly attached significance.

Jennie and Fiske were married in Berlin in mid-1880, not particularly long after Fiske left Iceland, but chronic illness had left its mark on her, and the marriage was considered unusual. Either Icelanders did not want to involve themselves in Fiske's personal affairs or they did not know about the marriage. Pétur Guðjohnsen, a student in the Learned School and a cabinetmaker, wrote to him years later nonetheless on 29 October 1890, congratulating him on winning the will case (chapter 22):

> . . . [A]nd now let my happiness be clearly seen regarding [the outcome], and I would like further to mention that all whom I have spoken with about this have also expressed happiness about it. This is nothing but a hope, though, that the Icelandic nation should be glad over the fortune and prosperity of this man who has shown it every goodness. Though the Icelandic nation dwell in cold climes, the hearts are warm all the same, and it trusts those who desire to be its friends.[17]

Pétur had been a little lad in Húsavík when Fiske landed there. Without success he sought to give Fiske something and offered to make some object as a souvenir. The object could, however, not be so large as to make transporting it difficult. Pétur remembered also that Fiske collected Icelandic plants in Húsavík and offered to dry and send to him an "herbarium Islandiorum."[18] After graduation from the Learned School Pétur had gone off to Copenhagen to study law, but that turned out a complete disaster and he began the study of music instead. For this he needed funds and asked Fiske for support.[19]

Fiske had not had the opportunity to go to the Faroe Islands, but in his correspondence there are letters from there. The men in power in Denmark were not, in the opinion of many, sympathetic toward the culture and traditions of the Faroese, and the latter had to struggle mightily to be able to express themselves in public in their own language. In a letter to Fiske they modestly requested from him, among other things, help in bringing out a newspaper in Faroese.

Fiske had good connections with parties who obtained Icelandic written works for him. In letters from these intermediaries the conversation was most often about books. Nevertheless they cover various topics, and many of the letters are amusing. Ólafur Davíðsson wrote vigorously and sent Fiske very instructive letters about daily life in Iceland, discussing people's work, cultural matters, publishing, poetry recitals, and stanza repetitions through which people amused themselves in the evenings. Also, how stories were narrated:

> Then all are silent, save the one who recites the story. It is almost equally men and women who recite stories, as these women have learned from men and women in their youth, and these women have learned anew the stories in their youth and thus have the folktales gone from person to person; but sometimes young people recite the stories they have read in foreign, especially Danish books.[20]

At Fiske's request Ólafur compiled a long document on *kvöld-vökur* (evening wakes)[21] and winter work of ordinary people in the evenings, and there he cited various factors regarding the circumstances of land and nation. He produced a fine report on the status of his countrymen in cultural and educational matters, and in his informative letter to Fiske of 22 March 1880 he stated:

> Now the reading room has emerged among us school lads, and you have the most part in its establishment, with your gifts of books and newspapers. All the lads thank you cordially for them. This reading room can be for amusement and benefit for us schoolboys, if we know how to use it, and it is desirable that it should be so.

Grímur Thomsen wrote Fiske in English from Bessastaðir on 6 August 1895 and was pleased that Fiske liked his "Dante" that he had sent him not long previously; Fiske had replied forthwith. According to Grímur's letter of 8 February 1880, Carpenter was still in Iceland. ". . . [H]e is a modest, amusing and exceedingly sympathetic young man," wrote Grímur, and added:

> Every Icelander, I as well as others, must be thankful to you for your good will and ready good wishes for this country. Yet all true improvement, all true progress, will have to come from within ourselves. . . . We ourselves shall have to learn to heft our weight, to display enterprise, forward momentum, stability, and thrift; and neither expect nor hope for any substantive help from abroad. Each nation, each man ought to be self-sufficient.[22]

Such letters displaying a friendly nature continued long to be sent. Þorsteinn Br. Arnljótsson, son of the Rev. Arnljótur Ólafsson at Bægisá, wrote on the 6th of September 1880:

> It was a very great pleasure to both my parents and us siblings when we heard that you were married, and wish for you and the lady of your heart a long and happy life. It was merely one of my sisters (I have six), Valgerður, who said, when she heard you had married, "It is sad that the professor married," and when my mother asked her why she was speaking this nonsense, she replied, "Because he will never more come to Iceland." It has got to be good that even children who have not seen a man but once should sorrow at not seeing him again.

Þorsteinn wrote Fiske more cordial letters. Fiske replied punctually, and it was noteworthy that he did not forbear to write the very young. On 2 March 1880 Þorsteinn wrote:

> Papa received from the library in Akureyri on my behalf one of the books you gave at the national holiday, titled Anderson *The United States Reader* [sic; he took great pains with the calligraphy of the author's name and the title] and I have read a little in it, but Papa is teaching me—Papa has many of your fine gift books here to read, and says he is soon to receive *Harper's Weekly* and more. In winter I shall have to go to the school at Möðruvellir and he says I should devote all my time to English and English books.
>
> The remarkable invention of Edison, your countryman, is immeasurably great, and what useful implements such men make, and perpetually while the world endures. It [must be] a pleasure to be a citizen of [your] nation, which has so many excellent people; I intend to see the United States when I am grown up, if you are there then. But the incident in Russia is the most remarkable event, the attempted assassination of the Tsar himself. It is good that did not succeed. . .
>
> Now I have nothing more, except that Skapti [Jósepsson, publisher in Akureyri] went on the wagon in the autumn, and has quite abstained since, so that he has become a new man.[23]

Þórsteinn was fifteen when he wrote this letter, and longed without measure to go to the school at Möðruvellir. Due to poor health he was unable to go, but he educated himself well on his own accord. Willard Fiske appreciated the self-motivated endeavor of young people, and sustained school pupils with word and deed—although he himself had earned no degrees in his school career.

Chapter 21

The Year with Jennie

Willard Fiske was quite satisfied with his Iceland trip and believed he had gotten to know land and nation considerably better. The ties he now had with Icelanders carried significant weight, especially when it came to acquiring books. He had also seen a nature, magnificent unlike any other, that was often as surprising as was the condition of a people that valued literature before anything else; but in Fiske's estimation, Icelanders had to draw closer to the outside world and learn something about the civilization of other nations.

Jennie McGraw was likely uppermost in his thoughts at this time, and he wished she had been able to come to know Iceland with him. He had wanted to share with her everything beautiful and memorable that he saw, everything special and splendid that he experienced. During the summer he composed a poem for her; it was dated July 1879. He called the poem "An Epistle from the Arctic Sea," and in it were these lines:

> Come to the North, O gracious queen,
> Come to the land of snow and sheen,
>   Come to the whiter zone!
> Come while the summer zephyrs blow,
> Come while the stellar flowerlets glow,
>   Come ere the light be flown!
> A royal welcome shall be thine—
> Posies of alpine blooms divine,

By dews celestial kissed;
Crowns with auroral gems bedight,
More lustrous than the chrysolite,
Sphered pearl, or amethyst;
Landscapes wherein no line is laid
Of pallor cold, or hueless shade;
And runic poets' lays,
That tell in rhymes of skaldic art
How dear thy image to my heart
Through all these darkless days.[1]

This poem, along with many others he composed to Jennie over a long time, she did not see until later. Truth to tell, she was quite unaware of his poems when he finally admitted her into the secret recesses of his thoughts. She knew he wrote poetry but had seen very little of it.

Fiske went from Iceland through Britain to Germany, meeting in Berlin Andrew D. White, his friend who had become United States ambassador there. Jennie was in Italy to mend her health. Willard wrote to her and decided thereafter to travel and meet her in Rome. He was restless and told Andrew White of his plan. White counseled his friend firmly to hasten, and lent him money for the journey. The reunion in Rome was quite happy, as Jennie and Fiske had not seen each other since she left on her European tour from Ithaca eighteen months before, in the spring of 1878.[2] From Rome Fiske wrote to White that he and Jennie had decided to marry, and he added that he had loved her much longer than White had suspected. White unequivocally urged him to wed. The couple undertook their journey and in Berlin they were married on 14 July in the presence of Andrew White and Judge Douglass Boardman, an old friend from Ithaca, together with but a few other friends.[3] Before the ceremony Fiske signed a document relinquishing rights to Jennie's property. Jennie later wanted to invalidate the signature, but he was unwavering. She asked him likewise to read over her will, but he declined. He paid not the least attention to Jennie's estate.[4]

Þjóðólfur on 28 July 1880 related that Fiske had married on the fourteenth of the same month in Berlin Miss Jennie McGraw, who was also from Ithaca. As it stated, "We can say we are certain all the many friends of the professor in Iceland heartily wish him the best in his life choice."

This was a fortuitous year in the life of Willard Fiske. He had come to the promised land after a nearly thirty-year wait and had been joined in wedlock with the lady he had loved for at least eleven years.

The fortune lasted briefly, as Jennie's health deteriorated steadily. They visited a lung specialist in Paris who confirmed that her lungs were very much in a bad way; he regretted he could offer neither a cure nor a palliative. They journeyed to several resorts in Europe that physicians had recommended, but all came to naught. Inexorably the consumption worsened. They fêted Jennie's fortieth birthday on 14 September in Paris; Willard was one year shy of his fiftieth. The autumn was chilly and damp; winter was approaching and Jennie was coughing steadily. They decided to journey south and sail up the Nile in the hope the warmer climate might strengthen her lungs. Willard Fiske had been before to Egypt, land of myth and enchantment, and was intimately familiar with it.[5] They commenced the journey in November aboard a vessel named *The Hope*, and on board in addition to them were the skipper, seventeen sailors, two cooks, three servants and a tour guide. All the crew were deeply solicitous in making the journey as enjoyable and comfortable as possible.

In the beginning the trip was truly an adventure for them both.[6] Jennie enjoyed the trip despite her illness and felt she was disappearing into a scene from the Old Testament. She identified with the history along the riverbanks where people were at work and play and thought she was viewing Biblical images akin to those she had had as a child. All seemed ancient and as if from another world.[7] During the sailing Fiske revealed the poems he had written to her many years before, and she was both amazed and deeply affected with the reading of them. The poems confirmed his feelings of years toward Jennie before their meeting in Rome.

Nothing warded off fate, however: Soon it transpired that Jennie could not clothe herself without assistance. She came down with a high fever and expectorated blood. Her husband was desperate. Jennie sensed death nearing and yearned to come home to Ithaca.

Breaking their itinerary, they hastened back to Alexandria and took first available passage across the Mediterranean, arriving at Venice. From there the destination was Paris, and when they arrived, Jennie had grown very weak; she needed to rest and strengthen herself for the sailing across the Atlantic. All available medications and other expedients were tried, but to no avail, and the patient worsened steadily. After a difficult sea crossing that seemed to them never to end, they barely made it to Ithaca, and when she arrived, she was nearer to death than life. Defeated by the White Death, Jennie McGraw Fiske succumbed 30 September 1881, just forty-one years of age.[8]

Before sailing for Europe, Jennie had engaged the well-known architect William H. Miller to sketch for her her dream house, and he received a free hand in the design of the edifice, which was known as the Mansion. The house was more magnificent than was known in Ithaca at that time; nothing was spared. Jennie was away during the entire construction, yet evinced great concern for the construction workers engaged in the task, their health and welfare. It was said that when the news came of how ill she had become, the workers' wives prayed together for her, believing their prayers were strong and would bring about her improvement.[9]

When the couple returned to Ithaca on 10 September 1881 the house was completely built and appointed with fixtures and considered especially magnificent, equally so inside and out. There Jennie had prepared for her husband and herself a distinguished home that most nearly resembled an art collection, as the beautiful furnishings and art works Jennie had bought in Europe decorated every room. "It surpasses all my expectations," she is said to have remarked when, ill to the point of death, she managed to see the house from a distance as she was driven through Ithaca up to the house of Willard Fiske on campus.[10] Her strength exhausted, she expired in her husband's house. The memorial service followed on 3 October in her splendid mansion.

The fate of this beautiful and luxurious house, well made in every respect, was nearly as sorrowful as Jennie's. Never used by its owners, it burned to ashes in 1906.

The remains of Jennie were borne to the mortuary chapel attached to Cornell University's Sage Chapel, not far from the

The magnificent house Jennie McGraw Fiske had constructed in Ithaca. The house was appointed with the most beautiful furnishings and works of art, but she did not live to cross its threshold.

bell tower she had herself donated some years before.[11] Willard, downcast, followed. The leafy forests around Ithaca were in their most beautiful splendor of autumn colors; their sylvan nuance appeared to him as if in flame, and the air precipitated light. This tender albeit difficult love story ended in Ithaca as it had begun. In full optimism and belief in life they lived passionately in many lands and experienced much together until forsaken by fate. They had scant time together, but used it well. Bowed but not broken, Willard Fiske continued on the path of life; the story has it that he had made an agreement with a certain florist to place a wreath of Marshall Neil roses on the tomb the fourteenth day of every month, commemorating their wedding date of 14 July 1880. The florist is supposed to have fulfilled this wish until Willard Fiske died in the fall of 1904.

Chapter 22

The Will Case

Now began a difficult time for the widower. He had by no means recovered after the death of his wife when he had to wrestle with the matter of inheritance, since within a month after Jennie's demise legal proceedings commenced with regard to the estate. In the history of Cornell University Morris Bishop compiled and published in 1962, he chronicled in the chapter "The Great Will Case" the events preceding and following Willard Fiske's estrangement from Cornell. That narrative suffices for much of the substructure for the present chapter, although Morris Bishop's perspective, sharpened at times by acid observations, invites cautious reflection.[1] The earlier, quasi-hagiographic study of Jennie's life offered by Ronald John Williams differs from Bishop's in its considerable reliance on Andrew D. White's autobiography (*Autobiography of Andrew Dickson White*, 2 vols. [New York: Century, 1905]) for a narrative of the controversy.[2] *The Diaries of Andrew D. White*, edited by Robert Morris Ogden (1959), which are selective rather than comprehensive, nonetheless offer, as does the *Autobiography*, a personal sense of President White's experience of the case. Horatio S. White's *Willard Fiske: Life and Correspondence: A Biographical Study* (1925) reproduces correspondence and other documentation supporting, in essence, the position of his biographical subject. The present chapter essays a summary of events based on these treatments.

Jennie's will, made in Berlin, surfaced only by chance after the funeral. Had Jennie died intestate, as she was to die without issue, her father's estate, by terms of his will, would have devolved on his brother's family.

The register of wills proved the document without legal delays. It was declared that the husband of Jennie had inherited three hundred thousand dollars; Jennie's relatives, Joseph McGraw and his offspring, were to receive five hundred and fifty thousand dollars, and Cornell University two hundred thousand for the library and fifty thousand dollars toward the expansion of McGraw Hall. The student infirmary would receive forty thousand dollars and the university Jennie's holdings in landed property. People were not all agreed on the value of the property, but it was clear the university's share appeared to be no less than a million dollars.[3]

Jennie's mansion was in the university's share. President White entertained the idea of repurposing the structure as an art gallery. Fiske was not in a position to maintain the house even on his augmented income, and thought the university might serve as its custodian.

The deterioration of relations after Jennie's death between Fiske on the one hand, and university officials and trustees on the other, assumes the aspect of a chilly vortex as each side behaved in ways that aroused the ire of the other. Prominent among Fiske's antagonists on the university side were Henry W. Sage, a founder and trustee; and Judge Douglass Boardman, executor of Jennie's will, who was seemingly exact and exacting with regard to the legal formalities surrounding Jennie's estate. Judge Boardman and Henry Sage ultimately opposed Fiske's request that he live in the mansion built for Jennie. Fiske determined to go abroad and in 1883 would opt to resign his appointments with the university, by spring 1882 "nettled," as Williams phrases it, "by the changing atmosphere" among the elements that financed and guided the institution.[4]

Stories circulated that Fiske's behavior on his earlier European travels had been worthy of criticism. These tales, Bishop suggests, may have sufficed to induce an estrangement.[5] Sage and Boardman may have possibly resolved to see that this, in their judgment, man of deficient reputation should "have none of dear Jennie's money if they could keep it out of his hands," as Bishop wrote.[6] On 12 May 1882 the New York State legislature approved a revised charter for Cornell University. Although chiefly a formality, the revision's fifth section removed any limit to the university's ability to receive and hold the property of private individuals, whereas a maximum of three million dollars (that the university could hold from any combination of private sources) had formerly existed.

Prior to Fiske's sailing for Europe in 1882, an upstate New York attorney rang Fiske to explain Cornell University could not accept Jennie's bequest under the existing charter. Revision of the charter would retroactively remove the hindrance. State law also proscribed a married woman from bequeathing more than half her possessions to charitable intentions if her spouse survived. The attorney moreover informed Fiske that Judge Boardman, the executor, had consciously failed to apprise Fiske of his rights, and that confidants familiar with the matter had likewise deliberately withheld this legal knowledge from Fiske.[7]

A furious Fiske petitioned to break the terms of Jennie's will in his favor before embarking for Europe in July. The courts quickly enjoined Judge Boardman from transferring estate funds to the university, and the Great Will Case wound through the state and federal judiciaries. Despite an initial loss, Fiske and the McGraw cousins of Jennie, likewise named heirs, would win at appellate levels all the way to the United States Supreme Court in 1890. ". . . [A] great pity, my dear Judge, and a great blunder, as I now look calmly back on it all," was Fiske's recollection of his being kept in the dark when those in the know about proposed legal changes ought to have "frankly explain[ed]" matters affecting execution of Jennie's will.[8]

Andrew Dickson White, the university president until 1885 and in great measure a benefactor of Fiske's, did not forsake his friend. He made overtures during the 1880s to reconcile Fiske with the university, having in mind its larger aims and the generous objectives Jennie had entertained for the institution. Similarly, Hiram Sibley, a charter trustee of Cornell University, visited Fiske in Florence in the same decade and subsequently encouraged him, albeit to no avail, to return to Cornell.[9]

President White's reflections on the case and its principals appear stark in his *Diaries*, perhaps no more so than at the close of 1888, after several lost appeals but preceding the university's ultimate loss before the United States Supreme Court. Reflecting on what he feared was the impending loss, White remarked (31 December 1888) on what he perceived to be the demise of the university, "the noblest structure of its kind ever attempted in our country." He ascribed blame to both Judge Boardman and Henry Sage, "whose stupidity, folly, and want of friendliness have caused this great catastrophe." This entry reflected the one he made a month prior (28 November), upon learning Cornell had lost another appeal, remarking that "certain excellent gentlemen were so stupid, at every point in the history . . ." and adding for emphasis: "Gegen die Dummheit streiten die Götter selbst vergebens."[10]

Andrew D. White was literally at sea when he penned his entry; he and Daniel Willard Fiske had embarked on a winter's sojourn in Egypt, landing at Alexandria on 1 January 1889. Fiske would inform White on 5 March that he had in his will bequeathed "to the University everything which should come to him from this suit and his library and provision for a librarian and Icelandic scholar in connection with it."[11]

On 19 May 1890, the U.S. Supreme Court ruled against Cornell University, but the decision stipulated that the school could use its endowment fund, which was totally in its possession, for any purpose whatsoever. After ample legal fees, some half a million dollars went to Fiske and about a million to the McGraw family. Thomas McGraw, Jennie's paternal first cousin, purchased the mansion; its art works and house furnishings were sold at auction on 19 February 1891, with the McGraw heirs purchasing most of the items. Later the Chi Psi fraternity occupied the property.[12]

The Great Will Case had taken nine years and shaken the life of Fiske. Nonetheless, he had come out well, as would eventually the university because of the endowment access mentioned above and because of Fiske's gifts and bequests of literary collections.

Cornell University lost ultimately nothing more than a measure of the common purpose and trust that motivated its founding families, and this loss was significant in terms of the animosity that came to the fore: a spite so sharp as to raise objection to the interment of Daniel Willard Fiske next to Jennie in the Sage Chapel crypt. The old animosity even survives in bronze.[13] When one enters the old university library—now Uris Library, part of the Olin-Kroch-Uris complex—the following text, inscribed on a shield above a splendid marble seat, informs the eye:

The good she tried to do shall stand as if it 'twere done. / GOD finishes the work by noble souls begun. In Loving Memory of JENNIE MCGRAW FISKE whose purpose to found a great library for Cornell University has been defeated. This house is built and endowed by her friend Henry W. Sage. 1891.

In the same year, Fiske assembled and sent to Cornell his small but remarkable Rhaeto-Romanic collection. Five years later, the library received his outstanding Dante collection.

Chapter 23

Collecting Icelandic Imprints

There is no doubt that Willard Fiske was much enchanted by Iceland, the Icelanders, and the literary life lived there, but the enchantment was without question closely tied to his passion for collecting books. A new chapter began in his life when he moved definitively to Florence. After the inheritance from Jennie devolved on him, he no longer lacked for funds to satisfy his passion, and worked energetically to come into contact with those Icelanders most likely to assist him in the purchase of books. Frequent and extensive correspondence had to occur for him to be able to collect what he desired, and from when he visited Iceland until he died, he had the opportunity to acquire an incredible number of Icelandic publications. Most of the Icelanders wrote to him in Icelandic, with individual exceptions in Danish or English.

Fiske bought Icelandic books and books dealing with Iceland mostly from Icelanders and from the bookseller Skandinavisk Antikvariat in Copenhagen. It would be possible to name many who assisted him with collecting, among them Ólafur Davíðsson, naturalist and compiler of folklore; and Jón Þorkelsson the younger, who later became the national archivist. Both were school lads in the Learned School the autumn Fiske was in Iceland. Halldór Hermannsson, who subsequently became curator of the Fiske Icelandic Collection, also worked much acquiring books for Fiske while he was in Copenhagen, sending them to him in Italy. Halldór was also an intermediary for the gifts Fiske sent to Iceland.

On the other hand, Fiske deliberately did not collect manuscripts, remarking that manuscripts, which a fortiori were unique, had to stay in their home.[1] Nonetheless several manuscripts entered the collection by happenstance, most as gifts to him; these are now securely kept in the Fiske Collection at Cornell along with other Icelandic materials that came to him.

In Fiske's correspondence preserved at Cornell there is a rather large number of letters regarding his acquisition of Icelandic books; and letters as well from Icelanders thanking him for all the gifts of books, pictures, statues, chessboards, and chess pieces and other items he sent to Iceland. To judge from the letters, it seemed to Icelanders a clear choice on the part of a foreigner, yet all the same somewhat strange, that he should strive to acquire Icelandic books. They knew that out in the wide world Old Icelandic literature had been published, but it caught their attention that Fiske should want to have all that had come out in modern Icelandic, the most diminutive printing no less than the great thick tomes. Fiske admired this small nation of eager readers that published more in print than he had dared dream. People were bidden and able to assist him in acquiring Icelandic works, much that likely would otherwise have become prey to destruction, and with the passage of time he succeeded in amassing much of Icelandic printed matter with the help of Icelanders at home and also abroad.

Fiske's systematic collecting went forward inter alia in that he sent several people lists of desiderata in keeping with the composition of his Icelandic catalogue,[2] to be described below; or in that he had a special interest for other reasons. These people were extensively involved with the compilation both in Iceland and in Copenhagen, and Ólafur Davíðsson had a direct hand for a time sending Fiske books: in 1887 he collected books and also searched systematically through descriptions of books on Iceland. Fiske also was interested in books on games other than chess, for example bridge. In addition he was a puzzle enthusiast and vocal about it; Ólafur was an expert in such matters, doing much to enlighten Fiske.

Fiske sent antiquarian booksellers booklists, and often enough they devoted themselves unbidden to find what he needed. It is clear they also had in mind that he receive quality with the

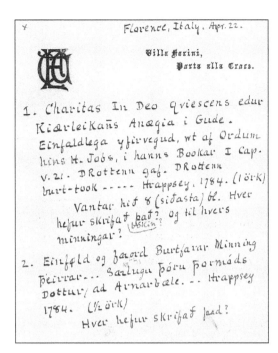

Fiske often wanted bibliographic information, and also wrote inquiring about specific books. This letter enumerates several desiderata.

item conveyed. Often one went from region to region, searching
throughout the land without ceasing until a good copy was identified in a private library. There were examples of reaching all the
way out to Hornstrandir in search of books for him.[3] Fiske paid
very well. He had the practice of sending his representatives ample
funds, and they themselves had then to subtract the amount that
acquired the desired works for them. When the balance began to
dwindle they informed Fiske, who sent more money. The collected
correspondence shows that nowhere did it begin to appear in his
thinking that some Icelandic material might be too expensive, and
with one exception, he never tried to lower the price.

He was quite offended when he received the New Testament
of Oddur Gottskálksson, printed at Roskilde (Denmark) in 1540,
truly a gem in all the history of Icelandic printing; he had stipulated obtaining the best and fullest copy procurable. Valdimar
Ásmundsson, founder and editor of *Fjallkonan*,[4] found a copy in
the estate of séra Eiríkur Briem in Hruni and sent it to Fiske,[5] who
was very disappointed because the copy was quite defective. He
had himself examined closely the copies in the Royal and university

VPJ

London, d. 31 Juli. 89

Kjære Herr.
Jeg skulde gjerne Kjöbe følgende af de Böger af hvilke De har godhedsfuldt tilsendt mig Titlerne:—

1. Eitt Lidet Stafrofs Kver. Skálh. 1695.
2. Lykprædikun H. Gysla Thorlaks Sonar. Hól. 1685. 12°
3. Forordning ahrarande Confirmation og Catechisation Hól. 1749
4. " " Hvis Datorne er 1749.
5. Tilskipan um Skrifta-Stoolen. Hól. 1749. Hvis den er visst tryht 1749.
6. Forordning um Taxta og Kauphöndlun. Hrappsey 1777.
7. Burtfarar Minning Þóru Þormóds Dottur. Hrappsey 1784.
8. Evangelisk-Kristileg Lærdoms-Bok. Leirár. 1811.
9. Lærdoms Bók. Vid. Kl. 1830.
10. Forordning um Kirgyllde. Hól. 1749.
11. " " Kyrkiu-Bakur. Hól. 1749
12. Nýjar Viku-Banir. Leirár. 1798.
13. Æfisaga Pauls Jónssonar. Vid. Kl. 1820.
De andre Titlerne besidder jeg.
Vil De være saa god at skikke de foregaaende, med en Regning, til

Letter (in Danish) from 31 July 1889, which shows Fiske's requests for specific books. Among others, he wanted the *Stafrófskver* (1695) and a funeral sermon from 1685.

min Adresse i Florens og jeg skal
strax sende Pengerne.

Jeg sandte Dem to Exemplarer af
Bib. Not. I, og er ledsen at vide
at De ikke har erholdt Dem. De
faaer et andet fra Florens.
altid med Agtelse Deres,

W. Fiske,
c/o Maquay, Hooker & Co.
Florence,
Italy.

libraries in Copenhagen and also the copy belonging to Rolf Arpi, a librarian in Uppsala, who had a considerable number of rare Icelandic items; and he came to the conclusion that this particular copy was quite inferior to them. Leaves were wanting and six of the leaves at the end were sorrowfully deteriorated; in addition, the binding was somewhat younger than the book. Accordingly Fiske refused to pay Valdimar the arranged price, and finally Valdimar lowered the price.[6] The New Testament is now one of the most precious objects in the Fiske Icelandic Collection at Cornell.[7]

An old friend of Fiske's from the Iceland sojourn, Jón Þorkelsson, proved by far most capable in exporting books. He wrote Fiske on 12 February 1887: "I just this minute received your letter and money order, for which I thank you. But the remittance is much too large, so you will need to see if you can allow me to do something more for you."[8]

Jón was born in 1859 and studied Old Norse at the University of Copenhagen after finishing in the Learned School. He defended his doctoral dissertation, "On Poetry in Iceland in the Fifteenth

Letter from Fiske to Valdimar Ásmundsson in which he expresses his dissatisfaction over the copy of the New Testament Valdimar had obtained for him.

and Sixteenth Centuries,"[9] in 1888, and it was considered a turning point, as Icelandic literature of later centuries had been disdained by Danish university men. He wrote poetry in his free time, publishing his verse under the pseudonym Fornólfur. The name, people thought, suited: the man was ancient in appearance, with an enormous, ancient-looking beard. Jón had an inextinguishable enthusiasm for medieval Icelandic studies and was a great bibliographer, exacting in everything regarding published editions. In addition, he had a prodigious memory and endlessly compared copies of books, pointing out to Fiske differences in editions. He went to book auctions for Fiske and truly for himself as well, as he himself had a very good library. Jón wrote Fiske long letters thoroughly describing auctions in Copenhagen and the winning bid for individual books. He weighed and pondered all items, himself asking if they were worth their price; much he thought was "tremendously expensive," as he said. He believed it important to be present himself at auctions and would not let others bid in his stead, as was generally the custom at the time.[10]

Some of the books Jón Þorkelsson and Ólafur Davíðsson purchased for Fiske were nowhere to be found in public collections at that time, not even in the Royal Library in Copenhagen, which nonetheless assumed responsibility for Icelandic materials after 1886. These colleagues were frequently in great spirits after acquiring works the library lacked. Occasionally Jón obtained a purchase option from a bookseller; he then let Fiske know and asked whether he ought to buy the item for him. As in former days he considered extensively the price and what would be fair given the scarcity and condition of the item for sale, and without hesitation he stated if he found the asking price too high.[11] Thus he often succeeded in bringing the sale price down.

Fiske also sought after all manner of pamphlets and various small-press publications, and frequently inquired about epitaphs. Of those Jón offered to Fiske for purchase were 302 epitaphs from 1833 or later and also 198 occasional poems from 1698 and downward, as he phrased it.[12] Jón attached such importance to Fiske's obtaining what he sought for the catalogue *Bibliographical Notices: Books Printed in Iceland 1578–1844*, which Fiske was compiling, that Jón sold even of his own books that he had in only one copy.

Ólafur Davíðsson brought together an enormous amount of material for Fiske in both Iceland and Denmark. The earliest letters from Ólafur in the Fiske correspondence are from the autumn of 1879, and there he reported on newly published books in Iceland. After graduation from the Learned School in 1882 Ólafur traveled to study in Copenhagen and then began to inquire about written Icelandic materials for Fiske. Ólafur compiled various attractive items during his Copenhagen years and sold them to Fiske. He also sold him a substantial part of his own collection, but then Ólafur was perpetually in financial straits. He made inquiries about Icelandic books in mainland Europe and ultimately managed to have sent some extremely rare books, which he thought Fiske longed to possess, from the bookseller Ludwig Rosenthal in Munich (originally in Leipzig). Then Ólafur succeeded in obtaining for Fiske sixteenth- and seventeenth-century printings from his cousin Jón Árnason, the folklorist, among them Andreas Musculus' *Bænabók Litel skrifud j Þysku Maale*, printed at Hólar 1597; *Biblia Parva* (Hólar, 1596); and *Antidotum* (also Hólar, 1597). All these were notable works. He also obtained the first edition of the *Passíusálmar* or (formally) the *Historia Pijnunnar og Daudans Drottins vors Jesu Christi*, from Hólar, 1666.[13] At an auction in Copenhagen he came across the *Grönlandía* of Torfaeus (Þormóður) Torfason for a more modest price than he had dared hope.[14]

Ólafur frequently sent large parcels to Florence, more often than not with scarce books, but not always reliably so. The shipments grew fewer and farther between, and in one letter to Fiske Ólafur declared he was ashamed of himself and wanted to compensate for the slothfulness by sending additional books, which he bade Fiske accept from him.[15] These books were the *Sálmabók* (Hymnal) from 1801; *Ein lijtel Nij Bænabók* by Þórður Bárðarson, printed at Hólar in 1730; and the oldest edition of *Harmonia Evangelica*, printed in Skálholt in 1687.[16] From 1891 it became again longer between letters and book consignments from Ólafur, and their relations dwindled substantially after that. In 1892 there developed a complete rift between them, likely because Ólafur was intemperate and began to owe Fiske money.[17] He failed to settle accounts regularly and Fiske could no longer trust him. At the beginning of the ninth decade of the nineteenth century Ólafur had been interested in coming to

Florence to work in Fiske's collection, Fiske then seeking a person with great knowledge of books and bibliography. Ólafur fit the bill well, until Fiske heard from Icelanders in Copenhagen that his hard drinking was beyond the bounds of propriety.[18] Jón Þorkelsson expressed concern about his colleague Ólafur in a letter to Fiske: "I have not seen Ó.D. any more . . . He has now sold what he had left in books to Jewish book peddlers here. It is a loss that wretched Ólafur has gone completely to the dogs, as he is very intelligent. I wrote a piece in *Berlingske Tidskrift* in recent days about his book on games, if that might be of some use to him. Do not let him know, nonetheless, that I have done that. He appears to believe the article is by pastor Feilberg, in Jutland."[19]

Ólafur was born in 1862, and after high-school graduation (as noted earlier) he sailed for Copenhagen. There he took a degree in philosophy and studied natural sciences at the university for a while before he quit his studies and began to give himself over completely to Icelandic folklore. Early in life he had become enchanted by the occult power of folktales, and while he was in the Learned School he became acquainted with Jón Árnason, his cousin, becoming very devoted to and learning much from him. According to Davíð Stefánsson frá Fagraskógi,[20] Ólafur's nephew by his sister, Ólafur had had for a time a considerable number of books. The majority of these Fiske had purchased and the rest had gone to waste while Ólafur lived in Copenhagen. Nonetheless Ólafur Davíðsson left behind his great quantity of transcribed folktales, and doubtless on that account saved many of them from oblivion.

Chapter 24

From Strength to Strength

Willard Fiske acquired books he had his eye on in various ways, and quite often he appears to have benefited from the help of Icelanders of his acquaintance (as the preceding chapter makes clear). It would be possible to digress considerably here on with whom he dealt and in what manner works came to him, but a modest sampling will suffice.

Sometimes Fiske received publications sent free of charge; for example, Tryggvi Gunnarsson sent him books from the Þjóðvinafélag without reimbursement; Tryggvi and Fiske had become acquainted aboard the *Diana* the summer Fiske was in Iceland.[1] A letter from Tryggvi dated 24 January 1890 states:

I am in receipt of your welcome letter of 21 January; only reproaching you that you have not indicated whether you are lacking any of the books of the Þjóðvinafélag in your library. On the cover of the almanac one can see what books the society has. It occurred to me that the reason for this is that you did not want to hope for books without payment; and that, I bid you, my dear sir, will not do: Icelandic books are nowhere better found than with you; and all Icelanders, Society members, and especially I think it very good if we can in some measure show that we take notice of your inherent benevolence toward the Icelandic nation.

Although Fiske did not mind paying for publications, it undoubtedly gladdened him to receive such items for the amity it showed him.

Nonetheless Fiske also received books sent as gifts from various people as a measure of thanks for all he sent to Iceland. Jón Árnason, first librarian of the Provincial Library (later the National Library),[2] whom Fiske had gotten to know well on his Iceland journey, sent him on behalf of the library copies out of the duplicate collection; Jón had compiled an index of all the books in the library in the millennial year 1874. The two bookmen had hit it off especially well and Jón Árnason had expeditiously put it forward with the library board that Fiske would be given ten to twenty confirmed duplicates from the library of those Icelandic books he had longed to possess.

Many more people wanted to show Fiske their friendly disposition. Bishop Pétur Pétursson and other men sent him their works, which Fiske accepted with gratitude and interpreted as a gesture of friendship. Poets also sent to him their books as soon as they were published, given the competition among them to acquaint him with their works.

There are many other examples of people giving to Fiske out of their own libraries. On 26 November 1886 Björn M. Ólsen wrote: "I am in conflict about a book I have, which is now very rare; it is a *Calendarium Gregorianum* [. . .]. Prentad a Hoolum, Af Marteine Arnoddsyne, Anno 1707."[3] This book he wanted to give to Fiske as a sign of friendship and appreciation for old time's sake, ". . . though the booklet is mildewed and not clean"—and Fiske accepted it with thanks. And on 25 March 1890 Björn sent him a number of the *Legislative Assembly Books* from 1713 to 1794, which he himself had. Fiske subsequently filled in the gaps from other sources and acquired all the *Alþingi Books* from 1696 to 1737 and later the *Legislative Assembly Books* through 1800, at which point the Alþingi was abolished for a number of years.[4]

The poet Þorsteinn Erlingsson invited Fiske to transact business with him.[5] He himself had quite a good library and was in a position to obtain works, yet it is not evident that much business went on between them. Fiske seems to have had more of an interest in receiving letters from the poet on the writing of poetry and other aesthetics.

Jón Borgfirðingur, the great bookman, invited Fiske to purchase all the Icelandic epitaphs from the years 1823 to 1889, a total of 520, for twenty-five aurar each.[6] Fiske saw a benefit in these small writings. Jón likewise offered him many other items, as he was impoverished and had to sell off what he had accumulated over time.[7] Jón had been an industrious collector, poverty notwithstanding, and was enormously well read and erudite; and after Fiske began working on his catalogue, Jón conveyed to him multifarious and useful data regarding one or another item in the history of Iceland, especially the history of printing, as he himself was a meticulous bibliographer. In a letter Fiske wrote to him from Florence in 1885, he asked for example whether it was possible that Jón Matthíasson, who was the first to print in Iceland, had gone with his printing press because of errors or other reasons into Húnafjörður rather than Skagafjörður, setting it up at Hólar in Vesturhópur and later printing the *Breviarium Holense* there.[8]

In possession of Magnús Einarsson, a watchmaker in Copenhagen, was a book that to him was most precious, but Fiske longed to purchase it from him. Magnús wrote Fiske, saying: "I have taken with your letter today and see that you are offering me 110 krónur for the book *Passio*, anno 1620.[9] The book is a legacy and I have preferred not to let it go for anything. At the same time I shall admit you deserve that I do you a favor, although it only comes instead of the family tree that I am aware caused you a lot of work to obtain, and you were not willing to put any price on." Magnús was not disposed to parting with the book but did so all the same, adding to the letter: "Perhaps you desire to buy some other books that I have and that I am not so insistent on keeping after I have just let that one go. Among them are *Viaticum* (Hólar, 1706), *Eitt Gylline Reiklelsis Altare* (Hólar, 1706) and *Hallgrímskver* (Copenhagen, 1770). I am willing to sell all these for seventy krónur."

The pastors Valdimar Briem and Steindór Briem—they who had the New Testament of Oddur Skálksson that Fiske purchased out of the legacy of Eiríkur Briem in Hruni—had more costly items and proposed to him also the purchase of the *Biblia Laicorum*, printed at Hólar in 1599. The copy was in very good condition and was complete. From the library in Hruni Fiske bought more works, including a poor copy of the Gradual printed at Hólar in 1697. Lacking were the title page and the first two leaves. Furthermore he obtained the *Guðrækilegar VIKU Bænir* (Thoroughly Godly weekly prayers) printed at Hólar in 1728, in good condition aside from its not being clean, though quite readable. From the collection he also purchased the *Lærdóms bók handa Unglingum* (Book of wisdom for the young), printed at Leirárgarðar in 1807. The copy was very unclean, though readable and "complete."[10] All were precious items.

In the year 1888 Ólafur Davíðsson offered Fiske the *Þess Islenska-Evangeliska Smábóka Félags Rit* (Works of the Icelandic Evangelical Pamphlet Society) (numbers 1–80) for sale.[11] They were in good condition, bound in eight volumes. Not resisting, he bought all the works and later had them bound in a quality binding. He further-more received information from Ólafur that the famous work *Crymogaea*, by Arngrímur lærði (the Learned) Jónsson,[12] printed in Hamburg in 1609, was for sale in a rather good copy. Fiske had acquired *Crymogaea* before, but indulged himself nonetheless in buying the book. In the same consignment he received the *Stutt Ágrip um Skálhollts-Stóls jarðasölu, ásamt Fasteigna-Pant* . . . (Brief Summary on the Land Sale of the Seat of Skálholt, along with Real Estate Selection), with more from Copenhagen published in 1785. It was unbound but legible enough. Fiske was quite satisfied with the purchases. In a similar respect, many attractive items from various Icelanders ended up with him; one may name among them a *Stutt aagrip um Jardeplanna Nytsemd og Ræktan* (Brief Outline of Land-Planning Use and Cultivation), compiled by Jacob Kofoed Trojel in Copenhagen in 1772.[13] One may also mention he was offered the book *Stutt Undirvísan um Vatnsmilnur, sem uppteknar vóru í Barðastrandar Syslu árið 1778* (Brief Undertaking on Watermills, Which Were Occupied in the Shire of Barðaströnd in 1778), by Bjarni Einarsson; it had been printed in Copenhagen by Johan Rudolph Thiele in 1781. With it was bound the *Búnaðar-Bálkur* (Agricultural Series) of Eggert Olafsson, which had been printed in Hrappsey in 1783.[14] At about the same time Fiske purchased the above-mentioned works, he also acquired the second edition of Björn Halldórsson's *Atli, eða Ráðagjörðir Yngismanns um Búnað sinn* . . . (Atli or Advices of a Young Man on His Agriculture), also printed in 1783 at Hrappsey, where much was produced in the years 1773–1786.

In every instance shipments of Icelandic books arrived, Fiske welcomed them, whether it was a matter of old or new material, scarce or abundant; always he sent generous payment for what he requested. Without doubt, good came out of the additional work for Fiske in shopping for Icelandic works, as many young men of education chose to assist him.

Jón Þorkelsson, mentioned earlier, wrote Fiske that he would be able to obtain for him Torfaeus' *Gronlandia antiqua* from 1706, a completely sound copy that he had compared with the one in the Royal Library.[15] This work by Þormóður Torfason was in great demand, but Ólafur Davíðsson had succeeded in finding one for him before, so it is evident that both these men performed thorough searching for difficult items. Jón also wanted to send Fiske *Jörgen Jörgensens Usurpation i Island*, by Schulesen (the Icelander Sigfús Skúlason), from Copenhagen, 1832. These were good copies, and he advised Fiske firmly to purchase the books, given their scarcity.[16] Fiske received all such advice with thanks and purchased all Jón mentioned, as he trusted Jón's critical judgment to the fullest.

In Copenhagen Jón succeeded in procuring for him Vídalín's *Postillur* (collections of sermons), both the first edition, printed at Hólar in 1718–20, and the fifth edition (Hólar 1744–45); as well as the collections of Vídalín's sermons from 1798.[17] He also sent Fiske clarifications on the work *Ein Nytsamleg Bænabook Sem lesast maa, a sierhvørium Deige Vikunnar Kuølld og Morgna* (A Useful Prayer Book that May Be Read Every Day of the Week, Evening and Morning), by Johann Lassenius, printed at Hólar in 1681. He said the copy was excellent and the book itself exceedingly rare; it was neither in the Royal Library nor in the University Library in Copenhagen. As it turned out, Jón bought the book for Fiske. Jón also sent him "Rabe Grosshandel's," as the book was referred to familiarly, although it was actually titled *Gross-Handels Omspørgende om den islandske Friihandels Fremgang* (Wholesale Inquiry on the Progress of Icelandic Free Trade). It was by Jacob Fromsen Rabe and published in Copenhagen in 1803.[18] Jón wrote on 19 December 1890: "This copy is especially rare, as it has the author's autograph."

Much more of interest was sent Fiske's way, and each consignment aroused his expectations, as it was of overriding importance to him to compile a comprehensive collection. *Huggunarsaltari*

In March and April 1900 were named here the books, with accompanying price, to be sent to Fiske next. The letter is from Jón Þorkelsson.

List of works Jón Þorkelsson offered for sale to Fiske. It is notable that small-press items are included among books and rare works.

Jón Þorkelsson at the close of 1899 writes to Fiske, offering these works for sale, for example *Eyrbyggja saga* (item 4), which was printed in Akureyri in 1882 and long sold out. The price is indicated.

(The Psalter of Solace), printed at Hólar in 1756, was also sent to Florence as well as the *Hugvekjusálmar* (Thought-Provoking Hymns) of séra Sigurður Jónsson at Presthólar, fifth edition, printed at Hólar in 1703.[19] Jón stated in the event that the title page was lacking, and one or two leaves at the end. "A copy of the title page I can have obtained for you from a tattered copy I have. This edition is unusually rare, and not in the libraries here. The date of 1703 is very remarkable and I think, naturally, not on any other Icelandic book, and it shows that the printing press had then come back to Hólar. Jón Borgfirðingur says it moved there in 1704, but he had not encountered this edition."[20] In the same package he included a very good copy of Hallgrímur Pétursson's *Passiusalmar*, the thirtieth edition, printed in Reykjavík in 1866, together with a good copy of *Fridreks-Draapa*[21] printed in Copenhagen in 1766. In the consignment was also the work *Christiansmal*,[22] which was published in 1783 in Copenhagen.[23] Then Jón sent Fiske all the Graduals

Invoice from Sigurður Kristjánsson, 22 March 1886. The variety of literature is wide, from *Guðrækilegar vikubænir* (God-fearing weekly prayers) to
Ljóðmæli Jóns Ólafssonar (Poems of Jón Ólafsson). Sigurður very regularly
sent invoices, which Fiske settled quickly.

published from 1655 to 1843, and that was a great catch.[24] Fiske had a great interest in the oldest examples of Icelandic printing, and the divine word was there in the first rank. Jón Þorkelsson easily obtained the Bible identified with Bishop Guðbrandur Þorláksson, as it was printed in a large number of copies in 1584. He also located the Bibles of Þorlákur and Steinn on behalf of Fiske.[25]

The consignments went out from Jón fairly regularly, and he always insured them but was nonetheless half-afraid they would be lost on the way to Italy. Therefore he always asked Fiske for confirmation the parcels had gotten through. He stated in a letter of 9 November 1890: "I sent you the *Passíusálmar* [in multiple editions] 29 October last, addressed Lungo il Mugnone 3A, insured for two hundred francs. Please let me know at earliest convenience whether they have been delivered. I shall suffer for it if they have gone astray, especially the edition of 1704, since it is nowhere available."[26]

Jón also sent Fiske *The Primer*, printed at Hólar in 1745, and the Psalms of David from 1647, insured for five hundred francs, together with two rare works, *A Short Summary on Icelandic Yarnspinning* and *The Crater of Katla*.[27] Then he purchased *Key to Paradise*, printed in Skálholt in 1686, and it took him an entire year to bring down the price.[28] The copy was excellent and Fiske was very pleased with it.

Jón had his hands full otherwise, as he was known as a dedicated book enthusiast; and he thought at that time first of Fiske, his friend in Florence. In a letter of 26 February 1895 he stated having "a book in octavo that lacks a title page [but] appears printed at Hólar in 1599 as the preface ends with 'Written at Hólar the first day of January of the New Year 1599. Guðbrandur Thorlaks son.' The foreword begins with 'To all learned men and servants of God's word in the Hólar diocese.' *This book is not known from any other place, and is unable to be found anywhere.*[29] After what stands in the foreword is the book: 'Explanation and Translation of the Little Catechism of the Praiseworthy and Glorious Man of God, Martin Luther . . . Set Out from the Saxon Language, and from the Beginning Written by the Highly Learned Man Named Johann Aumann, Bishop of Syling in Saxonland [Germany].' In the book are wanting [signatures] Eiij, 5I, viij. Ends with the poem 'On Absolution, or The Key Power of the Christian Church,' and there seems little wanting after that. *In the book are many illustrations (woodcuts)* . . . [the book] is unicum."[30] Fiske wrote immediately and wanted by all means to buy the book. It was therefore sent off parcel post, and well insured.

In a letter from 10 October 1886, Jón wrote Fiske after having resolved several bibliographical inquiries: "Now this is most interesting: I have found two pamphlets printed before 1600 that are not on your list; they are the so-called murder-letter pamphlets of Bishop Guðbrandur [Þorláksson]."[31]

Jón Þorkelsson obtained the biography of Bjarni Pálsson, the country's chief medical officer, printed at Leirárgarðar in the year 1800.[32] He found it one of the most remarkable of the older biographies, and said not to know better than that it was extremely rare. Þorvaldur Björnsson, the pastor at Melstaður, had a complete copy of the Hymnal from 1589 and lent it to the Paris Exhibition of 1900. Jón inquired after the book on behalf of Fiske but Þorvaldur was reluctant to sell it. Jón estimated that it was the sole intact copy in the world.[33]

It is not too exact to say that Jón and the other collectors envied Fiske for being able to purchase whatever book he wanted. Scant resources, in particular, came in the way of the Icelandic book collectors' acquiring all they desired. Jón thought much of Fiske's Icelandic library and said in a letter of 8 December 1890 "that there is scarcely an expectation that an individual could crave another [such collection] and then more." Jón wrote more often in the same tone, for example on 6 December 1889: "I see it has become a great problem to procure books for you, as you have acquired nearly all . . . You have probably laid considerable sums into your library from the first until now."

Jón was also a zealous book collector but could not indulge himself in buying books in great style, and at times it occurred that people did not want to sell him a book before he stated that he was an intermediary for Fiske. Then he enjoyed great good will. This shows perhaps that Icelanders regarded works well paid if they came into Fiske's hands. It may be, however, that booksellers were also of the opinion that Fiske should have these works figuring in the compilation of the book catalogue he was working on, as the catalogue would then be achieved in a superior manner in terms of information recorded. The catalogue was considered a work of great necessity, and subsequently saw great use.

Jón went thoroughly over the lists Fiske sent him, correcting them and also transcribing a great amount for Fiske as he filled in copies that were damaged. For example, he transcribed title pages and described illustrations, but did not try to sketch them. From the letters of Jón one can see that he also transcribed stories and poems when it was not possible to obtain them in the original texts. In a letter of 18 September 1886 he says: "I am not yet finished with the transcription of *Gríshaldar saga* at all. You will receive it next month. I am unable to do so before then, and shall have to ask you to forgive." Of course he sent off the transcription.

Jón marveled at Fiske's extensive bibliographical knowledge, which was generally correct down to the minor points. Yet Fiske's penchant for collecting was not exclusively because of his passion for books, but also to fulfill his bibliographical ambition. His carefully wrought catalogue in Bibliographical Notices bears evidence of this, and of course he had to have the books at hand to compile the work.

Jón went often to the Royal Library in Copenhagen and examined copies and single editions in order to compare with the books he was concluding purchase for on behalf of Fiske. Comparing exactly and writing quickly, he found a difference no matter how small on the title pages if leaves were lacking in the books.[34] Good storage or shelter was available for Icelandic books in Hovedvagtsgade 2 in Copenhagen, where they awaited shipment to Florence.[35] With the help of three to four Icelanders in Copenhagen, most often students, all the Icelandic material was registered on cards and checked over.

In the fateful year of 1883, when Fiske left the United States definitively, he laid major emphasis on collecting Icelandic works. Much of the correspondence in the Fiske Icelandic Collection, as the preceding narrative shows, dwells at great length on collecting, and at times one can trace the story of individual copies—where they were found, who owned them previously, and of course whether they fetched the asking price. His representatives were careful, but Halldór Hermannsson related in the preface of the *Catalogue of the Icelandic Collection bequeathed by Willard Fiske*, which came out in 1914, that Fiske had never done bookkeeping on his purchase of Icelandic materials.[36] Accordingly it was not easy to trace the purchases, nor to see which ones were gifts and which were paid items. Halldór, who later assumed charge of the collection, was an extremely scrupulous man and saw to the major and the minor in relation to business transactions. Though some of the notes and invoices could have disappeared before Halldór began working for Fiske, these sources subsequently have offered a rather good picture of the transactions after Halldór began accounting for them. After the collection came to Ithaca and Halldór had responsibility for all acquisitions and likewise for care of the material, he was by contrast exacting in preserving all business correspondence and invoices.[37] That was also necessary given how rapidly the collection grew under the aegis of Halldór.

Though an exact accounting from Fiske himself does not exist, one may find amusing that his documents include receipts for well-known biscuits from Göteborg, Göteborg-kex, which he had sent from Sweden to Italy. During his 1896 trip to Sweden he had gotten to know this delicacy and indulged himself in ordering it regularly thereafter.

Sigurður Kristjánsson, a bookseller in Reykjavík, was very persistent obtaining books, and newspapers and journals no less, for Fiske. He obtained issues and numbers Fiske was lacking until annual volumes were complete, and regularly sent him lists of the material he had in his shop. Fiske was then able to indicate what he desired to purchase and have sent to Florence. Sigurður was most thorough in business and took on obtaining for Fiske rare books not available in his shop, for example both *Summaríurnar* (the Summaries, Summary of the New Testament and Summary of the Old Testament), printed at Núpufell in 1589 and 1591 respectively.[38] The *Summaries* are tremendously beautiful treasures in Icelandic printing, and are the only works known for certain to have been printed at the time the press was at Núpufell. He apologized for how damaged they were and asked Fiske to let them be repaired, but it is not known what came of that. It is rather unlikely there had been great damage during their time in storage and repair.

Sigurður usually wrote Fiske in Danish. In July 1891 he wrote: "I have the pleasure of sending you by post a good copy of the poems of Hallgrímur [Pétursson] 1755 that I had the fortune to obtain. It is of great rarity and the National Library has until now been unable to find a copy of this edition."[39]

In the preface to the *Catalogue of the Icelandic Collection* (1914), Halldór Hermannsson states that Fiske had increased his holdings considerably in the summer of 1899, noting that during that year he had received eight hundred to nine hundred volumes of books and three thousand pamphlets and other minor printings. Fiske had then taken up temporary residence in Copenhagen and Uppsala with a sojourn in Göteborg and was thus able himself to make an effort practically to rake together printed items on the journey. He was quite cognizant that all minor press material was important for casting light on history, topography, producer goods, commerce, language, customs, and culture of the country, as this material was sought after by scholars wanting to plumb the depths of their topics. Almanacs were also on his wish lists, and in one shipment he received eight from Sigurður Kristjánsson, who had done much to collect them for him.[40]

In Iceland men traversed the breadth and width of the island to obtain specific books for Fiske. Often it was difficult to assemble complete annual runs of newspapers and periodicals; individual numbers could be worn out or unusable, but always everything was tried to have every single snippet in good shape.[41] All kinds of material did not turn up in bookshops, for example occasional poems, epitaphs, school and business reports, and the like. This is material that disappears before it comes to light, but no less important and worthy, and Fiske laid it on his agents to obtain it for him. Depository laws that took effect in 1886 required all printed matter to be placed in Icelandic libraries and also in the Royal Library in Copenhagen, but there must always have been some shortage here. The bookseller Sigurður Kristjánsson nonetheless made a remarkable effort to have printers take from, and sell to Fiske, all the small printings that came off the presses. That did not go as well as it should, and Sigurður did not obtain all of them. Fiske paid his obligations to Sigurður richly but also very often sent him gifts, to which the letters bear witness. One time the parcel from him contained eight chessboards and chess sets and four pocket boards.[42]

Printing in Iceland had matured just before the mid-nineteenth century, when the one press on the island was moved from Viðey to Reykjavík. In the wake of this move more people gained access to printing, which had the effect of making publishing flourish. Actually, there was an explosion in publishing, so much did printed works multiply. One of the printers Fiske had relations with was Einar Þórðarson, who came into possession of a speed press in the autumn of 1879.[43] Einar ordered the press from London and completely reworked it for printing conditions in Iceland, and publishing activity grew considerably.[44] The new machine was said to print five times faster than the fastest printers on the best manual press, with one man or two small boys assisting; but the hand press needed two full-grown men.[45] These were therefore improved conditions for the work of publishing. More works were now printed than before, and the print runs greater, which for Fiske facilitated acquisition.

There is an amusing story about Fiske's diligence in book collecting. During his Icelandic sojourn he apparently had come into a little church out in the country and saw there a copy of Guðbrandsbiblía, which was printed at Hólar in 1584. Fiske longed eagerly to possess the volume and offered a high price for it, but pastor and vestry were unwilling to sell, thinking it unsuitable to sell a Bible. Fiske, however, did not give up. Noticing there was no organ in the church, he offered to see to it that the church acquired one in exchange for the Bible. This was tempting, and people were accordingly on the verge of accepting the offer when they remembered that no one in the vicinity knew how to play the instrument. The man with the will of steel then had the idea of ameliorating his offer by proposing to support the pastor's son's organ studies in Reykjavík. This offer was not possible to refuse, and Fiske received the Bible.[46] Jón A. Hjaltalín assisted in purchasing a harmonium and sending it to Iceland from Scotland; it cost twenty pounds.[47] The story has been widely circulated, and the organ is sometimes transformed into a church bell. It may not matter; the story shows Fiske was a provident man, and practical, and gave in not at all when it came to books.

Chapter 25

Icelandic Students Assist

In the 1880s great stories about the Fiske Collection in Florence came to Iceland, and it was thought singularly noteworthy that a foreign man of means had such interest in perfecting a collection of Icelandic works. The collection, which Fiske maintained at 11 Lungo il Mugnone in Florence, had now become extensive, and he had to have assistance with it. There was no way to copy and refresh the old card files Fiske had made in Copenhagen; thus he invited two young Icelandic students to come to Florence in 1899 to work on the collection.

From letters to Fiske it is evident fewer young Icelanders, adventuresome and eager in their knowledge, received work then wanted to, as very often he was asked whether he wanted assistance with the collection. It may be pointed out that Fiske moved slowly on employment matters and was discriminating. Sigfús Blöndal, then twenty-four years old, who later became a librarian with the Royal Library in Copenhagen, enthusiastically sought work with him, and Björn M. Ólsen undertook to speak on his behalf with Fiske. Nonetheless he did not receive the post, and it was rather because Sigfús was then combatting illness than that Fiske had no faith in him.[1] Hannes Þorsteinsson, later national archivist, had great enthusiasm,[2] but was not appointed to the work, since he was married. Fiske frowned on the idea that a librarian should need to look after his young wife along with the work.[3] Vilhjálmur Jónsson, a postal clerk in Reykjavík and the son of Jón Borgfirðingur, asked him for work with the collection and stated Björn M. Ólsen was eager to give him his recommendation.[4] Vilhjálmur read Germanic studies at the University of Copenhagen, but did not complete his degree. He was not so fortunate as to obtain the post.

It was Sigfús Blöndal who suggested Halldór Hermannsson from Völlur in Rangárvellir to Fiske; Halldór was then studying law in Copenhagen,[5] and Fiske hired him to work with the collection in 1899 along with Bjarni Jónsson from Unnarholt in Árnessýsla, who was also studying in Copenhagen. Hiring Halldór proved to be a sound step for the collection, as the man was well suited to the task. Fiske had then become too ill to attend to it well, and from summer 1900 he was more often away from Florence, far and wide in Europe, for his health. The two men sought leave from their studies at the University of Copenhagen,[6] and Bjarni and especially Halldór made good use of the sojourn in Florence. Their service with Fiske was good, and he was very satisfied with their work. On occasion he gave them vacation, and they took the opportunity to travel throughout Tuscany, among other places journeying in July 1900 up to the mountains to the summer paradise of Vallombrosa, not far from Florence and a renowned summer resort. The place was agreeable and Halldór wrote that up on the heights blew a nearly Icelandic wind.[7] They went likewise on their vacation in August, when the heat was the worst, to the city of Viareggio and afterward to Livorno; both cities are on the Tyrrhenian Sea, where it was somewhat cooler. From there Halldór went to Bagni di Lucca and Bjarni went to Pistoia and stayed with the Banchi family, whose acquaintance the Icelanders had made in Florence. Thus they returned, refreshed and glad, to work on the collection two weeks later, as it was without compare to have the opportunity to explore a bit around Italy.[8]

The colleagues enjoyed their sojourn in Florence, then inexhaustibly enchanting with cultural and artistic history. They shared equally receiving packages from Sigurður Kristjánsson, Jón Þorkelsson, and others who regularly sent material to the collection; reviewed the card index of desiderata; and found a place for them. Much of what came into the collection was sent out to the most capable bookbinders in the city, as Fiske was particular about the appearance and endurance of his books.

Bjarni worked only a brief time in Florence and returned to Copenhagen the year after, late in 1900, and completed his studies in law. After he returned to Copenhagen he was equally ready to assist Fiske in the acquisition of Icelandic works. Halldór, on the other hand, stayed longer and worked for Fiske more or less the last years of the latter's life. He returned nonetheless to Copenhagen in 1901 to resume studies because he was not prepared to cease with them definitively. Halldór then journeyed around Germany with a brief stay in Heidelberg; he thought it good to come to this university town. He was in Copenhagen for parts of the years 1901–02 and worked much with editions of works on chess; he was equally submerged otherwise in work for Fiske and in constant correspondence with him even while attending simultaneously to one thing or another.

Halldór was a workhorse, collecting material, translating and reading proofs and even making himself available to fashion new terms that might be used in chess.[9] He considered many words and concepts, but based them on the word "chess" itself.[10] In a letter to Fiske he was contemplating the word "self-checkmate" (sjálfsmát): "I prefer the word 'self-checkmate' to 'suicide-check-mate' (sjálfsmorðsmát) since the latter is tautological, and I have utilized the former word."[11] Yet his interest in creating neologisms focused not only on chess but also on the entire language, and he often wrote Fiske regarding his ideas about words and phrases. In a letter from 12 March 1901 he stated he had newly created an Icelandic word for the English "literary riddle," or "ritgáta" instead of "bóklega gáta," which had been used; he did not like the latter, as it was easy to misunderstand the term. Halldór also scouted museums to get wind of items they housed that were connected with chess, and found on his peregrinations antique chess pieces of various materials—silver, bronze, marble, wood, bone—all according to the economic conditions of the countries of origin and their possibilities for procuring materials. Some of what he found was very beautiful, well-made work crafted by hand. In countries where wood was plentiful, carved chess pieces were especially in circulation—delicate wood-carving that bore witness to the craftsmen—and often the wooden pieces were painted in a colorful manner. Marble chessmen raised no less his interest.

In mid-November 1902 Halldór again obtained leave from the university at Fiske's bidding to return to Florence. Fiske was then often absent and ever more often searching for various health resorts, but his illness worsened steadily. In 1902 he wrote Halldór that he could only get about with a measure of pain and was more or less confined to his bed. On 14 February 1903 Fiske wrote Halldór from a sanitarium in Naples, now considering at length future work on the collection. He wanted to appoint Halldór permanently, but Halldór had never intended to settle in Italy, though increasingly he found library work agreed with him. Halldór journeyed back to Copenhagen on 3 March 1903 but stayed briefly, returning to Florence.

One might say Halldór was Fiske's major mainstay in the Icelandic collection from the summer of 1899 through until Fiske died in the autumn of 1904, though with breaks. Michele Monzecchi, an Italian, was also available to assist Fiske in these last years.[12] He traveled with him, and at the last, when Fiske had become so ill he could hardly hold a pen, he wrote to various people as Fiske dictated. Ettore Sordi, also Italian, likewise performed various labors for Fiske, among others with the book collections.[13]

Above all, Fiske wanted to have a comprehensive Icelandic collection, and thus needed to look out for editions beyond Europe. In North America newspaper and book publishing was flourishing among the immigrants, and he wrote often to Canada in pursuit of Icelanders out west to get hold of Icelandic material. The bookseller Bardal in Winnipeg was helpful; so also was séra Jón Bjarnason, pastor of the Icelanders in Manitoba, diligent in sending him requested works concerning Icelanders there. Fiske wrote to Jón from Lungo il Mugnone on 12 November 1890:

> These days I am very busy reviewing my catalogue in Islandica specifically with the intent of having it printed next summer. The catalogue contains the titles of my entire collection, with notes. Here is a comprehensive catalogue out of my collection with all the Old Norse material and contemporary Icelandic literature, also foreign books that in some way concern Iceland and Icelanders. –That which is today called Islandica in collecting.

I am very thankful for all trifles such as funeral brochures, grave inscriptions, small poems, speeches or other small-press items printed in Icelandic in Winnipeg or elsewhere in America. I do not have a single grave inscription that has been printed in Winnipeg.[14]

In North America as well as elsewhere, everyone wanted to work on behalf of Willard Fiske, the friend of Iceland, doing the utmost to assist him in collecting to the utmost the printed works that appeared among Icelandic immigrants, which was considerable in quantity and bore positive witness to this "nation of books," as the Icelanders took their heritage with them and displayed much enterprise in the activity of publishing, both in books and periodicals. Thus they confirmed the Icelanders' love of books, which accompanied them wherever they went.

Chapter 26

State of the Libraries in Reykjavík

It was likely the Icelandic public were less than pleased when all the Icelandic books Fiske closed purchase on, the old with the new, were sent out of the country.[1] If one looks at the housing options and conditions available for preservation of books at this time, it becomes more understandable, however, why people allowed this without reproach.[2] Many people were thus quite satisfied that rare Icelandic titles should go to Florence, and likely saw them as better sustained in good and dry housing abroad than in crowded, inferior spaces in Reykjavík. We can also see how well stocked Reykjavík was in manuscripts and printed matter, as several so-called brokers were then learning.

In Iceland at this time there was truly no facility for collecting such material. The library in Reykjavík was a shambles and the District Library (Stiptisbókasafnið) had a housing problem. When Parliament House was completed in 1881, the books of the library were moved there; they had been two years in the library of the Learned School because of repairs on the cathedral.[3] Before then they had been in the cathedral attic in the damp, in a cluttered space. In 1879 the number of borrowers at the library was thirty and the number of books circulated 449; the year after the borrowers were only twenty and volumes lent 432.[4] The entire collection conveyed into Parliament House comprised thirteen thousand volumes of manuscripts and printed works.[5] An effort was made to hold the collection open three days per week, three hours at a time.

It was thought necessary to build a dedicated house for the collection, but the cost stood in the way.[6] According to the constitution of 1874, fiscal power was transferred to Iceland; it was determined to give the library a regular stipend from public funds, but until then the collection had received support only through monetary and book gifts of private individuals, Icelandic or foreign. Professor Finnur Jónsson wrote to Fiske about the poor condition of the library, which had become known as the National Library (Landsbókasafn), on 2 September 1903: books and manuscripts were in danger of being ruined, and moreover the staff was inferior. "Accordingly it is best that such ought not to continue longer under the circumstances. And whether the national treasury has the wherewithal to realize a sound and large enough house for the collection in near future, I doubt greatly. And the longer things endure, so more evident are the danger and damage the books are enduring. It is not necessary to point out how precious the manuscript collection is." Subesquently he described the reading room as being "nearly unusable."[7] Finnur's mind was set on the matter, and he considered frequently how a remedy might be suggested for it.

In the second and third paragraphs of the regulations the Icelandic authorities enacted for the library in Reykjavík on 2 February 1882, it is stated thus: "Anyone who is tidy in appearance and clean is permitted to use books and manuscripts of the national library in the reading room, whether to read them or copy from them. Such person shall present himself to the librarian to receive the book he wishes to use, returning it to him undamaged before he exits the reading room. One may neither write anything nor underscore in the books of the library." The rules are simple and clear. It says further: "In the reading room people must remain silent; the dictionaries of the library, and other books readers may wish to consult, shall be kept there; ink and pens will also be available there for readers to use."

Not until some years after the death of Fiske was a good house for the library built, and the books paid for. The elegant library on Hverfisgata[8] opened in 1909. Much was invested in the construction and the most capable craftsmen employed in the work.

In a letter of 20 August 1903 from Fiske, who was then situated in Copenhagen, written in a hand other than his own, it states he was concerned about the situation; it seemed to him likely that no other city in any country was in as great a need for the construction of a library as Reykjavík, the capital of Iceland. The two large libraries sheltered considerable material, the national library holding sixty thousand and the school library twenty thousand. The space of the national library was very small and difficult to use, and care of the materials nearly impossible. The school library was in a crowded space in a house that had been built at the instigation of an English friend of Iceland.[9] It was now so crowded that having a reading room there presented difficulties. The need for these two collections was great, as in them lay the chief opportunity for all Icelanders for instruction and enlightenment. Yet the proportion of students and readers there was higher than in any other country.[10]

Fiske also published in Copenhagen a pamphlet he called *Book-Collections in Iceland*. This was an introduction in which he mentioned the sorry state of libraries in Iceland. In it he reported on the two major libraries in Reykjavík, the National Library and the library of the Learned School; but also on smaller libraries in the country.[11]

After Fiske's death his large bequest to Iceland came to the library—around two thousand volumes comprising his collection on chess. So crowded had the library become that it was not possible to unpack the boxes; they were stacked unopened where they came to rest on the floor. This choice collection of books was thus in closed crates and difficult to use until the library found shelter in its building on Hverfisgata four years later.[12]

Chapter 27

Creating Bibliography

Meticulous bibliographers were not and are not everywhere to be found. Bibliography was always lofty in Fiske's thoughts, and Fiske—whose Dante, Petrarch, and Rhaeto-Romanic collections and not least his Icelandic collection were to arouse attention worldwide— put a great quantity of work into his catalogues. It is likely he derived a particular pleasure from bibliographical work, and of course he had the wherewithal to make special catalogues for his collections. The catalogues are still fully valid today.[1]

Bibliographical Notices I is Fiske's catalogue of *Books Printed in Iceland 1578–1844: A* [first] *Supplement to the British Museum Catalogue* of Thomas William Lidderdale (1830–1884), bibliographer with that institution.[2] The Fiske supplement covers material Fiske had but the British did not, although they had done their best to collect Icelandic material for years. The catalogue was printed in Florence by Le Monnier in 1886 and is in twenty-eight pages. Bibliographical Notices II and III were catalogues of his Petrarch Collection, an excellent compilation chiefly of the great Tuscan poet's works: as stated earlier, he did not stop with Icelandic catalogues.[3]

Fiske's next catalogue of Icelandic material was Bibliographical Notices IV, which covered the same and, once again, served to supplement the British Museum catalogue. The third supplement to the British Museum catalogue was Bibliographical Notices V, also printed by Le Monnier in Florence in 1890. Ettore Sordi, Fiske's assistant, also lent a hand in the catalogue. Fiske had come well along with Bibliographical Notices VI, but age did not permit him to publish that number.[4] That one came out under the aegis of G. W. Harris, Cornell University librarian, in 1907, three years after the death of Fiske, and is the fourth list of books printed in Iceland 1578–1844; aside from the list, it includes "a general index to the four supplements." Halldór Hermannsson finished this catalogue, which has forty-seven pages. The publisher is not named, although it has always been assumed the Cornell University Library had produced it.[5] In the preliminary note of the first supplement Fiske wrote a historically informed preface on the saga of Icelandic printing. He insisted considerably on that which appeared to be unusual, and discussed various entertaining matters such as decorations in books; woodcuts that could trace roots to Germany.[6]

Publication of the supplements laid a scholarly groundwork of indices for printed Icelandic matter, and Fiske was thus a pioneer in this field. He was surpassingly reliable and precise, describing items thoroughly, recording creator and title, outlining the contents and remarking on the origin and history of each book. He offered thereby a good and detailed overview of Iceland's printing history along with the bibliographical summary.

Fiske also compiled a catalogue he called *Icelandic Books of the XVIth Century*, printed in Florence in 1886. The list was based on the holdings of the Royal Library in Copenhagen and was printed with the intent of making known more widely descriptions of Icelandic books from this era in other collections.

Fiske's own books especially are at the foundations for his bibliographic catalogues, and he laid major emphasis more on those printed in Iceland rather than Icelandic material printed elsewhere.[7] Halldór Hermannsson later compiled the excellent bibliographies for the Fiske Collection that appeared in the Islandica series, and it is not for nothing that Halldór is considered the pre-eminent Icelandic bibliographer. He said of Willard Fiske that he had been a very erudite man, precise and meticulous in all he devoted himself to. He had a quick grasp of things and was most apt about everything concerning books, but tended to cease one project and take up another instead of finishing the work.[8] His restlessness accounted for his meager publication despite his diligence, enthusiasm, and energy. Nonetheless Fiske had been one of the most cooperative people Halldór had known, and what he accomplished in Icelandic bibliography had lasting value.[9] It was also quite clear to other colleagues what inestimable use Fiske made of his catalogues. In *Sunnanfari* Ólafur Davíðsson writes:

> Prof. W. Fiske is most kind and the most entertaining of men, as he has traveled very widely, both in North America and in Europe, Asia, and Africa, and thus can say much.[10] He is now middle-aged, around sixty, and rather unwell, but it would be desirable he live well and long still, so Icelandic bibliography may be enriched by benefiting from the excellent knowledge he has acquired in this field.[11]

Though Fiske thought his Icelandic collection the most valuable, far be it that he neglected his other collections. He worked diligently to compile as much material as possible, spending considerable money in the effort. In a letter of 10 September 1884 to the Danish national librarian, Fiske asked whether there were not Danish translations of the works of Petrarch, as he sorely was lacking them in his bibliography. He professed acquaintance with all the Swedish translations of Petrarch's works, but had found nothing of the Danish renditions: "You will forgive, I hope, the liberty with which I, from a lack of knowledge, give you so much trouble, as I have sought to no avail to obtain particulars on this matter in all my accessible bibliographic books. My collection of the Petrarchan literature (editions, translations, biographies, critical articles, etc.) is most likely the largest found (1800 volumes), and I intend to make of this catalogue a comprehensive Petrarchan bibliography."[12]

Not many years later Fiske was also seeking information on printed works by Dante in Denmark, as he was paying great attention to his growing Dante collection.[13] Willard Fiske sat seldom idle as a collector. Nonetheless, bibliographies are slow work, demanding undivided attention, and he did not survive to bring out as many catalogues as he had intended.

Nonetheless, Fiske had more irons in the fire. Of the books he published in Icelandic on chess, one can mention a work he edited, *Nokkur skákdæmi og tafllok eftir Samúel Loyd og fleiri* (Several chess game examples and game endings by Samuel Lloyd and others), and a small tome in Halldór Hermannsson's translation, *Mjög lítill skákbæklingur* (A very little chess booklet), which were printed respectively in Leipzig and Florence in 1901. He also produced a catalogue of contemporary Icelandic authors and their principal works, printed 1882–83;[14] in the year 1903, by then his health quite exhausted, he published in Copenhagen a practical little book under the title *Mímir: Icelandic Institutions and Addresses*.[15] For this project he availed himself, as so often before, of Halldór's assistance. He was very gratified to have published the work and thought it would come to be of use. *Mímir* contains various bits of good advice for those contemplating travel to Iceland and is a compact source of information. In the book Fiske urged people to such trips, though they could be strenuous here and there, and emphasized that the purity of the air and water was good for people. He also remarked somewhat on his tour around Iceland,[16] and one chapter was on the language and literature of the Icelanders. Then there was discussion on how best to come to Iceland and what one might expect regarding nature and culture. Following was a report on industries such as the collection, cleaning, and export of eiderdown. A historical survey was inserted into scenic descriptions of the land, with a discussion of Grímsey, which he had so longed to visit in his time, and its inhabitants. This work was uniquely informative and useful at a time when few books on Iceland existed for foreigners.

Fiske wrote to Halldór Hermannsson, who was then in Copenhagen, that he had not had before to fulfill orders for *Mímir* both to the United States and to Harrassowitz Publishing in Germany, and repeatedly had been asked about larger orders. Thus *Mímir* went over well, as there was lacking a work of this kind on the market on both sides of the Atlantic.[17]

Halldór stated in a letter from Copenhagen of 13 April 1904: "I have still in my keeping several hundred copies of the first edition of *Mímir*. What am I to do with them? Am I not to send part of them to Florence? It has been enough to print 1200–1500 copies." But by then several hundred were sold. Fiske was then staying in Paris and Halldór sent the remainder of the print run to Florence. From there it was distributed.[18]

Willard Fiske and Halldór Hermannsson were large-thinking men at work who truly put effort into producing this instructive book, which succeeded in improving the sparse choice of publications on Iceland in foreign languages.

Chapter 28

Grímsey Fascination

During his circumnavigation of Iceland in 1879 aboard the *Diana*, Fiske sailed past Grímsey and caught a fine view of the island. He scarcely believed people dwelled on the farthest sea and lived a largely civilized existence there.[1] Fiske's interest was aroused, and it caused him disappointment that he did not have the oppportunity to come ashore, have a look around, and meet the inhabitants.[2] Nonetheless he vowed to take the island under his protective wing, and the island occupied thereafter a secure place in his thoughts; he praised the people who lived there. This attachment has long awakened people's attention.

During many years he thought of Grímsey, longing to know how things were, and considered writing a book about the island and life there. Nothing resulted except to small measure: there is a chapter in *Mímir*, mentioned previously, the only item about the island that was printed. He was very thankful to Þorvaldur Thoroddsen, who sent him his scholarly essay, "Et besög paa Grimsö" (A visit to Grímsey, 1902), along with a hand-drawn, hand-colored map of the island.[3] In 1901 Fiske asked Matthías Jochumsson to obtain the following information from someone in Akureyri who knew well the conditions in Grímsey and was discerning:

1. How many families and houses were on the island.
2. Length and breadth of the island.

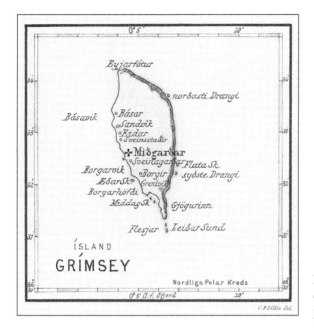

Handmade map
of Grímsey in the
possession of Fiske.

3. Style and construction of housing stock.

4. How was the church there.

5. Whether there were on the island animals, for example horses, sheep, cattle, or poultry.

6. How large was the harvest of down and how much was sold from the island.

7. Whether fish were exported from the island, and what quantity.

8. What sort of harbor was in the island, or what conditions for landing.

9. Whether there was provision for children's education.

10. Whether there were marriages between islanders and people on the mainland of Iceland.

11. Which were the nearest harbors and trading posts in the country, and how was shipping thence to the island arranged.

12. Whether the art of chess was much pursued in the island and who were the best players.[4]

Yet Fiske wanted more information, not least for his projected book. Two years later he wrote séra Matthías Eggertsson, the parish pastor in Grímsey and nephew of Matthías Jochumsson, setting out many questions in several paragraphs:

1. Does it happen often that people do not go between settlements in Grímsey because of the weather? On what type of paths do people go between settlements? How much are horses utilized in the island? Does it occur that people do not come to church on Sundays because of the weather? Do winter storms cause much damage to structures? Is there much snowfall? How long is the day when it is shortest and again when it is longest, from sunrise to sunset?

2. How large is the church? Is it heated? Does it withstand weather and wind? How many does it seat? From where is the altar-piece, how old is it, and of what is the picture? Is there a church bell or organ or baptismal font? How often is Mass said during the wintertime? How many life ceremonies, such as weddings, baptisms, and funerals, occur there annually? Are there many good singers? Are there graves around the church?

3. How goes it with the taking of birds and eggs? Are there many accidents with that activity? Are the birds trapped or shot? How are birds, eggs, and feathers paid for and later priced? How do people cook birds in the island? How many eider ducks are in the island and how much eiderdown is exported? Is there a greater catch in birding or fishing?

4. How many boats are in the island; are they large and how many fishermen are aboard? What species of fish are especially sought and where is the catch sold? Who are the owners of the boats? From where are provisions brought into the island and how long does it take to sail from the nearest harbor to the island? How many trips are made per annum between Grímsey and the mainland? Are wool and woolen goods sent out? Do the inhabitants pay some taxes?

5. How do the people live their social life? Is there much communication among people on winter evenings? How are elections to Parliament arranged on the island? How are the houses: are there ovens or fireplaces in them for heating and cooking? What type of lighting is in the houses? How are sports practiced? Is glíma practiced in the island? Are coffee and canned foods sent to the island? How is book possession by families arranged and which families have the most books? Which newspapers are bought? Has there been an emigration of people from Grímsey west over the ocean for settlement there [principally in Canada]? How many in the island know a foreign language and is some of the acquaintance in languages other than Danish?[5]

These questions were uppermost in his thinking, as he believed it was necessary to establish a library in Grímsey, and thus he wanted to know better the conditions in the island and how people spent their time.

The Island Library (Eyjarbókasafnið) in Grímsey has a unique position because of its origin, and the background is that Fiske had the idea of increasing the availability of books in the island along with other cultural activity.[6] On 1 May 1901 he wrote to Halldór Hermannsson from Bologna, stating he was thinking of founding a small general library in Grímsey. He asked Halldór not to share the idea with anyone, not even Bjarni Jónsson, Halldór's former colleague, nor his own brother, Jón Hermannsson, who was also corresponding with Fiske and was one of many who had been of assistance on one or another bibliographical matter.[7] His subvention of an island library had to be a secret.

Fiske had a definite idea. He wanted Halldór, who was then in Copenhagen, to have two bookcases made, plain but durable. Each of them had to be able to hold eighty to one hundred volumes, and they had to have wooden doors that closed tightly with a good lock. The lowest shelf had to be four to five inches from the floor and the clearance between the lower shelves high enough that books approximately octavo height, for example *Íslenskt fornbréfasafn,* could stand. Between upper shelves there could be less clearance. The problem would be to construct them without any luxury. The shelves could not be too large to fit easily in a dry place in the houses of Grímsey residents. He added that one of them could perhaps stand in the house of Árni Þorkelsson, a farmer in Neðri-Sandvík, and the other one in the home of the pastor or in the church.

Above the doors of the bookcases had to be inscribed, in gilt letters, "Eyjarbókasafn(ið) I." on the one and "Eyjarbókasafn(ið) II." on the other. Afterward he drew the bookcases in his letter as he wanted them to look and sent it to Halldór.[8] However, the bookcases in the sketch were labeled "Eyjabókasafn I and II."[9]

Halldór, who then was living in Linnésgade 26 in Copenhagen, answered him on 8 May 1901 and said he found the idea of establishing a library in Grímsey good; and that "The Island Library" was a well-chosen name. He later advised Fiske on which books to

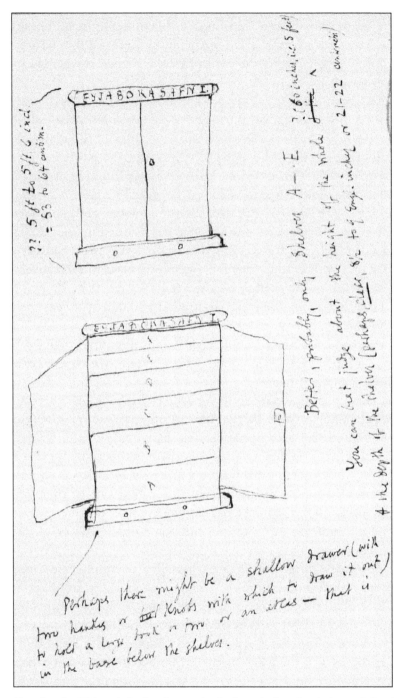

Sketches by Fiske of the bookcases he had made for the Grímsey Island Library (Eyjarbókasafnið). From his letter to Halldór Hermannsson.

The specially made bookshelves ready and standing in Grímsey. They were as well constructed as possible.

send with the bookcases: they ought to be Danish and Norwegian books and some would need to be about contemporary occupations such as fishing. Books on animal life, general scientific works, and books on health and the state of health were essential. Good novels and history would always be well received as reading material, along with language textbooks and dictionaries. He thought it regrettable that the encyclopedia *Salomonsens Konversations lexicon* was complete only up to the letter M, despite being the encyclopedia sought after in the Nordic countries.[10] Other good reference works, such as Hagerup's *Konversationslexicon*, which was new, could be useful, thought they were not the equal of Salomonsen's. Fiske had himself decided the Grímsey islanders would have Tégner's *Friðþjófs saga*, and Halldór succeeded in obtaining it from Malmö to send to Grímsey.[11] Regarding Icelandic books, Halldór thought it was a good idea to take those of the Icelandic Literature Society (Hið íslenzka bókmenntafélag). Finally he asked Fiske to compile a list of book titles in Danish from which he, Fiske, could choose.[12] He had by then ordered the bookshelves, which cost forty-five kroner each and were ready for sending to Iceland in June of that year.

All this was in accord, and when Halldór wrote to Grímsey and mentioned that the consignment was arriving, he still kept secret who the sender was, but most could now guess who it was. The gift was appreciated, as there was little of such value in Grímsey, and the residents received it with thanks. The bookshelves are still preserved today in Grímsey.

Fiske began publication of a chess journal in Icelandic in 1901and called it *Í uppnámi*, and a venue was chosen to report on this development. In the fourth issue from the year 1901 it states: "The Island Library in Grímsey, which we referred to in the previous issue, is now well on the way to what we wanted. Both bookshelves sent there have now been set up, one in the house of the pastor, séra Matthías Eggertsson, and the other in Sandvík with the son of Árni Þorkelsson; there they think them best preserved, as it is too risky to have them in the church, since people feared the books might be damaged by the humidity."[13] In the publication people were encouraged to send books to Grímsey, but solely bound ones, as there was no bookbinder on the island. Books in Icelandic or Scandinavian languages were naturally the most read, but the library then had some English, French, German, and Italian dictionaries, and grammar materials for the most part in Icelandic and Danish. Also in the collection were books with pictures, such as an album with printed pictures, photographs, and illustrated maps for the edification and entertainment of the inhabitants of this distant isle.

The idea also came to Fiske to finance an addition for the church rectory, and he mentioned it to Halldór.[14] Halldór considered this for a while and declared himself unable to answer with certainty how much it might cost to renovate the pastor's house, and he thus estimated the cost would be scarcely under one thousand krónur. He intended to inquire a priori about the condition of the house and to write to Fiske about that.[15]

Shortly after the death of Fiske, in the years 1905–1906, it was decided to build a schoolhouse on Grímsey; it was constructed with the funds Fiske gave to the islanders. Subsequently the Island Library was housed in the school, which in the islanders' everyday speech was called the old schoolhouse, all the way to 1967, when it was moved to the Cape community center.[16]

Fiske was incessantly thinking about chess, its history, and its positive impact on human cognition. Chess was in his estimation therapeutic, and those who played the game were likely to improve themselves in multiple fields. Chess had been carried early to Grímsey and Fiske knew there had been good players there before. Indefatigable in doing good for the Grímsey islanders, he sent a chessboard and chess pieces to each household in Grímsey with the intention that people should engage in chess whenever time permitted.

Later Fiske had considerable correspondence with several people on the island, among others séra Matthías Eggertsson. He received many warm, sincere letters equally from young and old inhabitants of Grímsey, and they must have been heartwarming. In the letters, which are preserved in his collection, people described for him daily travails; naturally, many of the letters were about the game of chess: who were the best players, which girls played, which youths were most promising; about chess tournaments and much besides concerning the art of chess.

Most of the surviving letters from Grímsey are from séra Matthías, who wrote personal letters and was most warm toward

Chessboard and pieces Fiske sent to séra Matthías Eggertsson in Grímsey. They are now in the possession of Haraldur Halldórsson, grandson of Matthías.

Fiske. In 1901 he wrote that he found it so unusual that strangers should have such interest in and benevolence toward Grímsey's inhabitants and that it warmed the hearts of the island's denizens to know of the good will Fiske sent from the lands to the south. (Fiske was then ensconced in Villa Landor in Florence.) Matthías thanked him for all the fine gifts he had sent to the island in previous years, saying it was a holiday when packages arrived. Warm thoughts and gifts were encouragement for the people and afforded them an increased measure of strength in the daily grind. Matthías wrote Fiske especially about the library in Grímsey. From there it is evident the concern for books and their treatment was great, and that it was thought inadvisable that picture books or other fine works should go out on loan because private dwellings could be worse than the church (where the library was then kept); but people should be welcome in the church to use the books.

The gifts from Fiske were well received and truly a window out on the wide world—not only for Grímsey islanders but also for the many Icelanders to whom he sent books and other gifts throughout the country. The fifth of July 1901 séra Matthías wrote from Miðgarðar in Grímsey:

It is so extraordinary that our remote island should in word or deed be shown some benevolence from our own countrymen, where heretofore their thoughts have been so extremely confused and absurd regarding the island and its inhabitants: all the more is one struck to the core when a foreigner in the summery and healthy southern clime of inhabited lands turns thoughts to the cold island in the icy sea with warm regard and scatters sunrays over the inhabitants, and though culture here is not on a high level, people here are not insensitive sticks or stones, and their hearts no less grateful for the good shown them in word or deed, than those others in the cultural mainstream.[17]

And on 1 February 1902 he wrote:

At the same time as I now, in the name of my parishoners, thank you for all the generosity you have shown our little community, I must thank you especially cordially for all the beneficences you have

shown me and my family. Never have I or mine lived a day of celebration as when the packages came from you. The second surprise
was that everything was so carefully chosen, just as if a good father
were sending to his child at a distance, and I cannot otherwise but
think daily about that, and the longer time passes, how cordially we,
husband and wife, find how inestimable consideration and good will
show themselves in the small and large items you have sent us. If
one can express it this way, it peeks through each and every hiding
place; out of every nook and cranny of the packets squints a glowing
elf urging a glance at life from the brighter side.[18]

Séra Matthías was bookish and most keen about the library,
seeing in it a possibility of widening horizons for people in the
island, not least for the young. In the same letter he wrote of the
library:

> Book circulation began promptly in the autumn, and Icelandic and
> Danish books have been lent out; no one here understands other
> languages yet, myself excepted. The picture books have not been
> lent out from the collection, as they would in little time be destroyed
> because of the poor housing; but when people have wished, I have
> shown them pictures in the church, and on last New Year's Eve
> there was held a general showing of them, and a great number of the
> inhabitants were present.

Many of Matthías' letters dwell on himself and his family in
daily travail, and they are a good source on the life lived in the
remote island at the turn of the century. On 29 April 1902 he wrote
Fiske a letter that moved him deeply. In it he related that on 15
April, in the midst of ice and snowfall, his wife had borne a son,
blond and blue-eyed, and asked in the the hour of celebration over
the newborn, well-shaped child whether Fiske would in any way be
opposed if they baptized the lad with his name, as his name was
so dear to them. They wished with all their heart that he should
receive the name of Fiske, whom they esteemed more than other
people. That request proved, of course, to be easily granted. It has
long been people's belief that fortune should accompany a name,
and like all parents, the pastoral couple took pains with the giving

of their child's name. Later more boys in Grímsey were baptized with Fiske's name, and his name still lives in Iceland.

Séra Matthías says more about himself in his beautiful penmanship than most Icelanders do in their letters. He reports much on the life of the residents and describes among other things the misfortunes of the islanders coming with provisions to the island from Húsavík in February 1902 when the sea ice was close to the land and a gale raged with a great snowstorm for three weeks. A bit more than a year later, on 23 April 1903, he wrote to inform Fiske that the commercial house of Ørum & Wulff in Húsavík had burnt to cinders on 26 November 1902, and nothing had been saved save a little bit of food:

> The shop manager, who is also the postmaster, wrote me that all letters and mailed parcels, among them a great deal of packages for Grímsey, which the manager says were from you, had burned, but the number or type of parcels is impossible to ascertain, as the postal registers also burned.[19]

One may assume other items of value had also been lost, but the islanders were likely accustomed to it since odds and ends disappeared at sea. Matthías also sent Fiske pictures from Grímsey and recounted for him chess life, going into detail about a particular game, as he himself was a good player. However, Fiske wanted more, and engaged the photographer Eiríkur Þorbergsson from Húsavík to go to Grímsey and photograph for him in late summer 1902. He was very satisfied with the pictures by Eiríkur, which were varied, showing landscape, houses, and people. The pictures of people are either group portraits or show people at work. Fiske remarked in a letter that Eiríkur's photographs, which are now preserved in the Fiske Icelandic Collection,[20] had been much better than he had anticipated, and that they had greatly augmented his knowledge of the island.[21]

Many people were curious about Grímsey, and foreigners journeyed there fairly often. Fiske received for example an unanticipated letter from Bernhard Hantzoch, an Austrian teacher, who wrote on 28 February 1904 that he had been in Grímsey and seen there with his own eyes a wall painting of Fiske in the church.

This showed that the islanders thought of him and esteemed him. In their midst was he a living force, though he was far away.

His trust with the islanders Fiske held all his life. The last gift shipment from him to Grímsey arrived some time after his death. In the consignment were five boxes with framed pictures, which Fiske had requested be placed with the residents of the island. Crates of books, chess boards, and chess pieces were to go into the library and the marble crucifix in the church. In his will it was declared that twelve thousand dollars should go to Grímsey to strengthen cultural life in the island.

Out of respect for Fiske, Grímsey islanders commemorate his birthday annually on 11 November with a gathering at the Cape social hall. Various other measures have also been taken to remember him, among others a monument that was erected in 1998.[22]

Chapter 29

The Charm of Chess

Chess has a long history in Iceland, and in Old Norse-Icelandic literature, chess players are mentioned. The game appeared in the Nordic world when it was still developing and the rules were not firmly established. In the world beyond Iceland and the North (in the last couple of centuries), chess was long played both in clubs and at home. Official matches and tournaments between countries were infrequent, but with the nineteenth century the playing of chess became

Fiske enjoyed playing chess with good friends on the grounds of Villa Landor in San Domenico, outside Florence.

international and chess competitions began to be held throughout Europe and the United States. Also at this time, people began thinking of publishing chess journals and books on chess. At the same time people's understanding of the game of chess deepened, and it received a higher regard than previously.

Fiske, who had been a chess player since youth, organized and took part in the first chess tournament in the United States in 1857, and afterward wrote thoroughly about the event, as previously mentioned. Always he wrote with great respect about chess, looking upon it as an art form.

Before Fiske came to Iceland, he had heard that the sport of chess had found a welcome among Icelanders on long winter evenings in the cold country, and thought that noteworthy.

The Chess Society of Reykjavík (Taflfélag Reykjavíkur) was founded on 6 October 1900. Fiske had shown great interest in furthering chess in Iceland, and in that measure had influence on the founding. When he received news of the society's founding, he began publishing, in Icelandic, books and various pamphlets on chess, covering all publication costs himself; and gave copies to the society for the furtherance of its activity.

Fiske enjoyed other games beside chess. He played cards often and thought it the best pastime.

He also published the journal *Í uppnámi*, as previously
mentioned, in the years 1901 and 1902, for a total of eight issues,
and the Chess Society benefited from the proceeds of its sales.
It was the first chess periodical in Icelandic and was intended to
awaken people's interest in the literature of chess and in academic
knowledge and practice of the game, as well as promoting its beauty
and nobility among Icelanders. The periodical was published in
Florence but printed in Leipzig. The editors for the first year were
Fiske and Halldór Hermannsson, but for the second and last year,
Halldór edited the publication alone. Sigfús Blöndal also worked
on the publication.

In the journal there are discussions of the art of chess, chess
examples and game closings are given, and young players
from foreign countries are introduced, in addition to historical
information about everything possible concerning chess, for
example how the game of chess appeared in the visual arts: a very
instructive publication, even for non-players.

The chess stories in the publication were by Fiske, but Halldór
Hermannsson translated them into Icelandic along with other
material Fiske wrote. Some of the stories had previously been

Mjög lítill skákbæklingur
(Very little chess booklet),
which Fiske published
in Forence in 1901.

published in English, but others appeared there for the first time. Several of the chess examples in the periodical had never been printed before. They were compiled from famous authors in various lands and published in recognition that an Icelandic-language chess journal had been founded.

Í uppnámi also discussed *hnefatafl* and other ancient board contests, and also puzzles and games. In addition, attention focused on what kind of reception chess had had in Iceland, among other things because of insularity, and how its history is unlike the history of chess in other countries. Valdskákin ("guard chess") is mentioned as an old and specifically Icelandic approach to chess that had never been practiced elsewhere.[1] In guard chess one may take out only unguarded pieces. The reading of the issues was informative and exceedingly good evening entertainment in winter. It was with some regret that Fiske ceased publication, but in the afterword of the last issue it states:

> With this issue, "Í Uppnámi" ends its publication run. To be certain, it has not aged, but this was not intended when it was founded; it was to be only the beginning of Icelandic chess literature, to bring it from a standstill, that more of the same genre should offer daylight, and moreover generally awaken people's interest in chess literature and an academic knowledge, and pursuit of the game, as well as working for the propagation of this beautiful, noble art among Icelanders.[2]

Thus was Fiske's goal attained, and although he and Halldór did not publish the periodical for long, they realized a significant circulation of the publication and kindled Icelanders' practice of chess. Fiske also wrote séra Matthías Eggertsson that the intention in publishing the periodical had from the beginning only been that of showing Icelanders a little collection on chess games and chess puzzles, along with education on the history of chess. When that had been accomplished, it became time to cease publication. He also mentioned that a fixed section on chess would be in one of the Reykjavík newspapers—one of the good ones.[3]

Fiske also published seventeen chess examples by William Orville Fiske, his younger brother. The brother was more artistically inclined and was thought quite musical. He played with the idea, for example, of composing a melody for Páll Ólafsson's poem "Sumarkveðja" (Summer greeting), which began with the words "Ó blessuð vertu sumarsól" (Oh blessed art thou summer sun).[4]

Fiske also utilized various other methods for the publication of chess examples, for example arranging to print envelopes with examples, and blank forms for writing on the chess table.[5] These stirred up little interest when they first came out, but later sold out and are now seldom seen and in great demand.

Willard Fiske's part would be overestimated late in the development of chess in Iceland, first with his publications and later with his collection of books on chess, which he bequeathed to the National Library of Iceland. He had long had the ambition that it should be the best collection of works on chess in the Nordic countries, as he said in letters to many people. In that connection one may mention his letters to Pétur Zóphoníasson, a powerful supporter of the Reykjavík Chess Society, where Fiske says he now had all the chess books that had been published in Scandinavia.

Fiske was at the same time very concerned about the Chess Society and that it should mature. Accordingly he sent the members many fine gifts, among them convenient pocket chessboards to have available when traveling, large and small chessboards and

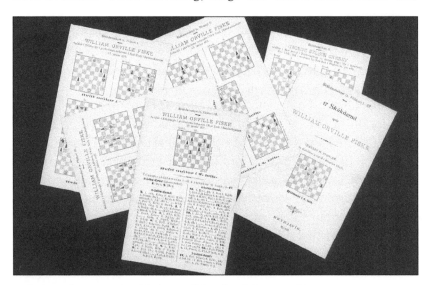

Fiske greatly enjoyed publishing all kinds of chess problems.

Envelopes with chess
problems became popular
and were sought after
by enthusiasts. Fiske
printed many examples.

chess pieces, some inlaid with marble or made out of other quality
material.[6] He also sent the society books about chess in addition
to twenty-five pounds for initial capital. With these funds he set
the stipulation that the principal could not be diminished and that
the payout should be used for the development of the society. The
investment was deposited later in the Icelandic National Bank[7] and
accrued well. All proceeds from the chess writings Fiske published
also went to the Reykjavík Chess Society at his behest.[8] With the
intent of thanking him for his support, Fiske was made honorary
member and director of the Reykjavík Chess Society at its general
meeting in October 1901.

In fact, Fiske sent chess gifts throughout Iceland, and this had
great influence on the interest of Icelanders in the art of chess. In the
years 1901 and 1902, one chess society after another arose among
Icelanders at home and abroad. These were the Chess Society of
Icelandic Students in Copenhagen; the Chess Society of Icelanders
in Winnipeg; and chess societies in Ísafjörður, Akureyri and
Bolungarvík, all founded in the winter of 1901–1902. The societies
in Stykkishólmur and Seyðisfjörður likewise were established. The
next winter were added those of Húsavík, Patreksfjörður, Eiðar, and
Keflavík. There were then ten chess societies in the country with
altogether some three hundred active members. Though most of the
societies died away afterward, Fiske became the first man to awaken
the general interest of Icelanders in chess and chess literature and
to give them the opportunity to get to know them; in addition

to which he became the first to lift Icelandic chess literature to a certain level of respect. He wanted Icelanders to have books on chess to learn from and to enjoy when they had nothing else to do or took time for entertainment, to which end the Reykjavík Chess Society strove.

On 5 December 1901 Halldór wrote to Fiske from Copenhagen that a chess society had just been founded called the Chess Society of Icelanders in Copenhagen (Skákfélag Íslendinga í Kaupmannahöfn). In it there were more than twenty members, and the society was growing. These were truly glad tidings. In the same letter he wrote further: "I have actually received in my hands the proofs for *Nokkur skákdæmi og tafllok III* [Some chess examples and game closings III]." He intended to roll up his sleeves and get them out, but said he could not do it slapdash. He wanted to take his good time to proofread and mentioned that Christmas was nigh and that in the far north people took ample holiday vacation.[9] Halldór was always meticulous and consistent in his work, and his labor served Fiske well. Halldór also undertook to be the middleman for what Fiske wanted to send to Iceland, whether books or material objects, and carefully saw to it that Fiske's bookplates were in the volumes sent to the National Library and the Island Library on Grímsey.

Fiske corresponded with many keen chess players, among them Þorvaldur Jónsson, a physician in Ísafjörður, who was a fanatical chess enthusiast. He was said at the time to be one of the best players in the country and the only Icelander who kept up with foreign chess and read about the game. Aside from being an excellent chess player, he was active propagating the art of chess in the Western Fjords. He mentioned often in letters to Fiske that he longed to visit him in Italy, as in fact so many other Icelanders had expressed; but few appeared to take on such travels. In 1901 Þorvaldur wrote to Fiske: "I have the satisfaction of having awakened considerable interest in chess among those who row out in Bolungarvík, where they often encounter inclement days, a large number of fishermen come together, who have nothing special to preoccupy them other than to row when circumstances permit. Several are quite good chess players, as may be expected."[10] Þorvaldur received from Fiske very many pocket chessboards, which he let go to interested people; they thought them the most useful items and easy to take with them anywhere. In addition, he received traditional boards and books on chess to distribute among enthusiasts in the western part of Iceland. To sit at the chessboard became the most desirable pastime in rough weather that kept fishermen ashore. Þorvaldur wrote Fiske often about promising chess players and reported that in the west of Iceland, girls and women were in no way second to men in chess. Fiske was able to rejoice that chess should reach a majority of both sexes.

Fiske also correpsonded for years at a time with the afore-mentioned Pétur Zóphoníasson, a merchant in Reykjavík, who was secretary of the Reykjavík Chess Society. Pétur was an instigator for establishment of an educational branch in the society, and it came to light that there was evident interest among young people who crowded in and studied energetically. Over forty lads benefited from chess instruction in the spring months of 1902, and they were said to make great and good progress.[11]

To awaken foreigners' interest in the chess of the Icelanders, Fiske wrote (among other items) a paper in the well-known German chess journal *Deutsche Schachzeitung* in 1901 on the Icelandic game of chess as it was then ("Das heutige isländische Schachspiel"). There he named the most significant chess players of the country, gave an account of the inhabitants of Grímsey and suggested there was a good chess book collection in the National Library. In further writings he acted to remind of the great interest in chess in Iceland.

All this was a great encouragement for chess enthusiasts, and Icelanders were thankful for Fiske's driving force and encouragement in his hobby, and wanted to show it. Otto Tulinius, in Akureyri, wrote Fiske a letter on 1 December 1902:

> In the name of the Akureyri Chess Society I hereby thank you for the packages of books you have sent to the society.
>
> Furthermore I am informing you that at the first meeting this year of the society you were elected unanimously an honorary member of the chess society: please know of a certainty that this was done because of the great interest and the great work you have realized to strengthen the art of chess here in Iceland, which bears such good fruit.

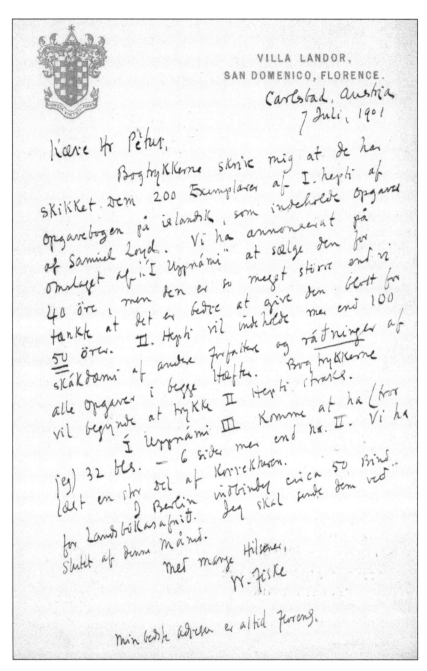

Letter from Fiske to Pétur Zóphoníasson in Danish. Fiske, in letters to Icelanders, alternated among Icelandic, Danish, and English.

One might believe this was felicitous news for Willard Fiske, and he wore himself out obtaining writings he thought might be useful in Iceland and sent them immediately. He had absolute faith this diversion would be both useful and fun for the Icelander.

As Fiske was a good chess player from youth and of all people the most knowledgeable about the history of the game, he longed to disseminate that history, and thus himself wrote quite a bit about his hobby.[12] Of his other works one can mention *Chess in Iceland and in Icelandic Literature with Historical Notes on Other Table-Games*, published in Florence by The Florentine Typographical Society in 1905, the year after his death. Horatio S. White, Fiske's friend; George W. Harris, Cornell university librarian after Fiske; and Halldór Hermannsson supervised publication of the book. Among other things, Fiske describes how chess was brought to Iceland and what changes it had undergone; and found much to indicate that the art of chess was practiced in Iceland in the days of Snorri Sturluson, and perhaps before then. It was known that medieval Icelanders ventured abroad and brought home with them games and arts, and that Hrafn Sveinbjarnarson, a well-educated poet, artist, physician, and legal scholar, had learned to play chess in the British Isles, continuing with it and teaching it to others after he came home. Fiske was very concerned about making this story understood, and his writings are detailed and enlightening for general readership. As discussion of chess is considerable in his collection of letters from people throughout the country, it may be supposed he was most happy to find a rapidly increasing interest in the topic among Icelanders.

Fiske having done his utmost to obtain good chess books, he had sooner than expected accumulated a handsome collection that preserved many rare works, and with the passing years he started thinking of a new location for it. He was moved by how well Icelanders had taken to chess, how far it had spread in the country, and how much it had been practiced wholeheartedly and ambitiously. Because he himself had pleasure playing chess in his leisure time, he knew for certain that the sport would be practical and suitable in the far north, where darkness hovers over long winter evenings and there is little for amusement. It affected him as before that Icelanders had so few means to become acquainted with the outside world, whether at work or at play.

Fiske decided in 1900 to give his chess book collection to the National Library of Iceland. The National Library was an agglomeration of various fields of study and it was likely the chess books would be well cared for there. The chess collection then numbered twelve hundred volumes. Before sending the books, he had them beautifully bound, as were most in the library left by him. The chess collection in the National Section (Þjóðdeild) thus has its own long history, and Willard Fiske was there in the main role, as often before.

In Fiske's gift of chess writings, there is a wide variety. There are a large number of works in many languages that treat chess history both ancient and modern, and that part of the gift is the most remarkable, since Fiske collected both large and small, even articles and papers on chess in newspapers and periodicals, isolated pictures, and relevant clippings. Nor did he confine himself solely to chess studies; he also collected both elder and younger literary works that dwelled on chess or in which chess comes in part into the narrative. Then he brought together quite a number of works on various genres of games, and gave them to the National Library. Finally, several manuscripts on chess accompanied his gift.[13]

In the special collections of the National Library of Iceland there are many rare works, and the chess collection equally arouses great attention among visitors. One can mention a famous work on chess from the sixteenth century by the Italian Horatio Gianutio della Mantia titled *Libro nel quale si tratta della maniera di giuocar' à scacch*, printed in Turin in 1597, and the first edition of *L'Analyse des échecs*, by the French chess master and composer François André Danican Philidor, considered a watershed work in the history of chess literature. Also mentionable are the works *Pascasii Iusti De alea libri duo*, the chess work of Iustus Pascasius published in Amsterdam in 1642 and bound in parchment; and the fifth edition of *Libro da imparare a giochare a Scachi et de Belissimi Partiti* by the Portuguese Damiano da Odemira, who flourished around 1500. This was one of the first works on chess to come out in print. The first edition was printed in Rome in 1512, and the work was subsequently reprinted at least six times in the sixteenth century. The language is chiefly Italian, but solved chess examples and game closings are also in Spanish. One may also mention a work by the author Joannes Aquila, *Opusculum*

The chess literature collection of Willard Fiske in a special collections space of the National and University Library of Iceland. One of the gems of the Þjóðdeild (National Section).

Enchiridion appellatum I. Aguilae: Ferme de omni ludorum genere, from Impressum Oppenheim 1516; the famous work *Il nobilissimo et antiqvissimo giuoco Pythagoreo nominato rythmomachia, cioe battaglia de consonantie de numer*, said to be by Francesco Barozzi and printed in Venice in 1572; and a work by Gregorio Ducchi, *La scaccheide*, published in Vicenza in 1586.

Fiske also sent the National Library several hundred books on subjects other than chess, and they have been distributed by relevant subject. Several manuscripts (as mentioned earlier) accompanied the gift, among others three attractively illuminated Persian manuscripts from the sixteenth and seventeenth centuries, written on Indian paper, as well as an exceeding beautiful vellum that is undated.[14]

All the books bear Fiske's bookplate, which is beautifully designed and enhances the value of each book. He invested great ambition in making his chess collection without peer, and at the time it was donated it was said to be the best library on chess in Scandinavia. The collection is now one of fifteen special collections in the National Section of the National and University Library of Iceland, and truly one of its crown jewels. Works in the collection are sought after by learned and lay, and a detailed catalogue has been compiled for it.[15]

Fiske prepared a bookplate that he wanted to place in all books sent to Iceland. Here is the casting for the bookplate.

The bookplate that was affixed inside every book.

Chapter 30

The Florence Decades

Let us return to the year 1883. As has been brought out earlier, the legal proceedings arising from the inheritance of Jennie McGraw were long and difficult, and affected people exceedingly personally; what is more, those who had lived harmoniously were now ill at ease. The malice and strong words with regard to Fiske resulted in his becoming exhausted in body and soul, and he resolved to leave Ithaca for good long before the Supreme Court of the United States handed down the decision in his favor. His mother, who still lived in Ithaca, was in reasonable health and the one person who now tied him to the place. After the conflict, Fiske did not wish to return to the United States. He had become sick and tired of the unbridled calumny surrounding him but traveled nonetheless to see his mother, and was present at her burial in 1897. She also enjoyed a long sojourn with her son in Italy, as their relationship was always close.

As his choice for a new place to settle in 1883, Italy was uppermost in Fiske's mind. He had come there on his trips to Europe and been enchanted by the land and nation, and it was not to Italy's detriment that the climate mollified the pains his rheumatism caused him. Florence, the city that became his first choice, had been capital of Italy for a few years, and bore many signs of being a high city of culture and the arts.[1] Authors and artists from all over sought to live in Florence. Fiske, who loved literature and the arts, could not have chosen a better city to enjoy a many-faceted civilization. He was thus well reconciled with his

View over San Domenico looking at Villa Landor. Fertile fields in the foreground.

decision and determined to have his fixed abode there. For the first five years he lived in the Villa Forini. G. P. Marsh, who has been mentioned before and who long ago had translated Rask's Icelandic grammar, lived previously in that house. In this location Fiske energetically collected Icelandic materials. In 1888 he moved his book collections to Lungo il Mugnone 11, where they were in more secure keeping, and closed on the Villa Landor[2] as his residence; it was named after its former owner, Walter Savage Landor, the English poet who long lived there and was well known for his writings and verse. Villa Landor was situated in a very attractive location named San Domenico, on the slopes below the village of Fiesole, with a magnificent view over Florence. The house is surrounded by vineyards and olive groves, and the area has indeed for centuries been fertile, being especially well disposed toward cultivation and known for the quality of its wine and olives.

It was likely not a coincidence that Willard Fiske, a man of literature, should settle there. The locale undoubtedly reminded him of the seven damsels and three men in Boccaccio's *Decameron* who sought refuge in the hills above Florence from the plague that then raged, and took turns relating stories to one another, ten original

Villa Landor, Fiske's residence in Italy. Contemporary photograph from his photograph collection.

Villa Landor now houses a Florence music school and stands to the side in the original image. The villa interior has been remodeled for use by the music students. Kristín Bragadóttir in front of the villa in 2004.

stories each day. Boccaccio was a favorite of Fiske's, and it was said he had long ago lived in the house.

After Fiske completed the purchase, he had the house and grounds renovated without spoiling any of the former charm of the place. The house had a long history of its own and it was difficult to restore it. Four spacious rooms were on each level when Fiske took possession. It was said the tower had been erected in or around 1300 and the house itself around the tower two centuries later.

Fiske wanted nonetheless to create a comfortable domicile à l'américaine with considerable luxury, scarcely known then among the bourgeoisie of the region,[3] and had a story added on to the house and the dovecote above the house remodeled in a manner other than it was originally.[4] Here Fiske was comfortable.

A large estate surrounded the house. Early in the seventeenth century the powerful Gherardi family came into possession of the property and lived from generation to generation. However, Walter Savage Landor bought the property in 1828. He had cypress and fruit trees planted on the grounds, which slope southward and are especially suited for agriculture. He was reputed to have the best olives, water, and wine in the region. There Landor wrote his *Imaginary Conversations*, for which he was best known, and also *Pericles and Aspasia*. Authors from Europe and America visited Walter Savage Landor at that location and a literary spirit hovered over the waters. Many artists and authors bought houses in San Domenico and settled there.

After the hermit in Villa Landor had installed himself comfortably, he permitted himself to let his thoughts wander toward the past. Now he thought that the poems he composed for Jennie as a young and love-struck man at home in Ithaca might be visible to all and began preparing their publication.[5] He had in his possession many love poems to Jennie, poems squirreled away but not forgotten. He decided also to have other poems accompany them, for example his odes to Icelandic nature.

The anthology, which came out in only fifteen copies in Florence in 1887, bears simply the title *J*, and the author is not identified on the title page.[6] The binding is especially beautiful, extensively gilt decorations on light-colored parchment, and black borders, again with gilt designs, above and below on the covers fore and aft.

Fiske was attentive to the surroundings of his villa and hired a gardener to look after the manicured grounds. The garden was still well mainatained in 2008. Florence is visible in the distance.

A scarlet lily is on the front cover, the red lily being the emblem of the city of Florence. –Symbols, thus, of what in life for him was most precious, *J* for Jennie and the lily for Florence. On the spine of the book is solely a gilt pattern, no lettering. The year is MDCCCLXXXVII, the place of publication Florence. The collation is 108 pages and the table of contents foremost. The paper of the book is well made and a large, red, luxurious J adorns the title page. The book was obviously produced as best as it possibly could be.

When Fiske's possessions were removed to Ithaca after his death, notable sources on his life in Italy accompanied them, among other things pictures he had had taken. On the flyleaf of a photograph album from the years in Florence is inscribed: "Views of the Villa of Walter Savage Landor, (in the commune of Fiesole, 1 ¾ km. from Florence) in which he wrote many of the *Imaginary Conversations*, now the property of Willard Fiske."

Fiske engaged a fair number of staff to assist him in Florence. In addition to those working on his book collections, he had a housekeeper, cook, and gardener. It was considered highly desirable to work for Fiske, and there are letters from several Swedes who wanted to place their offspring or other young people in his service.

Front cover of the book of
poems *J*, which Fiske published
in only fifteen copies in Florence
in 1887. It includes many
love poems to Jennie and, in
addition, poems he composed
during his voyage to Iceland.

Axel Andersson, "amanuens" in the University of Uppsala library, found, for example, a housekeeper for him. She was Beata Berling, the twenty-five-year-old daughter of the library's printer, Edvard Berling.[7] It was noted especially that Miss Berling was very well brought up and trustworthy, and Andersson ventured to guarantee that she would do well. Fiske hired her in 1897. Her sister Maria followed soon thereafter and became a chambermaid in the Villa Landor. This was a pathway for training young women and giving them an opportunity to see the world and make their way in it, and Fiske required ever more help in his large abode.

The arthritis that had afflicted Fiske for many years increased with time, and he also suffered a heart attack at least once. In 1889 he wrote Ólafur Davíðsson from Florence that his health was somewhat better after a sojourn in Egypt, not least because he had quit smoking. "I have not smoked a *whiff*[8] since April 12, 1888, now over a year. It was a dreadful task to break off."[9]

Fiske took his sickliness personally, as he was industrious and often worked a long day; but now he was ever more often prone to lying in bed because of poor health. He found accordingly that he was unable to travel alone and engaged the Italian Michele Monzecchi to assist him, which proved a great godsend. He worked with the library among other occasional tasks, journeyed considerably with Fiske, and assisted him in various ways, for example writing letters for his employer when the latter could no longer hold a pen because of the arthritis. They traveled together to Scandinavia, and in Gothenburg he assisted Fiske with the purchase of books in 1899. That year was fortuitous, and much Icelandic material was added to his collection.

Despite worsening health, Fiske engaged in lengthy trips, and in 1901 he undertook a voyage to Uppsala: a half-century had passed since he was studying there. He gave a lecture in Swedish at the university, discussing student life, and described many events from the time he was a young man there.[10] The lecture aroused considerable interest, not least because Fiske had not resorted to Swedish in the interval since his student days. In Uppsala he gave more lectures of cultural substance and, among other topics, discussed authors and their works. He was personally acquainted with Mark Twain, and had an opportunity to introduce him thoroughly to Swedes.

From 1902 Fiske mentioned ever more often in letters that his health was steadily worsening, and this is visible in his handwriting,

Fiske and his factotum Michele Monzecchi, who assisted him with the library, with correspondence, and on Fiske's voyages in his last years.

which heretofore had been smooth and legible. Occasionally he was unable to write himself, and then dictated to someone, signing his name underneath or even letting his initials suffice. Often it was Monzecchi who wrote, but once in a while a letter was typed. On 16 August 1904 Fiske wrote to Halldór Hermannsson from Lucerne: "You have already learned that as a correspondent I am a dead failure. The truth is that my health is almost as bad as bad can be. I am allowed neither to write nor read, and am almost forbidden to eat and drink."[11] He then asked Halldór and Bjarni Jónsson to come from Copenhagen to work in his collection, and mentioned he had found a place for them in a guesthouse, pensione Banchi, 54 Viale Principessa Margherita.

Traveling in Germany in September 1904, Fiske was suddenly taken ill, and saw it the best option to be hospitalized in Frankfurt am Main. After a brief stay he gave up the ghost on 17 September. Daniel Willard Fiske, friend of Iceland, was gone, not quite seventy-three years of age. His remains were transported to his former home town, Ithaca, where he was laid to rest alongside Jennie in the crypt of Sage Chapel on the Cornell campus. Some of those who were involved in the lawsuit and were opponents of Fiske were highly offended,[12] unable to reconcile themselves to the fact that the man whom they had thought an obstinate swindler should be laid to rest in the university chapel.

The news was brought to Iceland, and Icelanders sorrowed over the loss of their friend and benefactor. Many came forward to remember him, and among others, Jón Ólafsson wrote a reminiscence of him in *Skírnir*:

Professor Willard Fiske was barely of average height, at least in comparison with American men; he was thick-set and good-looking, dark in hair and beard (before he went gray), and exceedingly goodly in facial expression and intelligent in appearance. I remember his eyes as being gray. He was the most amiable man in every circumstance, placid and courteous, a good man and decent in every respect, as are nearly all Swedenborgians I have met. That was his faith, as it was his mother's. He was immensely erudite; every field of study and any common matter could captivate his mind. He was a happy man, amusing, steadfast, and loyal.

Fiske in advanced age. The portrait hangs in his special collection in the National Library.

No foreigner who has settled here has become known as well to Iceland as Fiske has. No foreigner has been more truthful in everything he wrote about Iceland. Neither foreigner nor Icelander has shown Iceland as great generosity in magnificent gifts. No foreigner, and few Icelanders, have had such a rock-solid faith in the future of Iceland, and no foreigner has loved Iceland so warmly as Professor Willard Fiske.

Willard Fiske was a doctor of philosophy (honoris causa); he was an honorary member of the Icelandic Literary Society, and doubtless he was honored by more societies. The king of Italy had decorated him, and finally in 1902 he became a knight of Dannebrog . . . Yet his most beautiful and durable honor is the memory of what he was and accomplished.[13]

Many others wrote about Fiske after his death. George W. Harris, earlier a colleague of Fiske's at Cornell and subsequently the university librarian there, wrote about him in *The Library Journal* for October 1904 under the title "Willard Fiske: Librarian, Bibliographer, and Bibliophile," in words of particular praise:

Generous and warmhearted, modest and unassuming, gifted with a winning manner, Willard Fiske easily found his way into men's hearts and made many firm and constant friends, whom he loved to gather round his board . . . In his bibliographical work he was insistent upon the minutest accuracy and indefatigable in following up every possible clue to the knowledge he sought. As a librarian, he had little sympathy . . . with those who look upon books as so many brickbats to be scattered broadcast as rapidly as possible. He had the greatest sympathy for the needs of earnest students, and took pleasure in encouraging beginners in the work of research. He loved books with a scholar's love, and his greatest desire was to have his collection used by scholars.

Those responsible for the Ithaca Reading Society in Reykjavík had a beautiful silver shield made in memory of this unusual man and sent to Cornell University, where it is now kept in the Fiske Icelandic Collection. On it is engraved in Icelandic:

Professor Dr. Willard Fiske.
From Ithaca, member of the reading society of
the Learned School in Reykjavík.

Wreath of sorrow,	Father of our society,
honor, and thanks,	promoter of culture,
lie thou on the departed:	passionate friend of Iceland.

Daniel Willard Fiske was well known and his death was widely noted, among other places in American, British, German, Italian, French, Egyptian, Danish, and Swedish papers. He was mourned by many. The Icelanders had lost their patron and godsend. No foreigner and few Icelanders had had as blind faith in the country's future, and in order to increase the knowledge of the nation, he worked to spread light over the land. He perceived very well that Icelanders had been too isolated and would not progress much farther without an augmented panorama and cultural formation. Icelanders likewise themselves knew they had to come up out of the depths, and the acquaintance with Fiske offered them an emboldened spirit and optimism.

Chapter 31

The Icelandic Collection

At the close of life of this remarkable friend of Iceland, there remained his worldly possessions, but Fiske had made his arrangements somewhat before his death. He made his will in the presence of witnesses on 11 April 1901, detailing in fourteen sections how his property should be distributed. He named first his brother's five children, who lived in the United States, and then his staff at Villa Landor. His servants were to have maintenance for one year following his death. Specifically mentioned were his secretaries and factotums, Ettore Sordi and Michele Monzecchi, who inherited considerable sums. Subsequently, his valuables were carefully divided up among various institutions.

Fiske stipulated in his will that Cornell University should inherit his special collections. In addition to the Icelandic books and the collections on Dante and Petrarch, he had collected books in the Rhaeto-Romanic dialects that are still spoken in isolated districts of Switzerland and Italy.[1] Fiske's interest in these dialects awoke in the summer of 1891 when he was in Tarasp, in the eastern part of Graubünden, taking the baths for his health; by chance seeing a book in Rhaeto-Romanic, he longed to see more of the same. That led to several buying trips in the alpine valleys of Switzerland, Germany, Austria, and Italy.[2] He also had a collection on runes, which also became for him a special interest. He wanted the special collections to be demarcated so they would not be integrated with other library collections, but that did not transpire with the Rhaeto-Romanic works.

Of the collections he stipulated for Cornell University, the Icelandic Collection is by far the largest. The origin of the collection may be traced all the way back to the middle of the nineteenth century when Fiske was a young student in Uppsala, and it is rich in old and rare books.[3] He collected from the beginning all that was printed outside of Iceland about Iceland and the Icelanders, and all that was available from the beginning of printing in the country. Stimulated by the Swedish surroundings, he commenced his collecting, and his enthusiasm never diminished. Most of the books were obtained in Iceland or in Denmark or even in Canada and sent via mail to Florence, where they were admired, read, bound in fine bindings, and taken into account for compilation of the catalogue. Afterward they were conveyed across the ocean and now stand on the shelves of the university library in Ithaca for the use and enjoyment of those who wish to acquaint themselves with Icelandic studies. –A magnificent remembrance of a man who surrendered to his love and passion for book collecting and remained perpetually faithful to his work.

In addition to bequeathing his prized possessions to Cornell, his special collections, he left the university a handsome sum, and thus in the end a portion of the inheritance from Jennie McGraw came home to the university library. In the will it was at the same time stipulated that the Icelandic collection should engage a librarian who would be compensated from his funds. He had to be born and bred in Iceland, be educated there, and have a recommendation from the principal of the Learned School in Reykjavík.[4]

Halldór Hermannsson fulfilled all the stipulations as Fiske had before requested of his workers, not least because he considered him to have great qualities, knowing well Halldór's methods and trusting him to the utmost. After Halldór retired in 1948, Kristján Karlsson assumed the curatorship, then Jóhann S. Hannesson, and then Vilhjálmur T. Bjarnar. Since then (the last mentioned died in August 1983), an Icelander has not discharged this office. Louis A. Pitschmann succeeded Vilhjálmur, with the title of Librarian of the Fiske Icelandic Collection, and then Professor P. M. Mitchell, emeritus from the University of Illinois but a Cornell alumnus and student of Halldór's, served as curator part-time. The present curator (since 1994) is Patrick J. Stevens, an American who reads Icelandic and Old Norse in moderation and also addresses other obligations in the library, notably collection development for Jewish Studies.[5]

In addition to paying the curator his salary from the inheritance monies, it was stipulated that works should be purchased for the collection and paid from Fiske's book funds; and a work should be published that promoted Iceland or materials in the Icelandic Collection. Among the duties of the curator was, accordingly, also publication of an annual volume on Icelandic material and the collection. The purpose was to inform English readers on multiple levels about Iceland and Icelandic literature.[6] Fiske saw how significant it was for Icelanders that correct knowledge of the land and its inhabitants be propagated among Anglophones. The Islandica series, which Halldór began publishing in 1908 and which has come out somewhat regularly since then, is thus at the instigation of Fiske.[7] In the first volume of Islandica was a bibliography of the Íslendingasögur, the Icelandic family sagas. Many well-wrought bibliographies subsequently saw the light of day, but the research of numerous scholars in Old Norse-Icelandic literature has also appeared in the series.[8]

On Fiske's initiative, a research collection at Cornell on medieval and modern Iceland came under way, one that was empowered to purchase, publish, and instruct, as Fiske had likewise intended support for teaching Icelandic. Thus came to be a little university community in Icelandic studies that earned respect. Halldór Hermannsson held the Old Norse-Icelandic teaching position in connection with the collection as long as his health lasted. His successors long had this teaching obligation, but now a specific position for teaching in connection with the collection has been discontinued. Graduate students in linguistics and medieval studies do, however, have the option to study Old Norse-Icelandic.[9]

It reflects well on Fiske that he placed his affairs, finances, and possessions in order to the effect that his successors need not be cast into doubt about how the terms of the will should be fulfilled. Here he went, as always, straight to the task.

Halldór Hermannsson, who knew the collection better than anyone else, saw to it that it should be especially well prepared

Halldór Hermannsson,
who worked for
decades with the Fiske
Icelandic Collection.
The portrait hangs in
Fiske's special collection
in the National Library.

for transport from Florence, and it was placed aboard ship along with the other special collections that were sent to Ithaca, arriving at journey's end in the spring of 1905. There Halldór received it and worked with it out of devotion his entire career, with the exception of one year, when he was invited to a position in the Árni Magnússon Collection in Copenhagen. Deciding to accept the position, he worked there for scarcely a year in 1925, when he determined to return to Ithaca.

Halldór found a place for the collection in Ithaca, classified it, and published a great catalogue of the collection in 1914. This catalogue, along with the supplements published in 1927 and 1943, has long been used as the Icelandic national catalogue.[10]

The collection grew considerably in magnitude in Halldór's time. When he completed the second supplement in 1943, there were just shy of twenty-two thousand items in the collection; there were more than eighty-five hundred at the move from Florence.[11] He kept a watch for publications that could enrich the collection, quickly procuring that which he deemed worthy. Here one can mention the *Calendarium perpetuum* of Bishop Þórður Þorláksson, which was printed at Skálholt in 1692; heretofore the collection had had a defective copy.[12] He likewise obtained the facsimile editions, published by Einar Munksgaard in Copenhagen, of Icelandic manuscripts, *Corpus codicum Islandicorum medii ævi*, and the facsimile printings of the first Icelandic books, *Monumenta typographica Islandica*, edited by Sigurður Nordal. He also purchased Danish translations of the Icelandic family sagas, in three volumes, titled *De islandske sagaer*, and illustrated with drawings of Icelandic saga locales and the Icelandic landscape. Halldór journeyed to Iceland in 1914 and bought quite a quantity of occasional poetry. Much was printed of such material, but it seldom went on the general market: purchasers had to be in the right place at the right time to obtain these small-press publications. In the preface of the first supplement to his *Catalogue of the Icelandic Collection Bequeathed by Willard Fiske*, which came out in 1927, Halldór stated that the catalogue contained a great quantity of ephemeral poetry, variously indexed by author or under a pseudonym, most often the latter. Often these would be mischievous or ironic poems about one or another event in the national life that aroused general interest—elections, scandals, or tension-raising matters of various kinds. These poems would show how it was easy for the Icelanders tto cast verses "on the slightest provocation (as did the skalds of old)," confirming they had received their share of the mead of Óðinn.[13] Halldór found it remarkable how publishing changed with the advent of the University of Iceland, seeing in its wake an increased submission of scholarly works and didactic material for performance and study.[14]

Halldór knew Fiske very well from long collaboration, and they became good friends. He always pronounced words of recognition regarding Fiske, and wrote this obituary:

> He began early to collect Icelandic books, and the collection has now become more extensive. First and foremost it is all printed Icelandic books, old and new, that have been collected, and much of it that has been printed in Icelandic and has not been for sale; but moreover there are also all literary works and monographs in foreign languages that touch upon and concern Iceland in part, its history, nature, government, and literature; furthermore there are

works about Scandinavia in that time, that the old sagas touch upon, about the Viking age, and so forth; so is the collection very rich as well in books on runes and runic studies . . . Fiske was of all people most competent in Icelandic bibliography, and no contemporary of his, in Iceland or outside of Iceland, could have surpassed him there. He published three issues in *Bibliographical Notices* on books printed in Iceland in the years 1578–1844 and the fourth issue was nearly ready for printing [at his death]. It is an entirely unique work in Icelandic bibliography; in it are discussed, however, only those books Fiske had and were not noted in the catalogue by Lidderdale of Icelandic books in the British Museum.[15]

The works Fiske brought together with great diligence form an exceptionally good collection. A characteristic feature of the collection is how good the orderliness of the works has been, and how well they have been cared for with repairs and bookbinding, wherein the ideas of the former owner, the aesthete Fiske, have been a guiding light. These treasures are kept underground in the vault of the university library.[16] There are precision control of temperature and humidity and a complete security system connected with campus police. The works have been catalogued online,[17] and one can search the collection for information on Icelandic literature and language from anywhere.

As mentioned before, it was Fiske's intention to bring together as complete a collection as possible, and later curators have followed conscientiously in his footsteps. In the collection is the corpus of Icelandic medieval literature, of books treating these works, and of the Old Norse-Icelandic language, medieval studies, and Norse mythology—Norse culture in all fields. Pains have been taken to collect new editions of works in these same areas from the beginning. There are few collections richer in such works. There are all the translations of the Eddas, skaldic poetry, and sagas that have been available; elder and younger grammars, chrestomathies, and dictionaries in Old Norse and modern Icelandic; moreover, works of foreign authors who have been influenced by Icelandic literature or captivated by it.

There are many of the older Icelandic printed works, some rare and others widely available, and only a very few lacunae exist in the sixteenth- and seventeenth- century editions, which may be said to be amazing. Nearly all editions of the *Passíusálmar* are in the collection.[18] At the turn of the nineteenth century, they were bound in a beautiful Italian binding. All the Graduals (*Almenn messusöngsbók með nótum*; Common Missal with Notes) are in the collection; they were printed a total of nineteen times, the last at Hólar in 1779; and also present are most other religious books. The New Testament of Oddur Gottskálksson from 1540 is a great gem in the Fiske Collection, one for which he paid much, as has been mentioned before. Björn M. Ólsen acquired for Fiske the *Catechismus* of Johann Spangenberg, printed at Hólar in 1610. Björn stated in a letter to Fiske: "Unfortunately it is not quite complete, but I imagine all the same you will think it a pleasure to have it. It does not exist in the British Museum; at least I do not find it in the catalogues."[19] Fiske also came into possession of the *Catechismus* by Peder Palladius, printed at Hólar in 1576, and another copy of this book was not known of at the time.[20]

Then there is in the collection a *Law Book of the Icelanders* (*Lögbók Íslendinga*, in this instance *Jónsbók*) from 1578, and Fiske was particularly pleased with that purchase. The *Law Book* was printed at Hólar by Jón Jónsson, the son of Jón Matthíasson, who was the first printer in Iceland. Of many other rare gems preserved in the collection, many copies are incomplete and smudgy, but that is a characteristic of early Icelandic books, as they were in constant use on farms, unlike antiquarian European books, which frequently reposed untouched on shelves for the embellishment of court libraries or cloisters more than for use by common people who would handle them with uneven care.

Printing was in its infancy in Iceland in the sixteenth century, and the seventeenth century was richer in printed items, for the most part religious books, in total about fifty in number. Seventeenth-century books were quite scarce and costly, especially books of a secular nature printed in Skálholt. In the year 1688 were printed four books on secular topics, *Landnáma*, *Kristni saga*, *Íslendingabók*, and *Grænlandssaga*, and Fiske acquired them all.[21]

Newspaper and periodical publishing of Icelanders in Iceland, and also in Denmark and Canada, flourished greatly from the close of the nineteenth century well into the twentieth. Halldór kept a special lookout for this material and improved the collection thereby, but some of the papers were short-lived, while others just scraped by. Many Icelandic periodicals and books were published in Copenhagen, although in Icelandic, as Copenhagen was important for the culture and education of Icelanders. There was the government administration and there the university, which attracted Icelandic students well into the twentieth century, and from which issued important cultural movements. It was important to keep up assiduously with printed material from there and augment the Icelandic collection.

Manuscripts in the collection are few, and those Fiske acquired came to him unbidden. For example, Jón Þórkelsson wrote on 3 July 1892:

> I am sending you now a few recent epitaphs I had in duplicate, and likewise am sending fragments on parchment, written in Iceland not later than about 1330, from a Latin gradual with musical notation. It came to me once wrapped around a book from Iceland. If you have not had anything of this kind before, it is still no worse than any such specimen. I have essentially nothing to do with it. I would like it that you overpay me on our last dealings, if you have no objection.

At issue were several krónur. Fiske laid no emphasis on the collection of manuscripts, and as has come forward already, he felt manuscripts had to be in their land of origin, as they were each of them unique.[22]

The collection is also very rich in Icelandic literature of the last centuries, works by Icelanders in other languages, and books about the history and natural history of Iceland. *Rímur* are also a weighty cohort, as much was published in the genre over the years. Minor works of various kinds—epitaphs, biographies, all kinds of orations, reports, memorial poetry, legislative bills, advertisements, forms, and occasional poetry—were material Fiske sought much after; these works are in their thousands in the collection, making it something of a unique agglomeration of ephemeral literature. The importunate question is whether that material would have been more or less lost if Fiske's passion and methodical collection of printed material had not intervened. The preservation of all material in the Fiske Collection is thus significant for Icelandic cultural history.

The collection on runes and runic inscriptions is one special compilation within the Icelandic Collection, and Fiske was especially set on that material. Halldór compiled a special catalogue of this collection, the *Catalogue of Runic Literature Forming a Part of the Icelandic Collection Bequeathed by Willard Fiske*, which was published in 1918. In the collection there is much that is rare; one can mention two runic staffs from Dalar in Sweden from the seventeenth century, runes carved in wood.

Work on the Icelandic Collection at Cornell proceeded in the spirit of Fiske and pursuant to his instructions. Its curators have seen to it from the beginning that newly printed material from Iceland was bought with the collection's disposable funds, and the Icelandic government has supported purchase of books for the collection.[23] Keeping up with evolving demands, videotapes, videodiscs, and audio books are now added. Nothing regarding Iceland and the Icelanders is irrelevant, but Icelandic materials on approval, as for example in the Icelandic Collection of the University of Manitoba, have never been resorted to. Nonetheless it can be mentioned that until the year 1977 the exchange obligation on printed items in Iceland was twelve copies, one of them sent most often to the Fiske Collection.[24] Furthermore, the national librarian of Iceland had the prerogative of sending surplus works to collections as he saw fit. Thus the long-prevailing arrangement was that works were sent to the Fiske Collection from the National Library of Iceland in so-called exchanges whereby the National Library received reciprocally two copies of each volume in the *Islandica* series. After 1977 the National Library purchased for some years Icelandic works for the Fiske Collection to maintain this literary exchange, continuing the practice until the National Library moved to the new facility in late 1994 and merged there with the library of the University of Iceland. Then the consignments to the Fiske Collection ceased.

Before Fiske died, he had brought together nearly all that had been published in Icelandic material, and the collection is the next largest outside of Iceland in Icelandic works; only in the Royal Library in Copenhagen is there a larger collection.[25] The Fiske image collection is also an invaluable source on the life and labors of Icelanders at the turn of the nineteenth into the twentieth century. The basis for the image collection derives from the British photographer Frederick W. W. Howell, who journeyed to Iceland around the turn of the nineteenth century and took pictures, but perished in his prime. Eiríkur Þorbergsson also accomplished considerably during a special journey to Grímsey, and managed to capture the spirit of the time—the landscape, dwellings, and working ways-- in pictures for coming generations.

Halldór and Fiske worked immensely well together; theirs was a meeting of the minds with like emphases and the same fields of interest. Books and chess were the principal interests: Halldór, who called chess the queen of all games, played Fiske regularly in Florence.

Recently documents have come to light that show many Icelandic works sank with the luxury liner *Titanic* on her maiden voyage in April 1912. That year one of Halldór's orders was filled and sent from Iceland to England, where it went aboard the ship, which lay at Bristol, ready to sail to North America. G. E. Stechert & Co., Dealers in Books and Periodicals in New York, which had branch offices in Leipzig, London, and Paris, oversaw fulfillment of the order. A letter, written 16 April 1912, was sent from the firm expressing regret that the shipment from Iceland, seven boxes of books and two packages of periodicals, had been lost with the *Titanic*. None of this consignment was insured, but the Stechert firm showed itself ready to come to some arrangement with the purchasers. A letter from 18 April 1912 states: "We discontinued marine insurance a few years ago and certainly never expected to have a loss on the newest and finest steamer ever built."[26] The Cornell Library agreed for its part not to seek compensation.

In the beginning of the tenth decade of the last century the Fiske Icelandic Collection was divided, with pre-1900 materials and rare copies from the twentieth century housed in the vault of the Rare and Manuscript Collections. The newer holdings are in the open stacks, chiefly in Olin Library, accessible to all. This was done for pragmatic reasons, but contrary to the wishes of Willard Fiske.[27]

From many perspectives, the Fiske Icelandic Collection is important and sought after by scholars far beyond Ithaca. Its documents are significant not merely in printed works and photographs, but also in the hundreds of letters to Willard Fiske and Halldór Hermannsson that cast light on history, literature, and these men's

FOUNDED IN 1872

G. E. STECHERT & CO.

DEALERS IN BOOKS AND PERIODICALS

Cable Address:
"Nymflex, New York."   **151-155 West 25th St.**   ALFRED HAFNER, Managing Partner

BRANCHES:
LEIPZIG: Koenig Str. 37.
LONDON: 2 Star Yard, Carey St., W. C.   *New York,* April 16, 1912.
PARIS: 70 Rue de Rennes.

Mr. Geo. W. Harris,
      Cornell University,
         Ithaca, N.Y.

Dear Sir:-

      We much regret to have to inform you
that 7 parcels from Iceland coming as enclosures
for your University Library have been lost on the
steamer Titanic on which we had several cases of
books and some bales of periodicals. We hope that
the parcels do not contain any rare items that
cannot be duplicated.

            Very truly yours,

Letter from G. E. Stechert & Co. regarding disappearance of a consignment of Icelandic works that went down with the luxury liner RMS *Titanic* 15 April 1912.

work in the field of Icelandic culture. Scholars from far and wide throughout the United States and Canada make use of the collection's holdings, whence the copious interlibrary loan.

Still today, the Fiske Icelandic Collection is a feather in the cap of Icelandic culture overseas, visited by scholars from wherever. Thus it is well maintained, and new material from Iceland is ordered regularly. It stands to be in coming years a guide for Icelandic studies in the Western Hemisphere, forever awakening memories of the large-minded man who followed his conviction and his passion.

Notes

All correspondence to Daniel Willard Fiske or Halldór Hermannsson archived in the Fiske Icelandic Collection is cited in the endnotes with reference to the correspondent and the date, without further elaboration.

Chapter 1

1. Bogi Th. Melsteð, *Willard Fiske: Æfiminning* (Copenhagen: Hið íslenzka Bókmentafjelag, 1907), 6. See also the *Memorials of Willard Fiske*, comp. Horatio S. White, 2, *The Traveller* (Boston: Badger, 1920), 17–28. (Horatio S. White was a friend and collaborator of Fiske's. In his will, Fiske requested that White assume custody of all his personal papers.)
2. His acquaintance with Icelandic matters is evident in many of Fiske's early letters.
3. The first English edition was published in 1758 under the title *The Natural History of Iceland: Containing a Particular and Accurate Account of the Different Soils, Burning Mountains, Minerals, Vegetables, Metals, Stones, Beasts, Birds, and Fishes: Together with the Disposition, Customs, and Manner of Living of the Inhabitants.*
4. Richard Beck, *Útverðir íslenzkrar menningar* (Reykjavík: Almenna bókafélagið, 1972), 25.
5. Halldór Hermannsson, "Willard Fiske and Icelandic Bibliography," *The Papers of the Bibliographical Society of America*, 12, 3–4 (1918): 97–106.
6. Rask's first Danish edition of his Old Norse grammar appeared in 1811 as *Vejledning til det islandske eller gamle nordiske sprog*. In 1832 (his year of death), both a *Kortfattet vejledning til det oldnordiske eller gamle islandske sprog* and an *Oldnordisk læsebog* were published.
7. Richard Beck, *Útverðir íslenzkrar menningar*, 9.

221

8. Originally published in 1840 by Chapman and Hall in London, with a large number of subsequent editions under varying titles through 1852 (the year Fiske returned to America from his Scandinavian sojourn) and well beyond.

9. William H. Carpenter, "Willard Fiske in Iceland," *The Papers of the Bibliographical Society of America*, 12, 3–4 (1918): 107. Carpenter refers to Carlyle's formula "land of frost and fire" while noting, aside from Fiske's "unusual knowledge of Iceland, its literature, and its history" acquired while in Sweden, his attention to "the actual conditions of the land and people of the present," the country's peripheral location notwithstanding.

10. Paul Henri Mallet's work was originally published in 1755, in Copenhagen, as *Introduction à l'histoire de Dannemarc, où l'on traite de la religion, des loix, des mœurs & des usages des anciens Danois*. Bishop Percy's translation first appeared in 1770 and again in 1809, but it is plausible Fiske initially saw the 1847 version (London: H. G. Bohn), which also included an "an abstract of the Eyrbyggja saga, by Sir Walter Scott" (see footnote 12 below).

11. Bogi Th. Melsteð, *Willard Fiske*, 5.

12. Halldór Hermannsson, "The Fiske Collection at Cornell," *The American-Scandinavian Review* (1915): 169–70. The "Abstract of the Eyrbiggiasaga; being the early annals of that district of Iceland lying around the promontory called Snaefells," was published in *Illustrations of Northern Antiquities, from the earlier Teutonic and Scandinavian Romances* (Edinburgh, 1814).

13. Sir G.W. Dasent's translations of Icelandic family sagas were *Njáls saga* (*The Story of Burnt Njal*, 1861) and *Gísla saga Súrssonar* (*The Story of Gisli the Outlaw*, 1866). Several scholarly publications and other translations preceded these two works.

14. For a succinct biography of William Morris, poet, printer, artist, and socialist, see Fiona MacCarthy, "Morris, William (1834–1896)," *Oxford Dictionary of National Biography*, online ed. Oct. 2009 (Oxford University Press, 2004); accessed 15 June 2016, http://www.oxforddnb.com/view/article/19322. The article notes Morris's voyages to Iceland in 1871 and 1873 and that he "was moved to find evidence of art and literature enduring in social conditions of such abject poverty," having seen not only Raykjavík and western regions referred to in several sagas, but also having crossed "the desolate, rocky interior of Iceland to Akureyri" at the head of Eyjafjörður in the north, a region not without its own cultural flowering at the time. Eiríkr Magnússon (1833–1913) was a librarian at Oxford from 1871 to 1909 and an important translator of Icelandic sagas and later folklore. (See *Íslenzkar æviskrár frá landnámstímum til ársloka 1940*, comp. Páll Eggert Ólason (hereafter *Íslenzkar æviskrár*), vol. 1 (Reykjavík: Hið íslenzka bókmenntafélag, 1948), 415–16.)

Correspondence from Eiríkr to Fiske is in the Fiske Icelandic Collection. The earliest collaborative saga translation by William Morris and Eiríkr Magnússon was of *Grettis saga*, published as *The Story of Grettir the Strong* (London, 1869). *Völsunga saga: The Story of the Volsungs & Niblungs, with Certain Songs from the Elder Edda* followed in 1870. Morris adapted from *Völsunga saga* and published in 1877 his *Story of Sigurd the Volsung and the Fall of the Niblungs*, which came out in a posthumous edition from the Kelmscott Press in 1898.

15. Bayard Taylor (1825–1878) was well known as a poet, translator (especially of Goethe's *Faust*), travel writer, lecturer, and diplomat. He was a non-resident professor at Cornell in 1869 and 1870 and well acquainted with Fiske. A biography of Taylor, accessed via the Internet 25 May 2016, appears at http://www.kennettpubliclibrary. org/taylor.cfm, noting that "[i]n early September 1869 Bayard accepted an emeritus position at Cornell University in German literature. For the next several years he delivered lectures on Goethe, Humboldt, Lessing, Schiller, and others."

16. See scattered references to Eiríkr Magnússon and Bayard Taylor in *Memorials of Willard Fiske*, comp. Horatio S. White, 3 vols. (Boston: Richard G. Badger, 1920–22).

17. The year 1874 was pivotal in Icelandic history. That year the Danish king granted limited self-rule to Iceland, a gesture that coincided with celebration of one thousand years of Icelandic settlement. Bayard Taylor visited Iceland during the celebration; his travel book *Egypt and Iceland in the Year 1874* (New York: Putnam, 1874) describes the events.

18. *Memorials of Willard Fiske*, 2, *The Traveller*, 79. Adam Gottlob Oehlenschläger (1779–1850) was Denmark's leading poet in his day. Essentially of the Romantic school, he turned to Nordic myth and legend for much of his work.

19. *Snorra Edda* is formally *Edda Snorra Sturlusonar* and is also known in English as the *Prose* or *Younger Edda*. The author, Snorri Sturluson (1179–1241), Iceland's outstanding medieval author, based the *Younger Edda* on the mythological poetry of the *Poetic* or *Elder Edda (Edda Sæmundar)*.

20. Halldór Hermannsson, "Willard Fiske," *Eimreiðin* 37 (1905): 370–77.

21. *Memorials of Willard Fiske*, 2, *The Traveller*, 69.

22. It is not clear how much Russian Fiske knew. His own assessment (see *Memorials of Willard Fiske*, 2, *The Traveller*, 97), in late 1852, suggests youthful confidence but minimal appreciation of the language's difficulty. Nor is it clear how well Fiske mastered the Arabic alphabet, although he taught Persian at Cornell and acquired some speaking knowledge of Egyptian Arabic during his visits there in the 1880s and 1890s (Horatio S. White, *Willard Fiske: Life and*

Correspondence: a Biographical Study (New York: Oxford University Press, 1925), 60–61 (Persian); 85, 157–76 (Egypt and Fiske's interest in Arabic)). Fiske's fluency in Danish, German, Italian, and Swedish at various stages in his life is incontestable.

23. The "Fjölnismen" were a group of young, educated Icelanders in Copenhagen who published *Fjölnir*, a periodical in Icelandic that was especially influential in shaping Icelandic nationalism and national opinion through articles on a wide range of topics pertaining to Iceland. *Fjölnir* was also a literary journal, publishing (among others) numerous poems by Jónas Hallgrímsson (1807–1845), the great Romantic poet of Iceland and a founding "Fjölnisman."

24. *Memorials of Willard Fiske*, 2, *The Traveller*, 96.

25. Þórunn Sigurðardóttir correctly referred to this in "Ástríðufullur Íslandsvinur: Bréf Daniels Willards Fiske til Gísla Brynjúlfssonar 1855" (A Passionate Friend of Iceland: Letters of Daniel Willard Fiske to Gísli Brynjúlfsson, 1855), *Tímarit Máls og menningar* 67, 3 (September 2006): 32–43. Gísli Brynjúlfsson (1827–1888) was named associate professor in Icelandic Studies at the University of Copenhagen in April 1874 and held the post until his death.

26. *Memorials of Willard Fiske*, comp. Horatio S. White, 1, *The Editor* (Boston: Badger, 1920), 96–99.

27. *Memorials of Willard Fiske*, 2, *The Traveller*, 31–35.

28. Ibid., 43. This passage is from Fiske's letter to the *Syracuse Star*, dated "Copenhagen, Dec. 30, 1850."

29. Bogi Th. Melsteð, *Willard Fiske*, 7. This is also evident from a great number of Fiske's letters.

30. Lund University, founded 1666, traces its academic roots to the fifteenth century. The library was founded at the same time as the university and is one of the largest in Sweden, serving since 1698 as a permanent center for legal deposit of Swedish publications.

31. Esaias Tegnér (1782–1846) was Sweden's most acclaimed poet in his time. His best-known work is *Frithiofs saga* (1825), a long poem based on the Old Norse-Icelandic *Friðþjófs saga frækna* and widely translated. He was an alumnus of the University of Lund and served some years there as a professor of Greek.

32. Visby, on the Swedish island of Gotland, was a major trading center in the High Middle Ages and exercised significant influence in the Hanseatic League. See for summary reference the *Britannica* article at http://www.britannica.com/place/Visby, accessed 25 May 2016.

33. *Memorials of Willard Fiske*, 2, *The Traveller*, 83–84.

34. Daniel Willard Fiske to Carl Christian Rafn, 3 September 1851, Det Kongelige Bibliotek, NKS 1599, folio. There is also a narrative of this in *Memorials of Willard Fiske*, 2, *The Traveller*, 102.

35. Ibid., 92.

Chapter 2

1. Sven Widmalm, "Vetenskapens och teknikens värld (1700–1900)," in *Gyllene Äpplen: Svensk idéhistorisk Läsebok*, ed. Gunnar Broberg, 2nd ed. (Stockholm: Atlantis, 1995), 2:794–97.
2. *Memorials of Willard Fiske*, 2, *The Traveller*, 91.
3. Ibid., 90.
4. The numerous letters with these descriptions are, among others, to Caroline, his mother and to his friend, Charles Dudley Warner.
5. Åke Davidsson, *Uppsala universitetsbibliotek 1620–1970: En bildkrönika* (Uppsala: Almqvist & Wiksell, 1971), 24. This manuscript is DG (De la Gardie) 11, 4to. See Halldór Hermannsson, *Icelandic Manuscripts*, Islandica 19 (Ithaca, N.Y.: Cornell University Library, 1928), 21. Queen Christina abdicated in 1654.
6. King Gustav I Vasa (1496–1560) reigned 1523–60 and was the founder of the modern Swedish kingdom who also accepted the Lutheran Reformation.
7. *Memorials of Willard Fiske*, 2, *The Traveller*, 98.
8. William H. Carpenter, "Willard Fiske in Iceland," 107–15.
9. This was part of the Swedes' self-perception as a major power. Götiska förbundet (The Swedish Alliance), founded 1811, sought its ideological grounding in the Old Norse cultural heritage, thus placing its imprint on the thinking of people in Uppsala when Fiske was living there.
10. Principally in the seventeenth and eighteenth centuries.
11. *Memorials of Willard Fiske*, 2, *The Traveller*, 111.
12. Halldór Hermannsson, "Willard Fiske and Icelandic Bibliography," 98.
13. He describes this in letters to his mother and to his friend Charles Dudley Warner.
14. *Memorials of Willard Fiske*, 2, *The Traveller*, 95. The word "nation" is used thus in English, Swedish, and Icelandic. Swedish students belonged to the nation of their home region; foreign students chose the nation that best suited them. Fiske calls his Dalecarlia in his letters, but its name was in fact Westmannia Dalecarliaque, and it was founded in 1639.
15. Mats Bergman and Jan-Olof Montelius, *Nationshusen i Upsala: en beskrivning tillägnad Upsala Universitet vid dess 500-årsjubileum* (Uppsala: Upsala studenters jubileumskommitterade, 1977), 169.
16. Dalarna, "the Dales," a historic province and now a county in central Sweden.
17. Horatio S. White, "A Sketch of the Life and Labors of Professor Willard Fiske," *Papers of the Bibliographical Society of America*, 12, 3–4 (1918): 69–88.

18. Letters Fiske wrote in Swedish and that are preserved in the manuscript division of the Carolina Rediviva library all indicate that he had mastered the language well. Also preserved are two brief diaries, written partially in Swedish, in the Fiske Icelandic Collection.
19. Horatio S. White, *Willard Fiske: Life and Correspondence*, 340, 349; *Breve fra og til Carl Christian Rafn* (Copenhagen, 1869), 304; *Memorials of Willard Fiske*, 2, *The Traveller*, 110.
20. Ibid., 43.
21. Halldór Hermannsson, "Willard Fiske and Icelandic Bibliography," 98.

Chapter 3

1. In both "A Sketch of the Life and Labors of Professor Willard Fiske" and *Willard Fiske: Life and Correspondence* (74ff.), Horatio S. White remarks (and quotes other voices, including Fiske's) at length on Fiske's formation as a librarian. In the Astor Library, Fiske served under the direction of Joseph G. Cogswell, former librarian at Harvard, who before Fiske was also influenced "by foreign precedents and standards," specifically those employed at the University of Göttingen, in library organization. On the Astor Library itself, a non-circulating reference library eventually incorporated into the New York Public Library, see for example the history of the latter accessed 1 June 2016, http://www.nypl.org/help/about-nypl/history.
2. These occupations—chess and free-lance journalism—reflect lifelong interests, culminating in the instance of chess in Fiske's donation of his collection on the subject to the National Library of Iceland. As seen above, Fiske's youthful dispatches to American newspapers trace to his correspondence with family and friends. All three volumes of the *Memorials of Willard Fiske* testify to his journalistic roles as, respectively, editor, correspondent, and instructor (in courses offered at Cornell).
3. *Memorials of Willard Fiske*, 1, *The Editor*, ix–x.
4. In a university as such. However, Gustavus Adolphus College has taught Swedish since its founding in 1862. See summaries at https://www.stolaf.edu/depts/norwegian/nordic/colleges/colleges_sweden.htm, accessed 1 June 2016.
5. Morris Bishop, *A History of Cornell* (Ithaca: Cornell University Press, 1962), 15–17.
6. Ibid., 35. Bishop and White's autobiography infer White's acquisition of fluent French and German while he studied, traveled, and worked in Paris, Berlin, and St. Petersburg (serving as an American attaché in the last location). After Europe, he returned to Yale and completed a master's degree in history.
7. Then known as the "committee on literature"—Andrew D. White,

Autobiography of Andrew Dickson White, 2 vols. (New York: Century, 1905), 1:105.

8. Bishop, *History of Cornell*, 74.

9. Daniel Willard Fiske to séra Jón Bjarnason, 25 May 1874. Fiske Icelandic Collection. Fiske chiefly discusses Icelandic scholarly matters in this letter, and refers in passing to the forty thousand volumes in the Cornell Library. Professing comfort in reading if not composing Icelandic, he declares that "[a]n Icelandic letter is as precious to me as a draught from Mímirs brunn [sic]."

10. Andrew D. White, *Autobiography*, 1:343.

11. The original permanent installation was in the tower of McGraw Hall, although for the opening, the bells occupied a provisional "wooden tower" near the entrance to what is now Uris Library (ibid.). With the erection of the university library (now Uris Library) in 1891, the carillon was transferred to its adjoining, and iconic, campanile.

Chapter 4

1. Daniel Willard Fiske, *J* [poems dedicated to Jennie McGraw Fiske] (Florence: D. W. Fiske, 1887), 7. Here the poem is titled "At the Beginning."

2. Principally in the Old Northwest (Wisconsin, Michigan). See Ronald John Williams, *Jennie McGraw Fiske: Her Influence upon Cornell University* (Ithaca: Cornell University Press, 1949), 6ff.

3. Ibid., 14.

4. Lettie's full name was Mary Celestia McGraw; she and Jennie were paternal first cousins, daughters of McGraw brothers.

5. Williams underscores this secrecy in *Jennie McGraw Fiske*, 31.

6. Many letters bear witness to this occurrence.

7. Richard Beck, *Útverðir íslenzkrar menningar* (Reykjavík: Almenna bókafélagið, 1972), 82.

8. From 1869 onward Taylor regularly gave public lectures at the university, having been appointed a "non-resident professor of German literature" there. As Williams relates (p. 30), Fiske collaborated in the endeavor to bring Taylor to campus for a series of such lectures in the spring of 1875, and introduced him to Jennie. See also the guide to the Bayard Taylor papers, #14/18/1169, Division of Rare and Manuscript Collections, Cornell University Library, accessed 16 March 2015, http://rmc.library.cornell.edu/EAD/htmldocs/RMA01169.html.

Chapter 5

1. Caroline lived with her son in Florence from her widowhood in 1884 until 1891, when she returned to upstate New York. See, in Horatio S. White, *Willard Fiske: Life and Correspondence*, 7–8, an

"account of Mrs. Fiske's life reproduc[ing] substantially the facts of a notice published at the time of her decease, October 31, 1897."

2. Williams, *Jennie McGraw Fiske*, 31.

3. Ibid., 38.

4. Douglass Boardman (1822–1891) was a New York county and state judge, first dean of the Cornell law school, and a close friend and advisor to Jennie McGraw. See the Guide to the Douglass Boardman Papers, 1839–1891, #1622, Division of Rare and Manuscript Collections, Cornell University Library, which contains extensive correspondence. Accessed 7 June 2016, http://rmc.library.cornell.edu/EAD/htmldocs/RMM01622.html.

5. Williams, *Jennie McGraw Fiske*, 42. This visit to New York occurred in December 1877, seven months after Jennie's father's death.

6. Now Oslo.

7. The author specifies Lillehammer is in Guðbrandsdalur (Gudbrandsdal). The city is inland, northwest of Oslo and south-southwest of Trondheim.

Chapter 6

1. *Letters from High Latitudes: Being Some Account of a Voyage in the Schooner Yacht "Foam"* . . . *to Iceland, Jan Mayen, & Spitzbergen, in 1856* was first published in 1857 (London: J. Murray), and aroused considerable interest. The book became popular not least because of its literary value. Lord Dufferin (1826–1902) was formally Frederick Temple Blackwood, Marquis of Dufferin and Ava, his final promotion in peerage.

2. Lord Dufferin to Fiske, 10 November 1879.

3. Lord Dufferin to Fiske, 10 March 1874.

4. *Skýrsla um bækur þær, sem gefnar hafa verið Stiptisbókasafninu á Íslandi, í minningu þjóðhátíðar Íslands 1874* (Reykjavík: Prentsmiðja Íslands, 1874) records the books donated to the forerunner of the National Library of Iceland. In this report are found names of donors in America and also in Denmark, Sweden, and Norway. The most extensive entry lists for individuals and institutions are for Willard Fiske and Cornell University. In his 1914 catalogue of the Fiske Icelandic Collection, Halldór Hermannsson notes that Jón Árnason, librarian and pre-eminent Icelandic folklorist of his era, compiled and edited the report.

5. Séra Matthías Jochumsson (1835–1920) was to be a friend of Fiske's for the duration of the latter's life. Séra (the Icelandic honorific for ordained pastors and priests) Matthías was a major national poet (skáld) who authored the lyrics of the Icelandic national anthem ("Ó, guð vors lands").

6. *Þjóðólfur*, 14 Sepember 1874.

7. W. H. Carpenter, "Willard Fiske in Iceland," 108.
8. Jón Ólafsson (1850–1916) was a journalist, editor (of the journal *Skírnir*), and member of the Alþingi. He published a report on his Icelandic expedition to Alaska in 1875, although his scheme to establish a colony of Icelanders there did not materialize.
9. Jón Sigurðsson (1811–1879), known as Jón forseti because he was president of the Copenhagen chapter of the Icelandic Literary Society, was the pre-eminent figure in Iceland's non-violent struggle for independence from Denmark. Aside from his role as a scholarly literary editor, he developed a compatible orthography for the Faroese language. His birthday, 17 June, is now Iceland's Independence Day.

Chapter 7

1. W. M. Wilkingson, *A Handbook for Travellers in Denmark, with Schleswig and Holstein and Iceland* (London: John Murray, 1893), 98.
2. W. H. Carpenter, "Willard Fiske in Iceland," 111.
3. Sumarliði Ísleifsson, *Ísland: Framandi land* (Reykjavík: Mál og menning, 1996), 153.
4. Ibid., 198.
5. Ibid., 211.
6. William Dudley Foulke, *Biography and Correspondence of Arthur M. Reeves: Being a Supplemental Volume to Mr. Reeves'* "Finding of Wineland the Good: The History of the Icelandic Discovery of America" (London: Henry Frowde, 1895). See also concerning Reeves in *Sunnanfari* 2, 3B (Sept. 1892). Reeves' translation of Tegnér's poem (see chapter 1, footnote 31) was submitted as an undergraduate senior thesis ("Tegner's 'Frithjof's saga'") in 1878, and is in the holdings of Cornell University's Division of Rare and Manuscript Collections. The poem is partially translated metrically and partially rendered in a prose synopsis. Reeves also translated as *Lad and Lass: A Story of Life in Iceland* (London: S. Low, Marston, Searle, and Rivington, 1890) *Piltur og stúlka*, by Jón Thoroddsen (1818–1868), which was one of Iceland's earliest modern European novels.
7. The newspapers *Ísafold*, *Þjóðólfur*, and *Norðanfari* write about this. Further, Icelanders express themselves about it in letters to Fiske.
8. *The Finding of Wineland the Good*, published in 1890, was in its time a thoroughgoing compilation of saga manuscript sources on the Norse encounter with America. The text incorporates critical studies, translations, transcriptions, and photographs from the principal manuscripts: Hauksbók (AM 371, 544, and 675, all 4to), AM 557 4to, and Flateyjarbók (GKS 2005).
9. Letter from Björn M. Ólsen, 1 December 1892.
10. Deyr fé, / deyja frændur, / deyr sjálfur ið sama; / en orðstír / deyr

aldregi / hveim er sér góðan getur. This verse (in normalized Icelandic) is seventy-sixth of seventy-seven in the chapter of the poem called "Gestaþáttur" (Guest's chapter), online rendition accessed 9 June 2016, http://www.anomy.net/havamal/. This site includes transcriptions of two English translations.

11. The telegram conveying word of Reeves' death, not preserved in the Daniel Willard Fiske papers, reached Fiske in Cairo in late February. Correspondence in Fiske's papers (#13–1–348) indicates he immediately wrote to Reeves' mother to express his sympathy. Writing a postcard from Cairo on 4 March to his own mother, Fiske finds himself "still thinking of the sad telegram from Mrs. Reeves about the sudden death of her gifted son, Arthur. There was no other American so much in sympathy with my own studies as he, and I shall miss him greatly." Ten days later, returning to Italy and nearing Brindisi, he wrote again to his mother: "I can't help thinking of poor Reeves. Brief telegraphed accounts of the accident have appeared in the papers . . . The loss of Reeves is a terrible one when one thinks of his promise. He will be greatly regretted in Denmark and Iceland."

Chapter 8

1. *Willard Fiske in Iceland: Based on the Pocket Notebook Kept During His Sojourn There, 1879*, ed. P. M. Mitchell (Ithaca: Cornell University Library, 1989), 5.

2. Volcanic activity and uncertain agricultural conditions contributed to significant emigration from 1875. Most of these Icelanders went to North America, the majority to Canada, where the ethnic concentration of Icelanders remains pronounced in Manitoba. In a letter to Fiske dated London, 10 November 1879, and now in the Fiske Icelandic Collection, Lord Dufferin, Governor-General of Canada 1872–78, reminisced warmly about his own visit to Iceland and remarked that nothing offered "greater pleasure than . . . to welcome an Icelandic emigration to their new-found home in the Dominion."

3. A man's daily labor was valued at a seasonal high of gkr. (*gullkrónur*) 2.50 in the spring of 1879; the hourly wage was twenty-one *eyrir*. These values applied to Reykjavík and Eyrarbakki, a fishing village and trading post (and birthplace of the author) on the southwest coast. *Hagskinna: Sögulegar hagtölur um Ísland*, ed. Guðmundur Jónsson and Magnús S. Magnússon (Reykjavík: Hagstofa Íslands, 1997), 608. The Danish krone replaced the Danish rigsdaler as currency in Iceland from 1874 ("Icelandic króna," *Wikipedia*, accessed 19 June 2018, https://en.wikipedia.org/wiki/Icelandic_króna).

4. *Ísafold*, 18 July 1879.

5. Fiske apparently had better fortune nearing the Faroes on the return

trip. In his letter to Charles Dudley Warner (and Charles's wife Susan) of 12 November 1879, he mentions the ship "lying off and on outside the Faroes, and a day at Thorshavn, the capital of these islets." He does not indicate whether he came ashore at Þórshavn. (See on Warner in end note 13 of this chapter.)

6. See P. M. Mitchell's preface in *Willard Fiske in Iceland*.

7. Höfn is a village on the southeast coast of Iceland, and a direct sail northwest from the Faroes. From this point SS *Camoens* began a circumnavigation to the east and north of the island.

8. The sun does not set per se at the summer solstice in Iceland. Although the light turns to dusk at night about three weeks later, about the time Fiske was experiencing the "white nights," it is still quite feasible to read outdoors, unaided by lamps.

9. Daniel Willard Fiske to Caroline Willard Fiske, 12 July 1879. Daniel Willard Fiske papers, #13–1–348.

10. Fiske subsequently published the poem in his poetry volume *J*. The last line aptly portrays his intellectual attachment to Iceland and the Norse heritage and his simultaneous passion for Jennie, who was then in Europe and frequently on his mind. R. J. Williams (p. 49) refers to another "lengthy poem to Jennie" Fiske penned while in Iceland. The title is "An Epistle from the Arctic Sea"; it appears in *J* on pages 71–76. The closure commences with the line "Come to the North, O gracious queen . . ."

11. Daniel Willard Fiske to Caroline Willard Fiske, 12 July 1879. Daniel Willard Fiske papers, #13–1–348. Brekkubær was a property in Grjótaþorp, a neighborhood in Reykjavík.

12. Ibid.

13. Daniel Willard Fiske papers, #13–1–348. Charles Dudley Warner (1829–1900) was a close friend of Fiske's from their youth, and his classmate at Hamilton (from which, unlike Fiske, he actually graduated). He later became an editor, critic, and author. The first letter preserved in the Fiske correspondence at Cornell is a letter to Warner from Fiske in 1847. In two extant letters (also in the Daniel Willard Fiske papers, #13–1–348) to Warner dated 27 August and 12 November 1879 (after the voyage), Fiske describes in some detail his Icelandic sojourn and impressions of Icelanders, remarking on the banquets to which he was invited and on the evident culture among the people ("We have never been at a bær (farmstead) which didn't have a good library. We have seen in the most remote valleys private collections including . . . English books," he wrote in August).

14. The letters, which are several, long, and detailed, are preserved in the Division of Rare and Manuscript Collections in the Daniel Willard Fiske papers, #13–1–348.

15. *Willard Fiske in Iceland*, 2–4 for a narrative of the 1874 book donation; W. H. Carpenter, "Willard Fiske in Iceland," 108.

16. *Þjóðólfur*, 20 August 1879.
17. Matthías was in error on this degree; Fiske never earned a doctorate.

Chapter 9

1. Daniel Willard Fiske to Caroline Willard Fiske, 24 July 1879. Daniel Willard Fiske papers, #13–1–348. The letter was written from Akureyri.
2. Þórunn Sigurðardóttir, *Manuscript Material, Correspondence and Graphic Material in the Fiske Icelandic Collection*, Islandica 48 (Ithaca: Cornell University Press, 1994), 278. The photograph of Selfoss is preserved in the vault of Cornell's Division of Rare and Manuscript Collections along with the rare volumes of the Fiske Icelandic Collection.
3. D. W. Fiske, *J.* (1887), 78.
4. Ibid., 74. In the following stanza Fiske is transfixed by the unexpected brightness:

   > And O the light, the silver light,
   > More argent white, more pearly bright
   > Than any light that gleams!
   > It lumines heath and sea and sky. . . .

5. *Alþingisfrjettir* 2 [parliamentary news supplement in *Ísafold*], 16 July 1879, 5.
6. See W. D. Foulke, *Biography and Correspondence of Arthur Middleton Reeves* (London: Henry Frowde, 1895), xxii. The reference to the evening sky "prodigal in its colours and tints, and the bank of clouds around the setting sun, of a deep red copper, [throwing] a soft light over the narrow winding fjord" appears in a quoted letter from Reeves to his mother, not dated by Foulke but apparently written 24 July 1879.
7. The translation renders the reiteration of Reeves' name in the original.
8. Fiske held no such degree, having completed neither college nor university.
9. The water in the gorge is Fall Creek, which runs just north of the Arts and Sciences Quadrangle and descends to Cayuga Lake. The university still operates a hydroelectric station in the gorge.
10. *Norðlingur*, 11 August 1879.
11. Ibid., 25 August 1879.
12. Daniel Willard Fiske, [*Travels through Iceland*], entry dated 27 July 1879. (The diary is manuscript item 56 as enumerated in Þórunn Sigurðardóttir, *Manuscript Material . . . in the Fiske Icelandic Collection* (1994), supplied with the title *Travels through Iceland*. A description of this notebook appears on pp. 25–26 of *Manuscript Material*.
13. Ibid.; entry for Wednesday, 30 July.

14. *Ísafold*, 25 June 1879 and 10 June 1879.

15. *Þjóðólfur*, 19 July 1879.

16. Jón Hjáltason held the degree of candidatus theologicus (cand. theol.), roughly equivalent to a master's in theology and indicating eligibility to continue with a doctoral dissertation.

17. The *menntaskóli* in the Icelandic educational system retains students until the age of twenty and confers a degree roughly equivalent to an associate's degree in the United States.

18. The letter, written in an unknown hand, is preserved in the Fiske Icelandic Collection in correspondence from Jón Andrésson Hjaltalín (1840–1908), principal of the school at Möðruvellir, to Fiske. An English rendition accompanies the Icelandic original and appears to be in the hand of Jón Hjaltalín, who corresponded with Fiske in English.

19. One hundred aurar make one króna.

20. *Norðlingur*, 5 August 1880 and 17 August 1880.

21. *Þjóðólfur*, 10 October 1879.

Chapter 10

1. A photograph (image identifier number 1923.4.49) from the Frederick W. W. Howell Collection, taken from Akureyri harbor at the end of the nineteenth century, offers a sense of the village's still-compact size two decades after Fiske's visit. Accessed 22 June 2016, https://digital.library.cornell.edu/catalog/ss:269183.

2. Klemens Jónsson, *Saga Akureyrar* (Akureyri: Akureyrarkaupstaður, 1948), 106.

3. Konrad Maurer (1823–1902) visited Iceland in 1858. An outstanding scholar of German and Nordic legal history, he also took an interest in Icelandic folklore and published a collection of Icelandic tales as well as extensive legal and philological studies focusing on the Norse world.

4. *Norðlingur*, 11 August 1879.

5. Ibid. It seems Fiske feared any comment he made in the matter would breathe condescension.

6. Daniel Willard Fiske to Caroline Fiske, 18 August 1879.

7. *Norðlingur*, 11 August 1879.

8. Ibid.

9. Inquiry was made after these pictures in Richmond, Indiana, but they have apparently been lost.

10. *Lad and Lass* was published in London in 1890.

11. D. W. Fiske, [*Travels through Iceland*], entry dated Friday, 1 August 1879. Staying at the farmstead Flugumýri at the head of Skagafjörður in the north of Iceland, Fiske noted that "3 daughters [of the proprietor] sing & play guitar . . . Promised to send music (guitar) to daughters. R[eeves] & daughters sang in evening."

Chapter 11

1. Daniel Willard Fiske to Caroline Willard Fiske, 18 August 1879. Fiske also notes the visit extensively in his diary. Bægisá is west of Akureyri; the district is now traversed by the national ring road (Þjóðvegur). Two sectors, Ytri-Bægisá and Syðri-Bægisá, identify with this location. Jón Þorláksson (1744–1819), the poet and translator of Milton's *Paradise Lost*, associated with Bægisá, came to take up the parish there only at the age of forty-four. He is considered a pioneer in modern Icelandic poetry, his work prefiguring that of the Romantic era. Some of his verse reflects his liaisons with several women. (Eyþór Rafn Gissurarson, "Skáldið á Bægisá," *Menningarblað/Lesbók* (*Morgunblaðið*), 9 August 1997; accessed 28 June 2016, http://www. mbl.is/greinasafn/grein/347176/).

2. Daniel Willard Fiske to Caroline Willard Fiske, 18 August 1879. Fiske discussed Icelandic dress as he encountered examples and enthusiasts in the region of Þingeyrar, west of Hólar, remarking that "Reeves fell in love with" a farmer's daughter who "was kind enough to dress herself in the rich Icelandic costume for our benefit." At Bægisá, prior to Þingeyrar, the wife of the farmstead and her sister were "dressed in black silk, and looking very much like American ladies."

3. The reference is to the painter, artist, and cultural figure Sigurður Guðmundsson (1833–1874). An online site featuring biographical and archival information is available. Accessed 27 June 2016, https:// sigurdurmalari.hi.is/wiki/index.php?title=Sigurður_Guðmundsson.

4. Samuel Edmond Waller, *Six Weeks in the Saddle* (London: Macmillan, 1874), 34.

5. D. W. Fiske to séra Jón Bjarnason, 25 May 1874.

6. *Norðlingur*, 11 August 1879.

7. Öxnadalur is a long valley heading southwest from the Bægisá area; the national ring road now follows it.

8. D. W. Fiske, [*Travels through Iceland*], 31 July 1879.

9. Ibid., 2 August 1879.

10. Ibid.

11. Ibid. (The narration is also detailed in Fiske's letter of 18 August to his mother.)

12. Ibid.

13. Ibid., Borðeyri, Saturday, 9 August. Here Fiske jotted a note about a "[r]emarkable Danish linguistic boy here" named Thor Jensen. Perhaps the lad's capacities seemed noteworthy because of his age, but as the narrative of Fiske's journey shows, educated Icelanders had both considerable facility in languages and access to multiple literatures.

14. *Þjóðólfur*, 19 July 1879.

Chapter 12

1. Fiske speaks of this in his diary and also in letters to friends and relatives.
2. Klemens Jónsson, "Ýms atriði úr lífinu í Reykjavík fyrir 40 árum," *Skírnir* 87 (1913): 135–40.
3. *Þjóðólfur*, 25 June 1879.
4. W. H. Carpenter, "Willard Fiske in Iceland," 108–9.
5. D. W. Fiske, [*Travels through Iceland*], 1879. The diary entry for 16 August narrates his arrival by boat in Reykjavík.
6. *Ísafold*, 26 April 1881.
7. Fiske discusses this inter alia in the letter to his mother of 18 August 1879.
8. Séra Matthías Jochumsson (1835–1920) was one of Iceland's greatest poets of the late nineteenth and early twentieth centuries, a renowned hymnist who wrote the lyrics for Iceland's national anthem ("Ó, Guð vors lands»), a translator of multiple languages into Icelandic, and a newspaper editor. An ordained Lutheran pastor, he was nonetheless a religious skeptic. He endured health problems and personal losses, yet sustained important friendships in Iceland and abroad. See Kristín Bragadóttir, "Matthías Jochumsson," *Icelandic Writers*, ed. Patrick J. Stevens, Dictionary of Literary Biography 293 (Detroit: Thomson Gale, 2004), 246–59.
9. Matthías Jochumsson, *Sögukaflar af sjálfum mér*, 2nd ed., ed. Árni Kristjánsson (Reykjavík: Ísafold, 1959), 276. The Icelandic name of the archaeological society is Fornleifafélag [Íslands].
10. The importance of Þingvellir in the national and legal history of Iceland cannot be overstated. The official site (in English as well as Icelandic) for Þingvellir National Park (Þjóðgarðurinn á Þingvöllum) explores the history of Þingvellir from multiple perspectives, from the settlement of Iceland to the archaeology in situ. Accessed 1 July 2016, http://www.thingvellir.is/history.aspx.
11. Letter from Matthías Jochumsson, 27 June 1880.
12. W. H. Carpenter, "Willard Fiske in Iceland," 112.
13. Oddi in Rangárvallasýsla is the ancient seat of the extended family known as the Oddaverjar. The farmstead, with church, is in southwest Iceland, east past Selfoss, and off the national ring road (Þjóðvegur) between Hella and Hvolsvöllur.

Chapter 13

1. Daniel Willard Fiske to Halldór Hermannsson, 23 January 1902.
2. Matthías Þórðarson, "Fiskesafn," *Árbók hins íslenzka fornleifafélags* (1910): 93–97. See also Guðmundur J. Guðmundsson, "Egypsku

munirnir í dánargjöf Willards Fiskes," *Árbók hins íslenzka fornlei-fafélags* (1995): 49–74.

3. Daniel Willard Fiske to Halldór Hermannsson, 31 January 1902 and 18 February 1902; also one letter from DWF to HH from 1902, undated.

4. Many of the items Fiske gave the nation were on display in a collaborative exhibition of the National Museum and the National and University Library, held in the Library during 2005.

Chapter 14

1. Hilmar Finsen (1824–1886), a Danish government official, was governor of Iceland from 1873 to 1883 and also the king's representative in the Alþingi from 1867 (*Íslenzkar æviskrár*, 2:352–53).

2. I.e. the first session following the 1874 millennial celebration of the settlement of Iceland.

3. Eiríkur Kúld (1822– or 24–1893). The title prófastur (provost, archdeacon) is used in the Scandinavian Lutheran sense to designate a senior pastor administratively responsible for more than one parish (*Íslenzkar æviskrár*, 1:413).

4. Grímur Thomsen (1820–1896) was an important Icelandic poet and literary scholar and also an official in the Danish diplomatic service (*Íslenzkar æviskrár*, 2:105–6).

5. Garðar Svavarsson, a ninth-century explorer of Swedish extraction, was ostensibly one of the founders of Iceland (*Íslenzkar æviskrár*, 2:29–30).

6. Located in Reykjavík.

7. *Þjóðólfur*, 27 August 1879.

8. Interestingly, this proverb is of relatively recent origin, with earliest examples attested in the nineteenth century. See brief article on visindavefur.is, authored 4 July 2007 by Guðrún Kvaran. Accessed 6 July 2016, http://visindavefur.is/svar.php?id=6710.

Chapter 15

1. An important demographic feature outside larger Icelandic towns, from the late nineteenth century onward was migration from *sveit* to *þorp*, inland country to seaside village, whether seasonal or permanent. This movement coincided with a rise in the importance of commercial fishing.

2. The Learned School (Lærði skólinn), known during its history by several names; in its time the select national high school, and precursor of Menntaskólinn í Reykjavík. See the web site of Menntaskólinn í Reykjavík. Accessed 7 July 2016, http://www.mr.is/index.php?option=com_content&view=article&id=46&Itemid=28.

3. Jón Ólafsson, "Willard Fiske," *Skírnir* 79 (1905): 62–73.
4. Daniel Willard Fiske to Caroline Willard Fiske, 3 September 1879. Daniel Willard Fiske papers, #13–1–348.
5. Daniel Willard Fiske, *Mímir: Icelandic Institutions with Addresses* (Copenhagen: Martius Truelsen, 1903), 68.
6. 3 September 1879, cited in note 4.
7. Letter and name list from Jón Finnsson, 27 November 1879.
8. Letter from Jón Egilsen, 9 November 1879.
9. Letter from Jón Egilsen, 21 January 1898.
10. 3 September 1879, cited in note 4.
11. Daniel Willard Fiske to Caroline Willard Fiske, 10 September 1879. Daniel Willard Fiske papers, #13–1–348.

Chapter 16

1. Letter from Bogi Th. Melsteð, 28 November 1879.
2. Letter from faculty and students of the Learned School, 28 November 1879.
3. Letter from the directors of the reading society Íþaka, 27 June 1883.
4. Letter from the directors of the reading society Íþaka, 13 May 1895.
5. Letter from the reading society Íþaka, 29 May 1904. This "þakklætisávarp" (address of gratitude), as it describes itself, was no ordinary missive; it consists of four large sheets secured along a spine with a delicate cord. The calligraphy of the text shows skill and refinement in measure with the sentiments for Fiske evident throughout the text.
6. Vilhjálmur Þ. Gíslason, "Íþaka: Hálfrar aldar afmæli," in *Skýrsla um hinn almenna menntaskóla í Reykjavík skólaárið 1929–1930* (Reykjavík: Gutenberg, 1930), 1–11 (supplementary pages).
7. *Skýrsla um hinn lærða skóla í Reykjavík skólaárið 1879–80* (Reykjavík: Ísafold, 1880), 25.
8. Bjarni Jónsson (1809–1868) was headmaster (rektor) of the Learned School in Reykjavík 1851–68. (*Íslenzkar æviskrár*, 1:179)
9. Halldór Hermannsson, "Bókasöfn skólans," in *Minningar úr menntaskóla*, ed. Ármann Kristinsson and Friðrik Sigurbjörnsson (Reykjavík: Ármann Kristinsson, 1946), 174–75.
10. Charles Kelsall (1782–1857) was an English architect influenced by the study of the Greeks prevalent among British academics at the time. He donated in his will one thousand pounds for construction of Íþaka. David Watkin, "Kelsall, Charles (1782–1857)," rev. Annette Peach in *Oxford Dictionary of National Biography*, ed. H. C. G. Matthew and Brian Harrison (Oxford: OUP, 2004); online ed., ed. David Cannadine, April 2016, http://www.oxforddnb.com/view/article/37627 (26 May 2016 version accessed 28 December 2018); "Bókhlaðan Íþaka: Saga safnsins," http://www.mr.is/~aesa/ (accessed 12 July 2016).

11. *Saga Reykjavíkurskóla II: Skólalífið í Lærða skólanum,* ed. Heimir Þorleifsson (Reykjavík: Sögusjóður menntaskólans í Reykjavík, 1978), 120.
12. Letter from Björn M. Ólsen, 22 July 1881.
13. Letter from Björn M. Ólsen, 29 November 1883.
14. Letter from Björn M. Ólsen, 17 March 1904.
15. Kristín Bragadóttir, "Skalden och redaktören Jón Þorkelsson," *Scripta Islandica: Isländska sällskapets årsbok* 45 (1994): 3–20. See also Stefán Pjetursson, "Jón Þorkelsson þjóðskjalavörður," *Andvari* (1960): 195–215.
16. Letter from Björn M. Ólsen, 25 April 1904.
17. Sigurður Sigurðsson was appointed an adjunct in the Learned School in 1879 and held a teaching post therie until his death in 1884 (*Íslenzkar æviskrár,* 4:261).
18. *Ísafold,* 21 November 1879.
19. Ibid., 2 December 1879. The Icelandic name of this women's school is Kvennaskólinn í Reykjavík. The school, still in existence and now coeducational, is colloquially known as Kvennó. A history of the school, accessed online 3 August 2016, is at http://www.kvenno.is/ kvennaskolinn/skolinn/agrip-af-sogu/.
20. *Ísafold,* 21 November 1879.

Chapter 17

1. Jón Sigurðsson was to die in Copenhagen 7 December 1879.
2. *Þjóðólfur,* 20 August 1879.
3. Ibid.
4. W. H. Carpenter, "Willard Fiske in Iceland," 110.
5. Glasgow was constructed in 1863 and served as a commercial establishment and a theatre over the course of its existence. The wooden structure succumbed to the "stærsti bruni í sögu Reykjavíkur fram að þeim tíma" (largest fire in the history of Reykjavík up until that time). http://www.leikminjasafn.is/sagan/islensk-leikhus/ glasgow/, accessed 05 August 2015.
6. The poem was printed in folio. Steingrímur called it "Kvæði flutt Prófessor W. Fiske og herra A.M. Reeves í samsæti, er þeim var haldið 11. oct. 1879 í Reykjavík (Glasgow)" (Poem read to Professor W. Fiske and Mr. A. M. Reeves at a dinner held for them at Glasgow in Reykjavík, 11 October 1879).
7. Fiske and Reeves were to leave Iceland, but William Carpenter stayed on to continue his studies of Old Norse-Icelandic. (See the excerpt from *Þjóðólfur,* 31 October 1879, and W. H. Carpenter, "Willard Fiske in Iceland," 115.)
8. Daniel Willard Fiske to Jón Sigurðsson, 25 August 1852, Landsbókasafn Íslands—Háskólabókasafn, Lbs. 2590 4to.

9. *Norðlingur*, 14 May 1880. The poem is quite long, and difficult Icelandic; only the first stanza is offered here in a tentative translation.

10. The Stiptisbókasafn was forerunner of Landsbókasafn Íslands, now amalgamated with the library of the University of Iceland as Landsbókasafn Íslands-Háskólabókasafn.

11. Letter from the board of directors of the library predating the National Library (Stjórnarnefnd stiptisbókasafnsins í Reykjavík), 7 October 1879. Of these works, *Landnáma*, printed in Skálholt in 1688, was the first secular title (apart from law books) to come off the press in Iceland.

12. Andrew Dickson White was then on leave from the presidency of Cornell University. He welcomed Fiske at Berlin 8 November 1879. See *The Diaries of Andrew D. White*, ed. Robert Morris Ogden (Ithaca, NY: Cornell University Library, 1959).

Chapter 19

1. *Þjóðólfur*, 11 December 1879. The text is given in Icelandic. The original English text of the article in *The Times* of London has the byline "from a correspondent" and was filed 20 September.

2. Fiske wrote about Jón Sigurðsson inter alia in the New York *Daily Tribune* of 4 January 1880; the New York *Herald*, 9 January 1880; the *National—Zeitung* of 24 December 1879; and the *Kölnische Zeitung*, 23 December 1879.

3. On Icelandic literature and language, Fiske wrote in *The Nation*, 22 January 1880; *The Berkeley Quarterly*, 2 (1881); and *The Bulletin of the Library of Cornell University*, 1 (1882–83); among others.

4. (Gunnlaugur) Tryggvi Gunnarsson (1835–1917) apprenticed as a carpenter but became involved in commerce and was eventually appointed bank director of the national bank (*Íslenzkar æviskrár*, 5:32).

5. Letters from Tryggvi Gunnarsson, 5 February and 20 October 1897.

6. *Almanak hins íslenzka Þjóðvinafjelags um árið 1898*: 31–33; a portrait of Fiske also appeared in this number.

7. *Cornell Era* 12, no. 11 (28 November 1879): 135, 137.

8. Letter from Steingrímur Thorsteinsson, 12 February 1880.

Chapter 20

1. Þórunn Sigurðardóttir, *Manuscript Material . . . in the Fiske Icelandic Collection* (1994). The letters are organized broadly by recipient (Fiske, Halldór Hermannsson...) and then by correspondent in this catalogue, as in the collection itself; each entry provides free-text description of subjects entertained in the correspondence.

2. Letter from Jón Björnsson, 11 November 1891 (incidentally Fiske's

sixtieth birthday). Two other altarpieces painted by the queen are known, both in churches in Denmark.

3. John 4:13–14 [Jesus in conversation with the Samaritan woman]: "... Whosoever drinketh of this water shall thirst again: But whosoever drinketh of the water that I shall give him shall never thirst. ... " (The Official King James Bible Online, accessed 27 November 2014, http://www.kingjamesbibleonline.org/.) The Eyrarbakki church in question was the parish church of the author, a native of this village.

4. Letter from Jóhn Jóhannessen, 27 November 1895.

5. Letter from Einar Benediktsson, 18 July 1891. Einar Benediktsson (1864–1940) was to achieve fame as one of Iceland's most important modern (neo-romantic) poets.

6. Letter from Benedikt Gröndal, 8 February 1880. Benedikt (Sveinbjarnarson) Gröndal (1826–1907) was a leading Icelandic naturalist and author, and helped found the Icelandic Natural History Society (Hið íslenska náttúrufræðifélag).

7. The Rector mentioned here was the rector of Reykjavíkur lærði skóli, as Menntaskólinn í Reykjavík was officially known during the latter half of the nineteenth century. He was Jón Þorkelsson eldri (to distinguish him from the much younger scholar of the same name who was to become national archivist), who served from 1872 to 1895.

8. Benedikt Gröndal, *Dægradvöl: Æfisaga mín* (Reykjavík: Bókaverzlun Ársæls Árnasonar, 1923), 336–37.

9. Letter from Þorvaldur Thoroddsen, 6 February 1880.

10. Letter from Þorvaldur Thoroddsen, 1 August 1885.

11. Letter from Vilhjálmur Stefánsson, 10 June 1904.

12. Letter from Jón Þorkelsson.

13. Letter from Matthías Jochumsson. Oddi, from which Matthías was writing, is an ancient churchstead in the Rangárvellir area of the shire Rangárvallasýsla, southern Iceland. The early Icelandic historian Sæmundur fróði Sigfússon (1056–1133) was priest there. Jón helgi is a reference to the indigenous Icelandic saint Jón Ögmundarson (1052–1121), first bishop of Hólar, whose canonized status was never confirmed by Rome.

14. Letter from Matthías Jochumsson. Fiske had by then moved to Florence.

15. Letter from Páll Þorkelsson, 7 July 1887.

16. Letter from Finnur Jónsson, 13 May 1902.

17. Letter from Pétur Guðjohnsen. The will case is described chiefly in chapter 22.

18. Letter from Pétur Guðjohnsen, 1 February 1891.

19. Letter from Pétur Guðjohnsen, 25 August 1893.

20. Letter from Ólafur Davíðsson, 22 March 1880.

21. The *kvöldvökur* served the extended farmstead family (farmhands and

female servants included) as a venue for evening chores while listening to readings or recitations of sagas, poetry, devotional literature, or current events.

22. Letter from Grímur Thomsen, 8 February 1880.
23. Letters from Þorsteinn Br. Arnljótsson.

Chapter 21

1. D. W. Fiske, *J.* (1887), 75–76. These are the closing lines of the poem.
2. R. J. Williams, *Jennie McGraw Fiske*, 43.
3. Andrew D. White witnessed the civil cermony on 13 July, and was also present the following day at the "religious marriage at [the American] Legation," where he witnessed Jennie's will. *Diaries of Andrew D. White*, 206.
4. Ibid., 57.
5. Fiske had been to Egypt prior to this voyage, in the winter of 1867–68, and would visit multiple times at length again in his widowhood. See Horatio S. White, *Willard Fiske: Life and Correspondence*, 157–76 (chapter 11, "Egypt," including extensive discussion of Fiske's development of a Romanization scheme for Egyptian Arabic) and *Memorials of Willard Fiske*, 2, *The Traveller*, 206–31 ("Trip to Egypt and Palestine," Fiske's description of his travels and impressions).
6. R. J. Williams, *Jennie McGraw Fiske*, 59ff. Williams remarks that Fiske, during this honeymoon, "increased his knowledge and interest in the language which, in later years, took him back to Egypt . . . on a romantic but vigorous crusade for a modernized Egyptian alphabet" (p. 60). Fiske had already put his hand to substituting the roman alphabet for the writing of colloquial Egyptian Arabic. Too great a distance was thought to exist between the written language and the spoken vernacular, and was seen as a barrier to universal education. In 1891 Fiske would publish the textbook *An Egyptian Alphabet for the Egyptian People*; it is written in roman letters. (A second edition appeared in 1904. Documents on Fiske's work with Egyptian Arabic comprise "Series IV—Egyptian alphabet material" in the Daniel Willard Fiske papers, # 13-1-1165.) Fiske took up with the German grammarian Wilhelm Spitta's work of 1880, Spitta having died before the textbook came to be. Among others, Bogi Th. Melsteð relates this in his book on Willard Fiske.

    In addition, Fiske compiled on this voyage an extensive collection of ancient Egyptian objects that he later presenetd to the National Museum (Þjóðminjasafn) in Reykjavík.
7. Ibid., 59. Jennie remarked in a letter home, quoted by Williams, on "veiled women with water jars on their heads as if they had stepped out of Bible times."

8. Carol U. Sisler, *Enterprising Families, Ithaca, New York: Their Houses and Businesses* (Ithaca, NY: Enterprise Publishing, 1986), 69–84.
9. R. J. Williams, *Jennie McGraw Fiske*, 51.
10. Ibid., 65.
11. The mortuary chapel attached to Sage Chapel was completed in 1884. The tower reference is to the McGraw Hall tower, original location of the carillon Jennie donated.

Chapter 22

1. Bishop, *History of Cornell*, 224–32.
2. Williams, *Jennie McGraw Fiske*.
3. Andrew D. White states that "[Jennie] had left to the university very nearly two millions of dollars" with "more than a million and a half, for the university library." Andrew D. White, *Autobiography*, 1:419.
4. Williams, *Jennie McGraw Fiske*, 70.
5. Bishop, *History of Cornell*, 228.
6. Ibid.
7. Ibid.
8. Bishop, *History of Cornell*, 229; Williams, *Jennie McGraw Fiske*, 71; Horatio S. White, *Willard Fiske: Life and Correspondence*, 104ff. The letter was dated Florence 29 May 1890, and thus written ten days after the final US Supreme Court decision. Seemingly Fiske felt he had to explain himself to the erstwhile executor of his wife's estate, perhaps also thinking that much of the dust might have started to settle with the final resolution in hand.
9. Horatio S. White, *Willard Fiske: Life and Correspondence*, 102. Describing the conflict as "a mutual mistake and mutual misfortune to all," Sibley urged Fiske to "[c]ome back and share with us in the Glorious [sic] achievements of Cornell," stating this to be "the ardent hope and wish of your friend."
10. *Diaries of Andrew D. White*, 287.
11. Ibid., 288–89. Fiske's evidently brief, embryonic mention of a scholarly librarian in association with his Icelandic collection would come to full fruition with Halldór Hermannsson's arrival at Cornell in 1905, but even before then, Fiske's employment of Icelanders in Florence to assist in organizing and cataloguing the collection implicates an investment from his inheritance for the eventual benefit of the university library. Fiske's Petrarch collection would likewise go to the library. His small but notable Rhaeto-Romanic and far larger but no less notable Dante collections, not on the horizon in 1889, would precede his bequests, arriving at Cornell in the 1890s.
12. Williams, *Jennie McGraw Fiske*, 75.
13. See, for example, Bishop, *History of Cornell*, 232, where he also rehearses the inscription dedicating the library to Jennie.

Chapter 23

1. The preponderance of surviving Icelandic medieval vellum manuscripts found their way into major collections in the two centuries before Fiske began collecting. The Arnamagnaean Collection, compiled chiefly by Árni Magnússon (1663–1730) at the behest of the Danish crown and now shared between Iceland and Denmark, is by far the most emblematic for Nordic vellum manuscripts. The collections of Old Norse-Icelandic paper manuscripts, notably in the National and University Library of Iceland, are of remarkable significance inter alia for understanding the perpetuation of the Icelandic manuscript tradition up to the early years of the twentieth century.

2. Fiske's catalogue of Icelandic books appeared as the first and the fourth through sixth volumes of his *Bibliographical Notices* (Florence, 1887) under the title "Books Printed in Iceland 1578–1844." These volumes were conceived as supplements to the British Museum's *Catalogue of the Books Printed in Iceland from A.D. 1578 to 1880*, compiled by Thomas W. Lidderdale (London, 1885).

3. In a letter from Jón Þorkelsson dated 23 September 1899 there is discussion of a *Forfeðra bænabók* (Prayerbook of the forefathers) printed at Hólar in 1607, which was acquired from Hornstrandir, which as the northernmost peninsula (and now a nature reserve) in the Western Fjords is one of the more remote regions of Iceland.

4. Valdimar Ásmundsson, the publisher of Icelandic sagas, was sole editor of *Fjallkonan* ("lady of the mountain"; a feminine allegory of Iceland akin to France's Marianne, but thoroughly Icelandic) for its first eighteen volumes starting in 1884.

5. At this time five other exempla were known, of which one was in the possession of séra Helgi Hálfdánarson, in addition to the copies in collections according to Ólafur Davíðsson.

6. Letter from Valdimar Ásmundsson, 4 December 1898.

7. See the catalogue entry in Halldór Hermannsson, *Catalogue of the Icelandic Collection Bequeathed by Willard Fiske* (1914), 46, for a partial description of this copy's extraneous features, e.g. marks of prior ownership. Although the closing leaves (especially) of the volume show considerable wear, the book, while not perfect, is in reasonable shape given age and multiple transfers of ownership. The missing leaf from Matthew was long ago replaced with a leaf in manuscript that appears exact down to marginalia and catch-words—demonstrative of a pervasive Icelandic practice of curing textual defects in printed copies with manuscript substitutes.

8. Letter from Jón Þorkelsson, 12 February 1887.

9. Published as *Om digtningen på Island i det 15. og 16. århundrede* (Copenhagen: A. F. Høst, 1888).

10. Letter from Jón Þorkelsson, 27 April 1887.

11. In many letters from Jón Þorkelsson there is discussion of value, e.g. in the letter dated 17 October 1886.

12. Letter from Jón Þorkelsson, 26 October 1890.

13. Letter from Ólafur Davíðsson, 27 August 1887. The Fiske Icelandic Collection has a nearly comprehensive run of editions of the *Passíusálmar* from the first edition of 1666 through the close of the eighteenth century.

14. Letter from Ólafur Davíðsson, 12 May 1887. The full title is *Gronlandia antiqua, seu, Veteris Gronlandiae descriptio: ubi coeli marisque natura, terrae, locorum & villarum situs, animalium terrestrium aquatiliumque varia genera, gentis origo & incrementa, status politicus & ecclesiasticus, gesta memorabilia & vicissitudines: ex antiquis memoriis, praecipuè Islandicis, quâ fieri potuit industriâ collecta exponuntur.* The work appeared in Copenhagen in 1706. Þormóður Torfason (1636–1719) was prominent among Icelandic historians and authors of the seventeenth century and eventually became royal historian of the Dano-Norwegian kingdom.

15. Letter from Ólafur Davíðsson, 16 May 1892.

16. Letter from Ólafur Davíðsson, 15 March 1892.

17. Letter from Jón Þorkelsson, 2 March 1892.

18. As examples, one may mention letters from Jón Þorkelsson, 31 August 1890 and Tryggvi Gunnarsson, 7 May 1892.

19. Letter from Jón Þorkelsson, 29 November 1890.

20. Davíð Stefánsson frá Fagraskógi (1895–1964) was one of the most significant Icelandic poets of the first half of the twentieth century, and also a novelist.

Chapter 24

1. Letter from Tryggvi Gunnarsson, 26 May 1881. Hið íslenska þjóðvinafélag (the Icelandic Society of Friends of the Nation) was founded in 1871 by members of the Alþingi with the aim of promoting Icelandic culture and national identity. The first president was the scholar and patriot Jón Sigurðsson. The organization is still in existence. See https://www.thjodvinafelag.is/, accessed 8 January 2019. (The letter to Fiske from Tryggvi dated 24 January 1890, quoted from on the same page, is also in the Fiske Icelandic Collection.)

2. Stiptisbókasafn and Landsbókasafn respectively.

3. The original Icelandic reads: *Calendarium Gregorianum* Edur SA NJE STJLL, Uppa hvorn Gregorius 13de Pave i Rom, fann Anno 1582 fyrer Hialp og Liðveitslu Aloysii Lilii Stiornumeistara. Hvar med og fylgia *Islendsk Misseraskipte*, epter því sem þau hafa vered brukud á tveimur næst fyrerfarande 100 Aara olldum (Calendarium Gregorianum, or the New Style, which Gregory XIIIth, the Pope in Rome

established in the year 1582 through the help and assistance of the astronomer Aloysius Lilius. Accompanied by Half-Yearly Changes, according to their establishment over the next two centuries).

4. The Icelandic terms are, respectively, *Lögþingisbækur* and *Alþingisbækur*. See the *Catalogue of the Icelandic Collection bequeathed by Willard Fiske* (1914), 7, under Proceedings (of the Alþingi).

5. Letter from Þorsteinn Erlingsson, 21 December 1890. Þorsteinn (1858–1914) was an important poet, translator, and man of letters in Iceland at the turn of the century.

6. Letter from Jón Borgfirðingur, 28 March 1889. Jón Borgfirðingur (1826–1912) was an author and (largely self-taught) scholar who published in 1867 a *Söguágrip um prentsmiðjur og prentara á Íslandi* (Historical outline of presses and printers in Iceland) and in 1884 a *Stutt rithöfundatal á Íslandi 1400–1882* (Brief dictionary of authors in Iceland). He worked variously as a printer, publisher, and bookseller; for twenty-three years he also served as a police constable in Reykjavík. Fiske acknowledges him in his "Books Printed in Iceland 1578–1844" as "the well-known bibliographer." The epitaphs referred to are in Icelandic called *grafskriftir*; one may assume there were more marked graves than 520 created in the more-than-six-decade span indicated, but that the texts of these epitaphs were the ones that had been transcribed.

7. Letter from Jón Borgfirðingur, 25 March 1889.

8. Letter from Fiske, 15 April 1885. *Breviarum Holense* was the first work printed in Iceland, ostensibly in 1534; only fragments of it exist. Halldór Hermannsson refers to this 1534 work as "the so-called *Breviarium Nidrosiense*, the only book known to have been printed in Iceland prior to . . . the Reformation." See his *Icelandic Books of the Sixteenth Century (1534–1600)*, Islandica 9 (Ithaca, NY: Cornell University Library, 1916), i and 1. Húnafjörður lies west of Skagafjörður in northwest Iceland; error or weather could have affected sailing into the intended fjord. The episcopal seat of Hólar is about thirty miles east of Sauðárkrókur, at the head of Skagafjörður.

9. See Halldór Hermannsson, *Icelandic Books of the Seventeenth Century, 1601–1700*, Islandica 14 (Ithaca, NY: Cornell University Library, 1922), 86, for a bibliographical description of this work, an anonymous set of seven sermons on the Passion as related in Matthew. These were translated into Icelandic by Oddur Einarsson (1559–1630), bishop of Skálholt.

10. Letter from Magnús Einarsson, 19 January 1890.

11. Letter from Ólafur Davíðsson, 26 May 1888.

12. Arngrímur Jónsson lærði (1568–1648) was a pastor and scholar, and most notably author of *Crymogæa* (Hamburg, 1609), a history of and apology for Iceland. See, in *Lesbók Morgunblaðsins*, 10

November 1968, Haraldur Sigurðsson, "Arngrímur Jónsson lærði: Fjögurra alda minning 1568–1968." (http://timarit.is/view_page_init. jsp?pageId=3291928&lang=0, accessed 14 September 2016), for a consideration of his life and work.

13. Letter from Ólafur Davíðsson, 26 May 1888.

14. Hrappsey, an island and farmstead near Stykkishólmur in western Iceland, was significant as the location of the first printing press in Iceland not under ecclesiastical control (active 1773–94). See "Hrappsey" in Þorsteinn Jósepsson, et al., *Landið þitt, Ísland* (Reykjavík: Örn og Örlygur, 1980–85), 2:123–24.

15. Letter from Jón Þorkelsson, 25 May 1887.

16. Ibid.

17. Jón Þorkelsson Vídalín (1666–1720), a grandson of Arngrímur Jónsson, was consecrated Bishop of Skálholt in 1698. He is best remembered as a gifted preacher, and his vastly influential *Hússpostilla*, containing sermons for reading and study at home, first published in 1718–20, came out in thirteen editions before the mid-nineteenth century. The American scholar Michael Fell has translated some of these homilies in *Whom Wind & Waves Obey: Selected Sermons of Bishop Jón Vídalín*, American university studies, Series 7, Theology and religion, v. 195 (New York: Peter Lang, 1998). See also, in *Lesbók Morgunblaðsins*, 24 December 1940, Magnús Jónsson, "Smávegis um Jón biskup Vídalín."

18. Letter from Jón Þorkelsson, 29 November 1890.

19. Letter from Jón Þorkelsson, 10 July 1888.

20. Ibid.

21. The title transcription in the letter is *Fridreks-Draapa, um Sorglegan Alldrtila, dygdir oc Söknud þess Allrabetsta, nú Sælasta Konungs oc Herra Fridreks ens Fimta.*

22. *Christiansmál, edr Lof-qvædi um Hinn Hávoldugazta og Allra-milldazta Konung og Einvallzherra Christian hinn siöunda Konúng Danmarkar og Norvegs, Vinda og Gauta, Hertoga í Slésvík, Holsetu, Störmæri, Þettmerski og Alldinborg. Qvedit í Nafni hinnar Islenzku þjódar, á Norrænu, edr enn nú tidkada Íslenzka túngu med Látínskri Utleggingu og á fædingar-degi Konungsins, þeim XXIX. Januarii, Ar eptir Christs-burd MDCCLXXXIII í allra djúpuztu Undirgefni framborit af nockrum Islenskum Lærdóms-stundurum í Kaupmannahöfn, og Ordu-limum hins Íslenzka Lærdómslista Félags, er saman lögdu til útgefningar Qvædinu.*

23. Letter from Jón Þorkelsson, 3 December 1889.

24. Letter from Jón Þorkelsson, 17 October 1886. Incorporated in the letter is the list of Lutheran graduals (containing the order of the Mass) to which Jón refers; there are fifteen editions noted from this period, most of them printed at Hólar. It is not clear Jón was able to obtain these editions for Fiske, as the dates he gives in the list do not

correspond with the publication dates for graduals catalogued in the 1914 *Catalogue of the Icelandic Collection.*

25. See the 1914 *Catalogue of the Icelandic Collection,* 44–45. Þorláksbiblía was revised by Bishop Þorlákur Skúlason and Steinsbiblía by Bishop Steinn Jónsson. Both Þorlákur (1597–1656) and Steinn (1660–1739) were bishops at the northern episcopal seat of Hólar, and their editions of the Bible in Icelandic were both printed there. These editions are respectively the first and second revisions of the Icelandic Bible to follow the pioneering Guðbrandsbiblía of 1584. Both states of Þorláksbiblía were already in Fiske's collection at the publication of his Bibliographical notices 1 on *Books Printed in Iceland 1578–1844;* see entry no. 8 on this edition there. It is not clear whether Jón Þorkelsson obtained both states for Fiske.

26. The 1704 edition is indeed present in the collection and in the 1914 *Catalogue.* In the correspondence to Fiske, a second folder accompanies the voluminous correspondence of Jón Þorkelsson and contains invoices and lists of books. There is a list of *Passíusálmar* that plausibly accompanied either the letter of 9 November 1890 or the actual consignment. Although the initial entries in the list generally agree with the 1914 *Catalogue,* the two compilations diverge markedly as the years of publication progress. In some instances it is evident the *Passíusálmar* were issued under the covers of other compilations; these Halldór Hermannsson tends to note as separate editions. Both compilations merit further bibliographical study, but it is clear Jón Þorkelsson was able to dispatch to Florence a nearly comprehensive run of the editions through at least 1880.

27. Letter from Jón Þorkelsson, 20 November 1890. The Icelandic titles are respectively *Stafrófskverið, Davíðssaltari, Stutt Ágrip Um Islandskan Garnspuna, and Kötlugjá.*

28. Letter from Jón Þorkelsson, 20 March 1892. (*Paradísarlykill* in Icelandic.)

29. Italics in the original.

30. Skyring og Utþyðing hins litla Catechismi þess Loflega og Dyrdlega Guds Mans Martini Lutheri . . . utlagdan wr Saxnersku Maale, og j ønduerdu skrifadan af halærdum Manne sem heiter Johannes Aumannus, Superintendens til Syling j Lande Saxen. The poem is titled in Icelandic "Um Aflausnena, Edur Lyklavallded christelegrar Kirkiu." The copy Jón Þorkelsson describes is not the same as the copy described as item 3 in the fourth list of *Books Printed in Iceland between 1578 and 1844* (Bibliographical Notices 6). Whereas the copy Jón offered in his letter appeared to be without a title page and to have several leaves missing, the entry in Bibliographical Notices, which appears to correspond to the copy on the shelves of the Fiske Icelandic Collection, has an intact title page with the title proper *Biblia Laicorum.* The leaves purported missing in Jón's description

seem to be present. There is no leaf Q5, however; nor is there evidence of the poem "Um Aflausnena." The entry calls this copy "admirably preserved" and "everyway perfect," but there is no reference to the copy Jón offered there or in the collection catalogue of 1914.

31. Jón was later to edit and publish (1902–1906) "the unique copy [in manuscript] of these works in the Royal Library, Copenhagen" (*Catalogue of the Icelandic Collection*, 655–56). *Morðbréfamálið* (the murder letters affair) was a late sixteenth-century scandal involving ostensibly forged letters that implicated the grandfather of Bishop Guðbrandur Þorláksson in several homicides of family members in the late fifteenth and early sixteenth centuries. Confiscation of property and inheritance was a signal motivating factor. There is an Icelandic-language entry on the affair with pertinent bibliographical references (also to works in Icelandic) at https://is.wikipedia.org/wiki/Morðbréfamálið, accessed 14 December 2016.

32. The biography, by Sveinn Pálsson (1762–1840), is *Æfisaga Bjarna Pálssonar sem var fyrsti Landphysikus á Islandi*; it was compiled in 1799 and published in 1800 at Leirárgarðar við Leirá. Several copies of this first edition are in Icelandic libraries, but it does not appear in the records of the Fiske Icelandic Collection. Bjarni Pálsson (1719–1779), first chief medical officer of Iceland, accompanied Eggert Ólafsson (1726–1768) on a scientific survey of Iceland in 1752–57, co-authoring the resulting *Vice-lavmand Eggert Olafsens og Land-physici Biarne Povelsens reise igiennem Island* (1772).

33. Seven copies of this twelfth edition of *Evangelisk kristileg Sálma-bók, til brúkunar í kirkjum og heimahúsum* are recorded in Iceland. One copy is in the Fiske Icelandic Collection. (*Catalogue of the Icelandic Collection*, 398).

34. Of this many letters from Jón Þorkelsson bear witness, e.g. a letter dated 14 December 1890.

35. Letters from Sigfús Blöndal, 10 August and 6 September 1899.

36. The author adds, ". . . og einungis geymt einstaka reikning" (and only kept a single invoice). Although there may have indeed been more than one invoice preserved from Fiske's time, the picture Halldór gives in his preface (p. v) is telling: "[H]e never kept a record of his purchases, and the letters from his Icelandic correspondents are almost the only sources we have as to . . . acquisitions. . . . [T]he bills [from antiquarian booksellers and auctions] have in many cases been lost."

37. P. M. Mitchell, *Halldór Hermannsson*, Islandica 41 (Ithaca: Cornell University Press, 1978), 18–19.

38. Letter from Sigurður Kristjánsson, 28 November 1885.

39. Letter from Sigurður Kristjánsson, 18 July 1891. This work would be Hallgrímur Pétursson's *Nockrer Lærdoomsrijker Psalmar og Andleger Kvedlingar*. Three copies are recorded in Iceland, including

one in the National Library; one copy is in the Fiske Collection. Halldór Hermannsson notes (*Catalogue of the Icelandic Collection*, 465) the compilation "is popularly known as 'Hallgrímskver'" and was edited by Hálfdán Einarsson.

40. Invoice from Bókaverzlun Sigurðar Kristjánssonar, 28 November 1888.
41. Letter from Sigurður Kristjánsson, 25 November 1890.
42. Sigurður expresses thanks for this in a letter dated 7 July 1900.
43. *Þjóðólfur*, 11 September 1879.
44. Ingi Rúnar Eðvarðsson, *Prent eflir mennt: Saga bókagerðar frá upphafi til síðari hluta 20. aldar* (Reykjavík: Hið íslenska bókmenntafélag, 1994), 46.
45. *Ísafold*, 6 May 1879.
46. See note 25 above, which proceeds from the text to confirm acquisition of Guðbrandsbiblía and two other editions of the holy writ by Jón Þorkelsson. The story of a bargain of organ and lessons for a copy of Guðbrandsbiblía is cited, with an enigmatic reference for the source to "T. P. O'Connor's M.A.P. [Nov. 16, 1901, p. 485]," in H. S. White, *Willard Fiske: Life and Correspondence*, 178–79.

    The author, Kristín Bragadóttir, has suggested Fiske initially acquired two copies of Guðbrandsbiblía, eventually exchanging one copy for other works and keeping for the collection the excellent copy now there. Copies of this Bible were by no means scarce, being, Kristín notes, in nearly all Icelandic churches during the nineteenth century. Kristín stated she believes Jón Þorkelsson had no part in negotiations for the copy in the church. (Electronic mail message from author to translator, 3 Febrary 2016.)
47. Letter from Jón A. Hjaltalín from Edinburgh, 13 March 1880, wherein he displays considerable enthusiasm over sending off the organ with the first steamer from Scotland. The cost would have equaled perhaps USD 2,200 in 2016 (approximated via https://www.measuringworth.com/, accessed 21 December 2016).

Chapter 25

1. Letter from Sigfús Blöndal, 19 September 1899.
2. Hannes Þorsteinsson, *Endurminningar og hugleiðingar um hitt og þetta, er á dagana hefur drifið* (Reykjavík: Almenna bókafélagið, 1962), 159.
3. Letter from Hannes Þorsteinsson, 1 October 1890.
4. Letter from Vilhjálmur Jónsson, 10 February 1901.
5. Letter from Sigfús Blöndal, 5 September 1899. See Þorsteinn Jósepsson, *Landið þitt, Ísland*, 5:125. Völlur is a "landnámsbýli og kirkjustaður" (original settlement farm and churchstead) in southwest Iceland associated with protagonists in *Njáls saga*. From the nineteenth century, it was the seat of local sheriffs, including

Hermannius Johnson [sic] (1825–94), Halldór's father. The reference also describes Halldór as "forstöðumaður hins mikla safns íslenskra bóka sem kennt er við Willard Fiske" (curator of the great collection of Icelandic books named after Willard Fiske). See also P. M. Mitchell, *Halldór Hermannsson*, 13ff., recounting that Halldór had grown up in a home with a good library before his departure in 1892 to attend the Learned School in Reykjavík.

6. Letter from Halldór Hermannsson, 3 December 1899.
7. Letter from Halldór Hermannsson, 16 July 1900.
8. Letter from Halldór Hermannsson, 20 August 1900.
9. Letter from Halldór Hermannsson, 24 August 1900.
10. Letter from Halldór Hermannsson, 28 May 1900.
11. Letter from Halldór Hermannsson, 16 July 1900.
12. Michele Monzecchi came from an impoverished Italian family in Fiesole and had worked at Villa Landor. Fiske "informally adopted" Monzecchi and supported the young man's education, eventually leaving him a bequest. Horatio S. White, *Willard Fiske: Life and Correspondence*, 219.
13. Ettore Sordi served as assistant or secretary to Fiske from the earliest years of the latter's sojourn in Florence until 1904. In the preliminary note of *Books Printed in Iceland 1578–1844: A Third Supplement to the British Museum Catalogue*, Bibliographical Notices 5 (Florence: LeMonnier Press, 1890), 4, Fiske offers "thanks, for intelligent aid in reading the proofs, to my secretary, Mr. Ettore Sordi." The Daniel Willard Fiske papers, #13-1-1165, include correspondence from Fiske to Sordi from 1883 to 1904, with some breaks. Consisting often enough of postcards but including also texts of telegrams and conventional letters, and composed by Fiske chiefly in Italian, the correspondence conveys a working relationship focusing on books and contacts with various persons of Fiske's acquaintance. Occasionally the salutation to Sordi is "carissimo," although the overall sentiment is businesslike.
14. Daniel Willard Fiske to séra Jón Bjarnason. Although a relatively sparse miscellany of Fiske's letters to his correspondents is in the Fiske Icelandic Collection, eight letters from Fiske to the pastor, including this one, were returned to the collection in 1955. See Þórunn Sigurðardóttir's *Manuscript Material, Correspondence, and Graphic Material in the Fiske Icelandic Collection* (1994), 187–88.

Chapter 26

1. Letter from Jón Þorkelsson, 15 November 1890.
2. Letter from Ólafur Davíðsson, 2 October 1886.
3. The cathedral in question is Dómkirkjan í Reykjavík, which has served as the national cathedral of Iceland since the merger of the dioceses

of Hólar and Skálholt in 1801. The structure, dating from its initial completion in 1796, underwent renovation in the mid-nineteenth century. The cathedral is adjacent to Alþingishúsið (Parliament House).

4. Jón Jacobson, *Landsbókasafn Íslands 1818–1918: Minningarrit* (Reykjavík: Prentsmiðjan Gutenberg, 1919–20), 126.

5. Ibid., 127.

6. Jón A. Hjaltalín points this out in a letter written in the Advocates' Library in Edinburgh to Fiske that 27 May 1874; many other correspondents later voice the same opinion.

7. Letter from Finnur Jónsson, 2 September 1903. The manuscript collection to which Finnur refers is likely the compilation of (chiefly paper) manuscripts that Landsbókasafn (the National Library) had acquired by the turn of the century. It was established in 1846, although some of its holdings are medieval in origin. (See, for further description, https://landsbokasafn.is/index.php/efni/handrit/handritasafn, accessed 12 May 2017.) The following quote is from Finnur's subsequent letter to Fiske of 9 September 1903 ("næstum óbrúkandr" in the original, although "óbrúkandur" appears difficult to confirm as standard Icelandic; one might have anticipated "óbrúklegur").

8. The building is now Safnahúsið, formerly Þjóðmenningarhúsið (House of Culture).

9. This "English friend of Iceland" would be Charles Kelsall (1782–1857), mentioned in chapter 16, who donated funds for construction of the school library that came to be known as Íþaka in recognition of Fiske's contributions to the collection.

10. Daniel Willard Fiske to Andrew Carnegie, 20 August 1903. He states literally: "It seems to me not unlikely that no town in any country stands so much in need of a library-building as does Reykjavík, the capital of Iceland. Of the two largish public libraries one (the National Library) contains about 60.000 volumes, and the other (the College library) nearly 20.000. The National Library is so crowded into the lower story of the contrasted parliament building, as to make its use and administration very difficult. The College library occupies a small structure, built many years ago by an English benefactor, which is now so crowded with books that there is no longer space for a reading room. It must be remembered that the demands upon these two collections are very great, since they are the chief sources of information for the whole population of the island, in which the proportion of readers and students is larger than in any other existing community."

11. With regard to smaller libraries outside Reykjavík, Fiske gives a brief but effective sketch of their situation at the beginning of the twentieth century: small public libraries located in the principal districts and settlements, and several private libraries of significance in possession of writers, scholars, and clergy. Notable also is the establishment,

through acts of the Alþingi in 1886 and 1895, of a legal deposit requirement for books printed in Iceland, with copies destined for libraries there and in Copenhagen. In closing, Fiske notes Icelandic book production in North America, chiefly in Manitoba, and also weekly Icelandic newspaper circulation.

12. Jón Jacobson, *Landsbókasafn Íslands 1818–1918*, 192.

Chapter 27

1. The validity of Fiske's catalogues, particularly the Bibliographical Notices pertaining to the Icelandic Collection, derives from two factors. They chronicle the growth of Fiske's collection of imprints (1578 through 1844) and, as the subtitles of each indicate, they stand as "[s]upplement[s] to the British Museum Catalogue" that covered the years 1578 to 1880. There is a hint in the preliminary note of the first supplement that Fiske, though pronouncing the British Museum catalogue "excellent," wanted to state his pre-eminence in the field. In listing the works in his library that "do not exist in the Library of the British Museum," he constructs an understandable rationale for restricting his own coverage in the bibliography to pre-1845 titles, but underscores thereby the more comprehensive nature of his anti-quarian holdings. See page 3, introductory paragraph.

   The second factor is the comprehensive detail deployed in the bibliography. Not only are title pages meticulously transcribed, but also extensive, not to say overwhelming annotations in fine print on history and content complement most transcriptions. Halldór remarked in the preface of his *Catalogue of the Icelandic Collection* (1914) that had one adhered to the format of the Bibliographical Notices in publishing a comprehensive catalogue, the sheer volume would have increased six- or sevenfold and been too "minute in detail" and too cumbersome to use. Although Halldór is correct on the issue of scalability for purposes of publication and utility, Fiske seems clearly to have approached the Bibliographical Notices project from the perspective of exhaustive erudition for a limited, defined subset of the collection.

2. *Catalogue of the Books Printed in Iceland, from A. D. 1578 to 1880: In the Library of the British Museum* (London: Printed by W. Clowes, 1885).

3. The second issue of Bibliographical Notices was not a catalogue of Fiske's own Petrarch holdings, but rather a *Hand-List of Petrarch Editions in the Florentine Public Libraries* that he compiled in 1886 "for [his] own convenience." Clearly the exercise was designed to gain a more effective understanding of the history of Petrarch's works in print, relying on the reasonable assumption that Florence would possess most editions in its institutions. The second bibliography

focusing on Petrarch is Bibliographical Notices III, *Francis Petrarch's Treatise* De Remediis Utriusque Fortunae: *Text and Versions* (1887). Its prefatory note shows that Fiske did break ground in compiling this bibliography for *De Remediis*, and many, though not all, editions listed were already in his collection.

4. The subtitles specify respectively *A Third Supplement* and *A Fourth Supplement to the British Museum Catalogue.*

5. ". . . issued by Mr. Fiske's Executors": p. 4 (preliminary note by G.W. Harris). Aside from revising and completing the work, Halldór Hermannsson compiled the general index covering all four volumes.

6. Guðbrandsbiblía (1584) has, aside from the woodcut title page, woodcuts deriving from the biblical narrative; evidently Bishop Guðbrandur Þorláksson imported these, and Fiske's suggestion that "wood engravings . . . in popular religious works are . . . of German origin" (p. 3) seems reasonable. See also the description of the "Bible of Guðbrandur Þorláksson" at http://web.archive.org/web/20041105070936/http://www.kb.nl/gabriel/treasures/country/Iceland/iso2.html, accessed 24 May 2017, which attributes decorative initials and ornaments (bókahnútir, which Fiske defines) to Bishop Guðbrandur.

7. Halldór Hermannsson, "Willard Fiske and Icelandic Bibliography," 106. Halldór does point out that "also in certain other lines which are not exclusively Icelandic," for example "Scandinavian mythology and runology," the collection is unsurpassed. The difficulty is not with the collector and his vision, but more perhaps with our tendency to think of Iceland as a small nation-state rather than as Fiske seemingly perceived it: the center, by virtue of its literary production, of the Norse world.

   Fiske focused overwhelmingly on contemporary literary production in Iceland alongside his antiquarian purchases, but an exchange of correspondence with séra Jón Bjarnason shows an unambiguous interest in Icelanders in North America. See Þórunn Sigurðardóttir, *Manuscript Material . . . in the Fiske Icelandic Collection* (1994), 85.

8. See the following footnote, especially with regard to Fiske's ""restlessness" and "tendency to work intermittently or to start on something new before he had completed what he had been working on."

9. Literally, "Fiske was a man of wide and accurate knowledge, and painstaking in everything to which he devoted himself. He was very quick in understanding things and in discerning the important and essential points when dealing with books. He worked hard at times and with enthusiasm on any subject he took up, but he had a tendency to work intermittently or to start on something new before he had completed what he had been working on. This was due to a certain restlessness, and it explains why, in spite of his enthusiasm and energy, he published little. But he was one of the most agreeable

men to work with I have known. And what he has done for Icelandic bibliography is of permanent value" (Halldór Hermannsson, "Willard Fiske and Icelandic Bibliography," 106).

10. Ólafur Davíðsson is, strictly speaking, correct, as Fiske spent considerable time in Egypt and also traveled (in 1868) to and through Palestine. However, he did not penetrate farther into either continent.

11. Ólafur Davíðsson, "Prófessor Willard Fiske," 10.

12. Daniel Willard Fiske to Chr[istian Walther] Bruun, 10 September 1884, Det Kongelige Bibliotek, NKS 3681 4to. Håndskriftsamlingens Brevbase (http://www.kb.dk/da/nb/samling/hs/Bestil/brevbase.html) accessed 22 June 2018.

13. Fiske began acquiring his Dante collection in April 1892 while pursuing items for his Petrarch collection, but stated that "the pleasure of collecting [really] began in the summer of 1893, and went on for three years" in its initial phase. Theodore Wesley Koch, *Catalogue of the Dante Collection Presented by Willard Fiske*, vol. 1 (Ithaca, NY: Cornell University Library, 1898–1900), iii-iv ("Introductory" composed by Fiske).

14. Bogi Th. Melsteð, *Willard Fiske*, 15. This brief bibliography, which appeared in *The Library of Cornell University*, vol. 1 (1882–83): 78–82, 110–14, was titled "The Living Authors of Iceland." See the catalogue entry in Halldór Hermannsson, *Catalogue of the Icelandic Collection* (1914), 156.

15. Mímir was "[a] mystic figure of wisdom" whom Óðinn consulted. See Andy Orchard, *Dictionary of Norse Myth and Legend* (London: Cassell, 1997), 113. The mythological narrative of Mímir's fate is rather more gruesome than Fiske's use of the name as the title of his directory would suggest.

16. D. W. Fiske, *Mímir*, 53–69.

17. Daniel Willard Fiske to Halldór Hermannsson, 2 May 1904.

18. Mímir came out in one edition and received reviews on both sides of the Atlantic. See the catalogue entry in Halldór Hermannsson, *Catalogue of the Icelandic Collection* (1914), 157.

Chapter 28

1. There are at least three islands off the Icelandic mainland named Grímsey. One is in the Vestfirðir (Westfjords) just off Drangsnes and is a natural attraction for its birds. (See https://www.westfjords.is/en/town/index/grimsey, accessed 14 January 2019.) A second is not far from Stykkishólmur in the mouth of Hvammsfjörður, which empties into Breiðafjörður. This Grímsey is a mere islet or skerry, unmarked on typical maps of the region among the many islets there (electronic communication from Kristín Bragadóttir, 24 November 2018). The

Grímsey that fascinated Fiske is in the north, some twenty-five miles off the mainland, and lies on the Arctic Circle. A summary description with references is at https://en.wikipedia.org/wiki/Grímsey, accessed 05 June 2017. Húsavík, where Fiske first alighted in Iceland, lies south-southeast of Grímsey.

2. D. W. Fiske, *Mimir*, 67.

3. In *Geografisk Tidsskrift*, 16 (1902): 204–10.

4. Daniel Willard Fiske to Matthías Jochumsson, 12 March 1901. In the Fiske Icelandic Collection, there is also a list of questions, differing from the ones recorded here, that Fiske sent, possibly to Þorvaldur Thoroddsen. See Þórunn Sigurðardóttir, *Manuscript Material . . . in the Fiske Icelandic Collection* (1994), 40 (entry 99, item 1).

5. Daniel Willard Fiske to Matthías Eggertsson, 21 January 1903, Landsbókasafn Íslands—Háskólabókasafn, Lbs 4868 4to.

6. The bookplate designed for the library uses the term Eyjarbókasafnið, followed by Grímsey, followed by the year of the founding, 1901. Space allows for inscribing an accession number.

7. Daniel Willard Fiske to Halldór Hermannsson, 1 May 1901.

8. Daniel Willard Fiske to Halldór Hermannsson, 4 May 1901.

9. In a letter from Copenhagen (3 June 1901), Halldór explains the necessary orthographic corrections: "There are three bad errors in the first word [Eyjarbókasafnið], r is left out, o in stead [sic] of ó, and d in stead of ð . . . [moreover] in the word 'Grímsey' there lacks accent [sic] upon the i. (í). [sic]."

10. Letter from Halldór Hermannsson, 8 May 1901.

11. Letter from Halldór Hermannsson, 25 September 1901.

12. Letter from Halldór Hermannsson, 8 May 1901.

13. *Í uppnámi: Íslenzkt skákrit* (1901): 107.

14. Letter from Fiske, 27 April 1901.

15. Letter from Halldór Hemannsson, 8 May 1901. Literally: "To your question about the expences [sic] of putting the clergyman's house in good order I cannot give any satisfactory answer, only I think it would scarcely cost less that 1000 kr., but I will try to get better information about the actual condition of the house and then I write you."

16. Félagsheimilið Múli in Icelandic. The center is a multipurpose community facility, having hosted a school, various social and civic groups, and a venue for the island clinic dependent on medical personnel visiting from mainland Iceland. See the article in *Morgunblaðið* (18 January 2001; http://www.mbl.is/greinasafn/grein/584046/, accessed 22 June 2017), which announced extensive remodeling of the building but made no mention of Eyjarbókasafnið.

17. Letter from Matthías Eggertsson, 5 July 1901.

18. Letter from Matthías Eggertsson, 1 February 1902.

19. Letter from Matthías Eggertsson, 23 April 1903.

20. The pictures are preserved in the Fiske Icelandic Collection and are catalogued in Þórunn Sigurðardóttir, *Manuscript Material . . . in the Fiske Icelandic Collection* (1994), 255–58.
21. Daniel Willard Fiske to Matthías Eggertsson, 21 January 1903.
22. This is confirmed in *Grímsey og Grímseyingar: Íbúar og saga*, ed. Helgi Daníelsson (Akranes: Akrafjallsútgáfan, 2003).

Chapter 29

1. *Í uppnámi* (1901): 34.
2. *Í uppnámi* (1902): 86 (afterword of the last issue).
3. Daniel Willard Fiske to Matthías Eggertsson, 21 January 1903.
4. These well-known lines are in the poem "Sumarkveðja" (Summer greeting) from 1877. Ingi T. Lárusson later set the words to music, which is the melody usually sung.
5. Pétur Sigurðsson, "Skrá um skákrit og smáprent um skák er Willard Fiske lét prenta á íslenzku og gaf Taflfélagi Reykjavíkur," *Árbók Landsbókasafns* (1950–51): 201–5.
6. Sigurður Jónsson, prison warden in Reykjavík, thanks him warmly on 6 December 1901 for such articles for the Chess Society as well as thirty pounds Sterling, which the society received from Fiske (Sigurður Jónsson to Daniel Willard Fiske, 6 December 1901).
7. The Icelandic National Bank, or Landsbankinn, was founded in 1885 as a public institution and still survives, albeit after considerable evolution and a particularly rough stretch starting with the financial crisis of 2008. For history, see https://en.wikipedia.org/wiki/History_of_Landsbanki, accessed 22 June 2017.
8. Bogi Th. Melsteð, *Willard Fiske*, 30–31.
9. Letter from Halldór Hermannsson, 5 December 1901.
10. Letter from Þorvaldur Jónsson, 6 February 1901.
11. Letter from Pétur Zóphoníasson, 12 May 1902.
12. Kristín Bragadóttir, "Willard Fiske og skákáhugi hans," in *Afmælismót Skáksambands Íslands og Friðriks Ólafssonar* (Reykjavík: Skáksamband Íslands, 1996), 31–35.
13. Finnbogi Guðmundsson, foreword to his *Skrá um erlend skákrit í Landsbókasafni Íslands* (Reykjavík: [s.n.], 1968).
14. These manuscripts are preserved in the Handritadeild (Manuscripts Section) of Landsbókasafns Íslands – Háskólabókasafns (the National and University Library of Iceland).
15. *Skrá um erlend skákrit í Landsbókasafni Íslands* (1968). In the catalogue are two supplements: "Skrá um skákrit og smáprent um skák er Willard Fiske lét prenta á íslenzku og gaf Taflfélagi Reykjavíkur" (Catalogue of works and pamphlets on chess Willard Fiske had printed in Icelandic and gave to the Reykjavík Chess Society), and also "Erlend skákrit í Landsbókasafni önnur en þau er Willard Fiske

gaf" (Foreign works on chess in the National Library other than those Willard Fiske gave). See also the foreword to the catalogue by Finnbogi Guðmundsson, the national librarian, in which he discusses Fiske and his gift.

Chapter 30

1. Florence was capital of the kingdom of Italy from 1865 to 1871. Its cultural status speaks for itself, and it may be that, aside from the climate, Fiske's established interest in Petrarch before 1883 attracted him to the city that was the cradle of the Italian Renaissance in terms of literature and the visual arts.

2. It is not clear that Boccaccio ever lived in the house Fiske purchased and named Villa Landor. Fiske remarks in a letter to Susan Warner (wife of his lifelong friend Charles Dudley Warner), quoted in Horatio S. White, *Willard Fiske: Life and Correspondence* (1925), 394, that "[t]he villa was built about the time Christopher Columbus was foolishly discovering America. . . Boccaccio's Affrico, a sweet streamlet, traverses the property. . . ." Nonetheless, the villa has had a distinguished history. The villa dates from at least the fifteenth century, if not the fourteenth, and was in the hands of a branch of the della Gherardesca family (and thus named Villa Gherardesca) before Walter Savage Landor purchased it in 1829. The property, now a music school, is known today as Villa La Torraccia. See https://it.wikipedia.org/wiki/Villa_La_Torraccia, accessed 29 June 2017.

3. Henrietta Irving Bolton, "A Florentine Villa: A Place that Recalls Boccaccio and Landor: Its Modern Owner," *New York Evening Post*, 24 March 1894, 32. (See citation in notes on illustrations in Horatio S. White, *Willard Fiske: Life and Correspondence* (1925), 480, where there are also several other references to published descriptions of the villa.)

4. See comments by Fiske in a letter to Charles Dudley Warner, 9 April 1892, quoted in Horatio S. White, *Willard Fiske: Life and Correspondence* (1925), 395–96, with reference to "add[ing] a half-story" and "raising the roof." See also Giulio Cesare Lensi Orlandi Cardini, *Le Ville di Firenze*, vol. 1, *Di qua d'Arno*, 2nd ed. (Florence: Vallecchi, 1965), 79–80: "Nella seconda metà dell'ottocento i Frisch la rialzarono d'un piano e ricostruirono al di sopra la colombaia con un aspetto ben diverso da quello originale." Although the description of the villa and its succession of owners clearly identifies with Villa Landor (Villa Torraccia), the author of *Le Ville di Firenze* twice refers to the solitary Fiske as "i Frisch."

5. Horatio S. White, *Willard Fiske: Life and Correspondence* (1925), 390.

6. Daniel Willard Fiske to Charles Dudley Warner, 27 February 1887. Daniel Willard Fiske papers, #13-1-1165.

7. Letter from Axel Anderson, 4 February 1897.
8. The letter is in English; emphasis of "whiff" is in the original.
9. Daniel Willard Fiske to Ólafur Davíðsson, 26 June 1889, Landsbókasafn Íslands—Háskólabókasafn, Lbs 1841 4to. The letter is not in Fiske's hand, except for the postscript and his signature. At this time it seems likely Ettore Sordi, whom Fiske describes with appreciation as his "secretary" in the preliminary note of *Books Printed in Iceland 1578–1844: A Third Supplement . . .* (1890), was writing out some of Fiske's correspondence.
10. The lecture, titled "Swedish Student Life," appeared in *Memorials of Willard Fiske*, comp. Horatio S. White, 3, *The Lecturer* (Boston: Badger; 1922), 1–59.
11. Daniel Willard Fiske to Halldór Hermannsson, 16 August 1904.
12. C. U. Sisler, *Enterprising Families, Ithaca* (1968), 80–84.
13. Jón Ólafsson, "Willard Fiske" (1905), 72–73.

Chapter 31

1. There are three (major) dialects of Rhaeto-Romanic: Romansh, Friulano, and Ladino. They are spoken by ethnic minorities in the Swiss, Italian, and Austrian Alps. Friulano is spoken by the largest group by far, with around half a million speakers in the Italian Alps (chiefly the region of Friuli Venezia Giulia). Romansh is spoken in Switzerland, primarily today in two pockets on either side of Chur (see map "Language distribution in Switzerland," accessed 21 July 2017, http://www.about.ch/culture/languages/words_n_phrases. html). Ladino (not to be confused with the Judeo-Spanish calque) has proliferated the least, being spoken by residents of the Ladin minority; some linguists refer to it as GalloLadin. Speakers number some twenty thousand in the Dolomite Mountains of Italy as of 2007 (in the Trentino-Alto Adige/Südtirol region, due north of Verona; see also language density maps accessed 21 July 2017, http://www. translationdirectory.com/articles/article2503.php), but information on language distribution and use in this area is incomplete.
2. In the catalogue of the Rhaeto-Romanic Collection, Fiske lists sixteen dialects and notes the dialect for individual bibliographic entries. In the instance of Romansh in particular, these dialects may correspond to individual cantons or valleys more than to clear linguistic distinctions.
3. These early purchases would have included, for example, *Ólafs saga Tryggvasonar hin mesta*, printed at Skálholt in 1689. This imprint is the first listed in an article on "Mr. D. W. Fiske's Collection" that appeared in the *New York Evening Post* on 27 April 1857, possibly written by Fiske himself. The Fiske Icelandic Collection preserves a typescript copy of the article conveyed to Halldór Hermannsson

by Horatio S. White on 23 June 1918. See Þórunn Sigurðardóttir, *Manuscript Material . . . in the Fiske Icelandic Collection* (1994), 22 (item 51).

4. P. M. Mitchell, *Halldór Hermannsson*, 19.

5. Louis A. Pitschmann served as Icelandic librarian from late 1983 into 1986. His dissertation (University of Chicago, 1975) was "a critical edition with a philological commentary" of *Þýzkalands saga*. Professor (emeritus) P. M. Mitchell, retired from the University of Illinois Urbana-Champaign, subsequently served as curator of the collection (then a quarter-time position) into the first months of 1993. Stevens assumed the role of curator in March 1994. The Fiske Icelandic Collection has also hosted visiting curators, including the Icelandic scholars Stefán Karlsson and Einar Gunnar Pétursson.

6. P. M. Mitchell, "The Fiske Icelandic Collection," *The Icelandic Canadian*, 49, 4 (Summer 1991): 8–12.

7. The series continued publishing, albeit at more extended intervals, during the last decades of the twentieth century, and underwent changes in editorial organization. The publication in 2008 of Islandica 53, *"Speak Useful Words or Say Nothing": Old Norse Studies* by Joseph Harris, edited by Susan E. Deskis and Thomas D. Hill, marked a departure for the series into (among other, traditional options) volumes of collected essays (by one or several authors) and online open access. These measures intended to bring the scholarship in *Islandica* more rapidly and flexibly to its readership. The sixtieth volume of the series, *Language of Power: Feasting and Gift-Giving in Medieval Iceland and Its Sagas*, by Viðar Pálsson, appeared in June 2017.

8. Islandica volumes 6, 7, 8, 10, 11, 12, 15, 16, 17, 18, 21, 22, 25, 29, 32–33, 34, 36, 39, 41, 42, 43, 45, 46, 49 – all from the twentieth century. Of course, several of the bibliographies, notably volumes 9 and 14 of the series, contain valuable, critical introductions to literatures of specific centuries or genres. Þórunn Sigurðardóttir's *Manuscript Material . . . in the Fiske Icelandic Collection* (1994), volume 48 of Islandica, is essential for comprehending the range of non-book holdings in the collection. Publication of essay volumes and of several monographic studies focused on specific sagas or literary themes (and in one case, on the *Icelandic Baroque: Poetic Art and Erudition in the Works of Hallgrímur Pétursson*, by Margrét Eggertsdóttir) has proceeded apace in the early decades of the twenty-first century.

9. At present, both undergraduate and graduate students may study Old Norse. The course is under the aegis of the Department of Linguistics and is cross-listed in Medieval Studies. Since 1984, an Icelandic graduate student in linguistics has been the course instructor. Therefore, students receive instruction from a native speaker of the modern

language who, well acquainted with Old Icelandic literature from years of *menntaskóli* and university, is able to convey the grammar, syntax, and significance of selected Old Norse-Icelandic texts. In recent years, faculty and graduate students have participated in an Old Norse reading group (in emulation of J. R. R. Tolkien and E. V. Gordon). In academic years 2015–16 and 2016–17, undergraduates also participated in this group.

10. The 1914 catalogue and its two supplements, along with the *Catalogue of Runic Literature* (1918), derived authority from the sheer comprehensive scope of acquisition that drove the Fiske Icelandic Collection from ca. 1850 through the first three decades of the twentieth century. The Bibliographical Notices and the preliminary cataloguing in Florence, principally by Bjarni Jónsson (for a year) and Halldór Hermannsson, were essential to the evolution of a coherent if succinct catalogue; see the preface of the 1914 *Catalogue* for a narrative justifying content and format. The success of the *Catalogue* as an effective bibliographical reference is evident from its use during the past century by antiquarian booksellers as a standard reference.

11. "8,600 volumes, including pamphlets"--Halldór Hermannsson, *Catalogue of the Icelandic Collection* (1914), p. v.

12. *The Catalogue of the Icelandic Collection bequeathed by Willard Fiske: Additions 1913–26*, comp. Halldór Hermannsson (Ithaca: Cornell University Press, 1927), p. v.

13. Ibid., vi.

14. Of course, a great quantity of material found in the Catalogue and its supplements was the literature on Iceland and the Norse cultural space published in multiple languages abroad. As the twentieth century advanced, an increasing volume of publication went to literary criticism, with works in English from British and North American scholars taking their place alongside critical studies from the nineteenth and twentieth centuries in Danish and German as well as in other languages. Halldór Hermannsson notes also in the preface (p. v) to the 1927 supplement, among other reasons for an active Icelandic press, an "increase in [Icelandic] scholarly works [since] research, historical, linguistic, and literary, ha[d] been greatly promoted by the establishment of the National University in 1911."

15. Halldór Hermannsson, "Willard Fiske," *Eimreiðin* 11 (1905): 107–8.

16. The vault is in the lowest level of the subterranean Carl A. Kroch Library, which houses the Division of Rare and Manuscript Collections and the Asia Collections.

17. Cataloguing the collection, more accurately migrating catalogue data to the online environment and Library of Congress classification, is a work in progress. Two significant retrospective projects to address cataloguing (and preservation, in the latter instance) occurred in the years 1977–80 and 1995–97. The projects produced several thousand

online records that reduced but did not eliminate the number of Icelandic Collection books without online representation in the Cornell Library holdings. In the second decade of the twenty-first century the effort to secure online representation of the Cornell Icelandic holdings continues. Data from leitir.is, formerly gegnir.is, the excellent Icelandic national bibliographic catalogue online, have significantly facilitated this work, although the scope and content of Icelandic and American bibliographic records are not entirely congruent.

18. According to the *Catalogue of the Icelandic Collection* (1914), all twenty editions of the *Passíusálmar* through 1780 are in the Fiske Icelandic Collection. After the tenth edition (1735) through the end of the eighteenth century, publication of the hymns occurs several times under the title *Psálmabók* or *Flokkabók* in conjunction with other hymns. See the entries in the *Catalogue* for notes by Halldór Hermannsson on edition numbering, especially p. 464.

19. Letter from Björn M. Ólsen, 1 February 1886 (original in Icelandic).

20. The book was still considered *unicum*, i.e. the only copy known to exist, per the assertion of Einar Gunnar Pétursson during a visit to the Fiske Icelandic Collection in 1994.

21. Equally scarce with regard to Icelandic printing in the sixteenth century was accurate information on books. Halldór Hermannsson noted that forty-two editions could be identified through physical copies as printed in Iceland prior to 1601. Even considering variations in counting methodology, the number of surviving imprints from Iceland (Hólar and Skálholt) for the seventeenth century Halldór estimated at 168. These numbers exclude overseas imprints in Icelandic, e.g. the crucial Roskilde New Testament of 1540. Numbers after the eighteenth century increase steadily and then exponentially by the close of the nineteenth century. (See Halldór's *Icelandic Books of the Sixteenth Century (1534–1600)* (1916), xii, and *Icelandic Books of the Seventeenth Century, 1601–1700* (1922), xi, Islandica 9 and 14 respectively.

22. Iceland in Fiske's time having no facilities for conservation and storage of manuscripts, institutions in Denmark—the Royal Library, the Arnamagnaean Collection—housed the lion's share of Old Norse manuscripts on vellum. Compilations of paper manuscripts, including those of Jón Sigurðsson forseti, were under way in the nineteenth century in what was to become the National Library of Iceland.

23. The Alþingi generously allocated approximately three thousand dollars per annum to the Fiske Icelandic Collection for the purchase of Icelandic books through 2008. The stipend quietly and understandably ceased in 2008 during a time of severe economic distress for Iceland.

24. In pre-Internet days, the National Library was thus fulfilling a significant mission in terms of disseminating publications to where they were likely to be utilized.

25. The holdings in the University and Royal Libraries of Denmark reflect Danish rule over Iceland, the residence in Copenhagen of much of the Icelandic scholarly community from the sixteenth through the nineteenth centuries, and the active printing of works in Icelandic there well into the nineteenth century.

26. The correspondence from G. E. Stechert & Co. is in the Cornell University Library records, 1868–1947, #13-1-17 (box 12), and spans some thirty years from 1884 to 1914.

27. Fiske had stipulated with good reason that the collection be separate from the general stacks of the library. This arrangement, well intended for facilitating the specialized research the collection offers, encountered evolving principles of stack management that, not without risk, opened Olin Library to a larger research community, including undergraduate students and the general public. Access for impaired users joined equitable scholarly access to circulating materials as a concern. The ultimate decision was to integrate the circulating holdings of the Icelandic Collection into the Olin Library stacks instead of trying repeatedly to identify separate shelving. This initiative paired shelf integration with a simple technique to afford the collection its separate identity: cataloguing records identify all Icelandic Collection books specifically as belonging to the Fiske Icelandic Collection. It is thus possible to identify the holdings in the collection in a virtual manner.

Bibliography

Books and Contributions to Periodical Literature

Alec-Tweedie, Mrs. (Ethel). *A Girl's Ride in Iceland.* 3rd ed. London: Horace Cox, 1895.

Benedikt Gröndal. *Dægradvöl: Æfisaga mín.* Reykjavík: Bókaverzlun Ársæls Árnasonar, 1923.

Bergman, Mats and Jan-Olof Montelius. *Nationshusen i Upsala: En beskrivning tillägnad Upsala Universitet vid dess 500-årsjubileum.* Uppsala: Upsala studenters jubileumskommitterade, 1977.

Bishop, Morris. *A History of Cornell.* Ithaca, NY: Cornell University Press, 1962.

Bogi Th. Melsteð. *Willard Fiske: Æfiminning.* Copenhagen: Hið íslenska Bókmentafjelag, 1907.

Bolton, Henrietta Irving. "A Florentine Villa: A Place that Recalls Boccaccio and Landor: Its Modern Owner." *New York Evening Post,* 24 March 1894.

Böðvar Kvaran. *Auðlegð Íslendinga: Brot úr sögu íslenzkrar bókaútgáfu og prentunar frá öndverðu fram á þessa öld.* Reykjavík: Hið íslenzka bókmenntafélag, 1995.

The Cambridge History of English Literature. Suppl. vol. 3, *A History of American Literature: Supplementary to the Cambridge History of English Literature,* edited by A. W. Ward and A. R. Waller. Cambridge: Cambridge University Press, 1921.

Carpenter, William H. "Willard Fiske in Iceland." *The Papers of the Bibliographical Society of America* 12, no. 3–4 (July–October, 1918): 107–15.

Conable, Charlotte Williams. *Women at Cornell: The Myth of Equal Education.* Ithaca: Cornell University Press, 1977.

Davidsson, Åke. *Uppsala universitetsbibliotek 1620–1970: En bildkrönika.* Uppsala: Almqvist & Wikström, 1971.

Fiske, Willard. *Book-Collections in Iceland.* Offprint. Copenhagen: Martius Truelsen, 1903.

Fiske, Willard. *Books Printed in Iceland 1578–1844: A Supplement to the British Museum Catalogue.* 4 vols. Bibliographical Notices 1, 4-6. Florence, 1886–1907. (Vol. 4 published in Ithaca.)

Fiske, Willard. *"Bréf Willards Fiskes til Íslendinga."* Edited by Nanna Ólafsdóttir. Letters in English translated by Finnbogi Guðmundsson. *Árbók* (Landsbókasafn Íslands) n.s. 8 (1982): 28-68.

Fiske, Willard. *Chess in Iceland and in Icelandic Literature: With Historical Notes on Other Table-Games.* Florence: The Florentine Typographical Society, 1905.

Fiske, Willard. *Chess Tales & Chess Miscellanies.* Edited by Horatio S. White. New York: Longman Green, 1912.

Fiske, Willard. *J.* Florence, 1887.

Fiske, Willard. *The Lost Manuscript of the Reverend Lewis Rou's "Critical Remarks upon the Letter to the Craftsman on the Game of Chess" Written in 1734 and Dedicated to His Exellency William Cosby, Governor of New York.* Florence: Landi Press, 1902.

Fiske, Willard. *Memorials of Willard Fiske.* Edited by Horatio S. White. 3 vols. Boston: Gorham Press, 1920-22.

Fiske, Willard. *Mímir: Icelandic Instructions with Addresses.* Copenhagen: Martius Truelsen, 1903.

Fiske, Willard. *The Reverend Lewis Rou and the Missing Manuscript.* Florence: Landi Press, 1902.

Fiske, Willard. [*Travels through Iceland*], 1879 (notebook containing diary entries, bibliographical notes, notes on Icelandic vocabulary and grammar, and gravestone inscriptions).

Foulke, William Dudley. *Biography and Correspondence of Arthur M. Reeves . . . Being a Supplemental Volume to Mr. Reeves' "Finding of Wineland the Good: The History of the Icelandic Discovery of America."* London: Henry Frowde, 1895.

Grímsey og Grímseyingar: Íbúar og saga. Edited by Helgi Daníelsson. Akranes: Akrafjallsútgáfan, 2003.

Guðmundur J. Guðmundsson. "Egypsku munirnir í dánargjöf Willard Fiske." *Árbók hins íslenska fornleifafélags* (1995): 49-74.

Gullander, Bertil. *Linné och Uppsala: Glimtar från en tid av kamp och framgångar.* Stockholm: Almqvist & Wiksell, 1978.

Hagskinna: Sögulegar hagtölur um Ísland. Edited by Guðmundur Jónsson and Magnús S. Magnússon. Reykjavík: Hagstofa Íslands, 1997.

Halldór Hermannsson. "Bókasöfn skólans." In *Minningar úr menntaskóla,* edited by Ármann Kristinsson and Friðrik Sigurbjörnsson, 171–76. Reykjavík: Ármann Kristinsson, 1946.

Halldór Hermannsson. *Catalogue of Runic Literature Forming a Part of the Icelandic Collection Bequeathed by Willard Fiske.* London: Oxford University Press, 1918.

Halldór Hermannsson. *Catalogue of the Icelandic Collection Bequeathed by Willard Fiske.* Ithaca, NY: Cornell University Library, 1914.

Halldór Hermannsson. *Catalogue of the Icelandic Collection Bequeathed by Willard Fiske: Additions, 1913-26.* Ithaca, NY: Cornell University, 1927.

Halldór Hermannsson. *Catalogue of the Icelandic Collection Bequeathed by Willard Fiske: Additions, 1927-42.* Ithaca, NY: Cornell University Press, 1943.

Halldór Hermannsson. "Willard Fiske." *Eimreiðin* 37 (1905): 358–77.

Halldór Hermannsson. "Willard Fiske and Icelandic Bibliography." *The Papers of the Bibliographical Society of America.* 12, no. 3–4 (1919): 97-106.

Hannes Þorsteinsson. *Endurminningar og hugleiðingar um hitt og þetta, er á dagana hefur drifið.* Reykjavík: Almenna bókafélagið, 1962.

Ingi Rúnar Eðvarðsson. *Prent eflir mennt: Saga bókagerðar frá upphafi til síðari hluta 20. aldar.* Safn til Iðnsögu Íslendinga 8. Reykjavík: Hið íslenska bókmenntafélag, 1994.

Jón Árnason. *Skýrsla um bækur þær, sem gefnar hafa verið Stiptisbókasafninu á Íslandi, í minningu þjóðhátíðar Íslands 1874.* Reykjavík: Einar Þórðarson, 1874.

Jón Helgason. *Íslendingar í Danmörku fyr og síðar: Með 148 mannamyndum.* Reykjavík: Íslandsdeild dansk-íslenzka félagsins, 1931.

Jón Jacobson. *Landsbókasafn Íslands 1818–1918: Minningarrit.* Reykjavík: Prentsmiðjan Gutenberg, 1920.

Jón Ólafsson. "Willard Fiske." *Skírnir* 79 (1905): 62–73.

Jón Þorkelsson. "Arthur Reeves." *Sunnanfari: Mánaðarblað með myndum* 2, no. 3B (September 1892): 33-34.

Klemens Jónsson. *Saga Akureyrar.* Akureyri: Akureyrarkaupstaður, 1948.

Klemens Jónsson. "Ýms atriði úr lífinu í Reykjavík fyrir 40 árum." *Skírnir* 87 (1913): 135–40.

Kristín Bragadóttir. "Íslandsvinurinn Daniel Willard Fiske: Ferð hans hingað til lands og söfnun íslenskra bóka." *Ritmennt* 9 (2004): 9–41.

Kristín Bragadóttir. "Skalden och redaktören Jón Þorkelsson." *Scripta Islandica* 45 (1994): 3–20.

Kristín Bragadóttir. "Willard Fiske og skákáhugi hans." In *Afmælismót Skáksambands Íslands og Friðriks Ólafssonar,* edited by Þráinn Guðmundsson. Reykjavík: Skáksamband Íslands, 1995.

Lensi Orlandi Cardini, Giulio Cesare. *Le Ville di Firenze.* Vol. 1, *Di qua d'Arno.* 2nd ed. Florence: Vallecchi, 1965.

Matthías Jochumsson. "A Mystical Vision." Translated by Willard Fiske. *Cornell Era* 12, no. 11 (28 November 1879): 137.

Matthías Jochumsson. *Sögukaflar af sjálfum mér.* 2nd ed. Reykjavík: Ísafold, 1959.

Matthías Þórðarson. "Skýrsla um viðbót við Forngripasafnið og þau söfn, er því eru sameinuð, árið 1909: . . . Fiskesafn." *Árbók hins íslenzka fornleifafélags* (1910): 93-97.

Mitchell, P. M. "The Fiske Icelandic Collection." *The Icelandic Canadian* (Summer 1991): 8–12.

Mitchell, P. M. *Halldór Hermannsson.* Islandica 41. Ithaca: Cornell University Press, 1978.

Nýárskveðja til Íslendinga frá Ameríku og Bretlandi hinu mikla. Edited by Þorlákur Ó. Johnson. Reykjavík: n.p., 1880.

Ólafur Davíðsson. "Prófessor Willard Fiske." *Sunnanfari: Mánaðarblað með myndum* 1, no. 2 (1891): 9-10.

Pétur Sigurðsson. "Skrá um skákrit og smáprent um skák er Willard Fiske lét prenta á íslenzku og gaf Taflfélagi Reykjavíkur." *Árbók Landsbókasafns Íslands* 7-8 (1950–51): 201-5.

Pfeiffer, Ida. *Nordlandfahrt: Eine Reise nach Skandinavien und Island im Jahre 1845.* Reprint. Wien: Promedia, 1991.

Richard Beck. *Útverðir íslenzkrar menningar.* Reykjavík: Almenna bókafélagið, 1972.

Richard Beck. "Willard Fiske: Aldarminning." *Eimreiðin* 37, no. 4 (1931): 358–77.

Saga Reykjavíkurskóla II: Skólalífið í Lærða skólanum. Edited by Heimir Þorleifsson. Reykjavík: Sögusjóður Menntaskólans í Reykjavík, 1978.

Sisler, Carol U. *Enterprising Families, Ithaca, New York: Their Houses and Businesses.* Ithaca, NY: Enterprise Publishing, 1986.

Smith, Albert W. *The Bells of Cornell.* Ithaca, NY: Cayuga Press, 1930.

Steingrímur Thorsteinsson. "By the Sea." Translated by Willard Fiske. *Cornell Era* 12, no. 11 (28 November 1879): 135.

Sumarliði Ísleifsson. *Ísland framandi land.* Reykjavík: Mál og menning, 1996.

Thor Jensen. *Reynsluár.* Vol. 1 of *Minningar*, recorded by Valtýr Stefánsson. Reykjavík: Bókfellsútgáfan, 1954–55.

Trollope, Anthony. *Íslandsferð Mastiffs.* Translated by Bjarni Guðmundsson. Reykjavík: Almenna bókafélagið, 1960. Originally published as *How the "Mastiffs" Went to Iceland* (London: Virtue, 1878).

Vevstad, Jens. "Boksamleren professor Willard Fiske." *Bokvennen* 5, no. 1 (1935): 1–4.

Vilhjálmur Þ. Gíslason. "Íþaka: Hálfrar aldar afmæli." *Skýrsla um hinn almenna menntaskóla í Reykjavík.* Suppl. (1929-30): 1–11.

"Vínfangatollur: Frumvarp frá Eyfirðingum. . . ." "Brennivínssala: Frumvarp frá Eyfirðingum. . . ." *Alþingisfréttir* (supplement to *Ísafold* 6) 2 (1879): 5.

Waller, Samuel E. *Six Weeks in the Saddle: A Painter's Journal in Iceland.* London: Macmillan and Co, 1874.

White, Andrew D. *Autobiography of Andrew Dickson White.* 2 vols. New York: Century, 1905.

White, Andrew D. *The Diaries of Andrew D. White.* Edited by Robert Morris Ogden. Ithaca, NY: Cornell University Library, 1959.

White, Horatio S. "A Sketch of the Life and Labors of Professor Willard Fiske." *The Papers of the Bibliographical Society of America* 12, no. 3–4 (1918): 69–88.

White, Horatio S. *Willard Fiske: Life and Correspondence: A Biographical Study.* New York: Oxford University Press, 1925.

Widmalm, Sven. "Vetenskapens och Teknikens värld (1700–1900)." In *Gyllene äpplen: Svensk idéhistorisk läsebok*, edited by Gunnar Broberg. Vol. 2. 2nd pr. Stockholm: Atlantis, 1995.

Wilkinson, W. M. *A Handbook for Travellers in Denmark, with Schleswig and Holstein and Iceland.* London: John Murray, 1893.

Willard Fiske in Iceland: Based on the Pocket Notebook Kept During His Sojourn There, 1879. Edited by P. M. Mitchell. Ithaca: Cornell University Library, 1989. Based on Fiske's [*Travels through Iceland*].

Williams, Ronald John. *Jennie McGraw Fiske: Her Influence upon Cornell University.* Ithaca, N.Y.: Cornell University Press, 1949.

Þórunn Sigurðardóttir. "Ástríðufullur Íslandsvinur: Bréf Daniels Willards Fiske til Gísla Brynjúlfssonar 1855." *Tímarit Máls og menningar* 67, no. 3 (Sept. 2006): 32–43.

Þórunn Sigurðardóttir. *Manuscript Material, Correspondence, and Graphic Material in the Fiske Icelandic Collection: A Descriptive Catalogue.* Islandica 48. Ithaca: Cornell University Press, 1994.

Newspapers and Periodicals (with relevant dates
for this narrative, or dates of existence)

Almanak hins íslenzka Þjóðvinafjelags um árið 1898.

Alþingisfréttir (supplement to *Ísafold* 6) 2 (1879)

Árbók Hins íslenzka fornleifafélags (1880–81)

Cornell Era 12, no. 11 (28 November 1879)

Í uppnámi: Íslenzkt skákrit (1901–2). Issue 1 edited by Willard Fiske and Halldór Hermannsson. Issue 2 edited by Halldór Hermannsson.

Ísafold (1874–1929)

Máni (1879–82)

Norðanfari (1862–85)

Norðlingur (1875–82)

Sunnanfari: Mánaðarblað með myndum 1, no. 2 and 2, no. 3B (1891–92)

Þjóðólfur (1874–80)

Correspondence

Letters from the following individuals to Daniel Willard Fiske or to Halldór Hermannsson are preserved in the Fiske Icelandic Collection:

Árni Friðriksson
Benedikt Gröndal
Bjarni Jónsson frá Unnarholti
Björn M. Ólsen
Bogi Th. Melsteð
Dufferin and Ava, Frederick Temple Blackwood, Marquis of (Lord
    Dufferin)
Einar Benediktsson
Eiríkr Magnússon (Cambridge)
Finnur Jónsson
Fiske, Caroline
Friðrik J. Bergmann
Gísli Brynjúlfsson
Grímur Thomsen
Guðbrandur Vigfússon (Oxford)
Halldór Hermannsson
Hannes Þorsteinsson
Jóhann Jóhannessen
Jón Árnason
Jón Bjarnason (Winnipeg)
Jón Björnsson
Jón [Jónsson] Borgfirðingur
Jón Egilsson
Jón Finnsson
Jón Hermannsson
Jón A. Hjaltalín
Jón Ólafsson
Jón Stefánsson
Jón Þorkelsson rektor [of the Learned School in Reykjavík]
Jón Þorkelsson þjóðskjalavörður [national archivist]
Magnús Einarsson
Magnús Stephensen
Matthías Jochumsson
Otto Tuliníus
Ólafur Davíðsson
Páll Þorkelsson

Pétur Zófoníasson
Pjetur Guðjónsson
Sigfús Blöndal
Sigurður Kristjánsson
Skapti Jósepsson
Tryggvi Gunnarsson
Valtýr Guðmundsson
Vilhjálmur Stefánsson
Warner, Charles Dudley
Þorvaldur Thoroddsen
Þórsteinn Arnljótsson

*Letters from Daniel Willard Fiske to the following individuals
are preserved in Landsbókasafn Íslands—Háskólabókasafn
(The National and University Library of Iceland):*

Árni Thorsteinsson
Grímur Thomsen
Jón Sigurðsson
Matthías Eggertsson
Matthías Jochumsson
Pétur Zóphoníasson
Steingrímur Thorsteinsson
Valdimar Ásmundsson

Illustrations: Index and Credits

Name Index

www.ingramcontent.com/pod-product-compliance
Ingram Content Group UK Ltd.
Pitfield, Milton Keynes, MK11 3LW, UK
UKHW041911060225
454777UK00001B/221